Categorization and Social Judgement

European Monographs in Social Psychology

Series Editor HENRI TAJFEL

E. A. CARSWELL and R. ROMMETVEIT
Social Contexts of Messages, 1971

J. ISRAEL and H. TAJFEL
The Context of Social Psychology: A Critical Assessment, 1972

In preparation

M. VON CRANACH and I. VINE
Social Communication and Movement

C. HERZLICH
Health and Illness: A Social Psychological Analysis

H. GILES and P. F. POWESLAND
Social Evaluation through Speech Characteristics

J. INNES
Bias in Psychological Research

EUROPEAN MONOGRAPHS IN SOCIAL PSYCHOLOGY 3
Series Editor HENRI TAJFEL

Categorization and Social Judgement

J. RICHARD EISER
University of Bristol, England

WOLFGANG STROEBE
University of Massachusetts, USA

1972

Published in cooperation with the
EUROPEAN ASSOCIATION OF EXPERIMENTAL
SOCIAL PSYCHOLOGY
by
ACADEMIC PRESS *London and New York*

ACADEMIC PRESS INC. (LONDON) LTD.
24–28 Oval Road
London NW1

US editions published by
ACADEMIC PRESS INC.
111 Fifth Avenue
New York, New York 10003

Library of Congress Catalog Card Number: 72–84352
ISBN: 0–12–235350–1

PRINTED IN GREAT BRITAIN BY
C. TINLING AND CO. LTD,
LONDON AND PRESCOT

Acknowledgements

We acknowledge with gratitude the helpful advice of Henri Tajfel, W. H. N. Hotopf and Lawrence E. Jones, and the support of the British Council, the Ford Foundation, the Medical Research Council, the Social Science Research Council and the University of London Central Research Fund, during various stages of the research on which this book is based. Most of the collaborative work was carried out when Wolfgang Stroebe spent a year at the University of Bristol and a year at the University of Sussex. We take equal responsibility for all parts of the work and our names therefore appear in alphabetical order.

September 1972

J. RICHARD EISER
WOLFGANG STROEBE

Contents

1

Introduction

A science fiction story, "In the Imagicon" by G. H. Smith, tells of life on Earth in the year 22 300, 100 years after a plague which had selectively destroyed male chromosomes and reduced the human male population to a few thousand. As a result, every man who survived found himself the centre of an eager and worshipful harem of women. Then the Imagicon was invented, a machine which made anything anyone imagined appear absolutely real. Surprisingly, it seems to have been the men rather than the women who made greatest use of the machine, so as to create even more exotic worlds than the one they lived in. This, however, only had the effect of making them increasingly bored and dissatisfied with their real lives and more and more addicted to the machine—except for the hero, who used the machine to create an imaginary world of cold terror, after which his real life appeared even more sensuous and luxurious.

Unfortunately, today's laboratories do not have Imagicons at their disposal. The kinds of situations we shall be describing, therefore, will be much more "down to earth", and the kinds of experimental conditions we shall be discussing, much less extreme. Yet, as we hope to show, even the relatively simple and restricted kinds of judgements made by subjects in a psychological experiment still reflect processes which are essentially the same as those depicted in the story. In short, experience is relative. A person's reaction to any object of judgement, be it a lifestyle or a lifted weight, depends on the standards against which that object may be compared. When these standards change, so will the person's reactions to the objects which he compares them with. However, it is also true that we do not simultaneously compare everything in our experience with everything else. We attend to certain stimuli and ignore others. We formulate hypotheses and draw inferences on the basis of only partial information. Experience, in other words, is not only relative but selective. It involves not only a process of comparison, but also a complementary process of categorization. We give names to different ranges of colours, even though colour is in fact a continuum. We know when to stop at traffic lights, even though the "red" light may look anything from scarlet to crimson.

In spite of the generality of such phenomena, however, there is surprisingly little agreement with regard to how they are to be explained. Although it is accepted that people's judgements of a given stimulus are affected by the context in which it appears, it is not always clear precisely which features of the stimulus context are responsible for the effects observed. Similarly, although few psychologists would deny that "people categorize", the precise effects and determinants of categorization are far less easy to define. These are questions which are of basic importance in almost any area of human psychology. It is almost commonplace to assert that a person's behaviour is not determined by stimuli as they "really" are, but depends on how these stimuli are interpreted by the person who perceives them; yet without any guidance on how such a process of interpretation takes place, this assertion frequently remains devoid of empirical significance.

The very generality of these judgemental processes makes it difficult to offer any single clear-cut definition of the term "social judgement". For our present purposes, however, we shall take it to include, on the one hand, the study of people's judgements of physical stimuli, in so far as these are influenced by socially communicated values and expectations, and, on the other hand, the study of people's judgements of "social stimuli", such as other people, their characteristics, their intentions, and the attitudes which they express. Such judgements may be considered from a number of different standpoints. A large number of studies have viewed them in relation to hypothesized individual differences in personality and cognitive style. We shall discuss this kind of approach only in passing, not because we feel it to be in any sense misconceived, nor because we wish to belittle the importance of individual differences, but because it appears to us in general to be of limited explanatory value merely to look for correlations between judgemental behaviour and measures of individual differences without also seeking to identify the factors by which such individual differences may be mediated in any specific situation. Similarly, social judgements have frequently been studied from the point of view of attitude scaling and psychological measurement. However, the development of sophisticated techniques of measurement does not *of itself* necessarily lead to a corresponding increase in one's ability to offer any general theoretical *explanation* of the phenomena one is measuring. We shall not, therefore, deal directly with the many methodological implications of this area of research, important though they undeniably are.

Instead, we hope to make our contribution elsewhere. Our main purpose will be to stress the generality of the cognitive processes which underly social judgements, whilst at the same time attempting to identify some of the factors which may influence these processes in particular conditions. We shall emphasize what we consider to be the essential continuities between judgements of simple physical stimuli on the one hand and social judgements on the other, whilst at the same time trying to do justice to the intrinsically *social* nature of social judgement.

We shall start, therefore, with a consideration of how people make judgements of simple physical stimuli, such as weights of different heaviness or lines of different length, when they are required to rate such stimuli along bipolar dimensions such as "heavy–light" or "long–short". This may seem a strange starting-point for what, after all, is supposed to be a monograph in social psychology, but we believe it to be essential for two reasons. Firstly, many of the approaches to social judgement which we shall be discussing in the later chapters of this book claim to be at least partly based on principles which are also supposedly operative in simple judgement situations, yet the accounts of psychophysical judgement which have been offered in support of this claim have often been over-simplified, and in at least one important instance, definitely misleading. Secondly, once a few such misconceptions are clarified, it is possible to argue that the close parallels between social and psychophysical judgement are based on much more than mere analogy, and, if this is so, then it is hardly good social psychology to ignore them.

Yet at the same time we do not consider our attempt to be reductionist. Unless one attends to the implicit social context in which social judgements are made, many of the results of social judgement experiments are uninterpretable. Unless one takes into account the individual's own system of values, and his apparent need to present himself positively to himself and others, then a comparison with psychophysical judgement will be unable to provide more than a partial explanation of the effects which one observes. As we shall see in the next two chapters, the three main theories which have been proposed to account for the relativity of judgement of simple physical stimuli, Volkmann's (1951) "rubber-band" model, Helson's (1964) adaptation-level theory, and Parducci's (1963) range-frequency model, apply in their unqualified form only to situations where all the stimuli presented to the subject are seen as relevant to the task of judgement, and where all the stimuli vary only in terms of the single physical attribute which the subject is required to rate. In social judgement situations, however, what is most interesting is often *which* stimuli the individual will choose to consider as relevant standards for comparison, and *which* stimulus attributes or dimensions will be those on which he bases his discriminations.

In Chapter 4 we shall move on to consider the question of how people make judgements of stimuli which vary simultaneously in terms of more than one attribute with particular reference to the analysis proposed by Tajfel (1959a). We shall see how, when faced with these more complex stimuli, subjects seek to simplify their experience through an act of categorization, accentuating in their judgements the differences between stimuli which fall into different classes. This will lead on to a consideration of a topic indisputably within the arena of social psychology, namely the effects of value on judgements of physical magnitude, in which we shall discuss not only the classic "new look" studies of twenty-odd years ago (e.g. Bruner and Goodman, 1947), but also more recent research such as that by Holzkamp (1965) and his colleagues.

We shall then proceed to a discussion of perhaps the most important single topic in this book, namely the question of how people make judgements of statements which vary in the degree of favourability or unfavourability of attitude which they express towards a given issue, and in particular, how such judgements are affected by the subjects' own attitudes towards the issue in question. This is reasonably close to Sherif and Hovland's (1961) usage of the term "social judgement", although our own interpretation of the phenomena in question differs in many important respects from theirs and although, unlike them, we shall not extend our analysis to a consideration of processes of attitude change. In Chapter 5 we shall review previous research in this area, and in Chapter 6 we shall present an interpretation of the effects of subjects' attitudes on their judgements which incorporates a similar line of reasoning to that proposed in Chapter 4 to account for people's categorization of physical stimuli which differ from one another in terms of value or some other superimposed cue. In doing so, however, we shall argue that it is also necessary to take into account factors for which no obvious parallel

exists in psychophysical judgement, in particular the evaluative connotations of the adjectives used to label the extremes of the judgement
scale along which the attitude statements are to be rated. We shall argue
that a consideration of such factors not only enables one to reconcile
apparently contradictory results in previous studies, but also allows one
to generate hypotheses, for which we shall present direct supporting
evidence concerning how subjects' attitudes and the evaluative connotations of the judgement scale labels may interact when they are
manipulated independently.

Finally, in Chapter 7 we move on from judgements of attitude statements to a consideration of attitude organization, cognitive consistency,
and related theories of phenomenal causality. Here what is essentially
involved is the question of how people appraise configurations of different
objects of judgement which they see as standing in particular kinds of
relations to each other. These theories bring out the important point
that individuals do not simply react passively to objects and events in
their experience: they actively attempt to structure their experience in
such a way as to render it predictable, meaningful and explicable. This,
we hope to show, is a common feature of all judgements, be they evaluative or descriptive, social or psychophysical.

2

Theories of Absolute Judgement in Psychophysics

Most of the problems with which we shall be concerned in this book are connected, directly or indirectly, with a particular method of psychological measurement, the so-called method of "absolute judgement". In many respects this name is misleading, since, as will be seen, judgements of this sort are not "absolute" at all, but vary considerably with the context in which they are made. Such variations, moreover, are anything but mere random errors of measurement. They are systematic effects the implications of which reach far beyond purely methodological areas of interest.

The usual procedure in an absolute judgement task is for the subject to be presented with a series of stimuli, one at a time, varying along some dimension of physical magnitude, which he has to judge in terms of their positions along some "psychological continuum" of apparent intensity. In tasks involving the judgement of lifted weights, for example, the subject is asked to report how "heavy" or "light" each stimulus feels in terms of a set of ordered categories, such as "very heavy", "heavy", "light" and "very light". The number of categories used varies from experiment to experiment. Sometimes only two categories are used (e.g. Johnson, 1944). When, as is more frequently the case, a larger number of categories is used, they are typically arranged in the form of a bipolar rating scale, with the extreme categories designated by such terms as "extremely heavy" and "extremely light" and with the intermediate categories marked off either by numerals or by such terms as "heavy", "moderately heavy", etc. Either way, an attempt may be made to measure the differences between the physical values of the stimuli judged in different categories.

An assumption of this method is that it is possible to derive from such judgements some measure of the "sensation" produced by each stimulus, and that from a comparison of these measures with the physical values of the stimuli one can relate the "psychological continuum" (e.g. apparent heaviness) to the "physical continuum" (e.g. weight). In other words, one can attempt to answer questions of the form: What is the relationship between weight and apparent heaviness? Since it attempts to discover the relationship between psychological and physical continua, this type of judgement is termed "psychophysical". When similar methods are used to determine subjects' reactions to attributes of stimuli that cannot be measured in strictly physical terms, for instance statements expressing points of view towards a controversial social issue, such judgement is termed "psychosocial", or, more commonly, "social".

As the title of this book implies, it is social and not psychophysical judgement with which we are primarily concerned. However, most of the explanatory models of social judgement are derived explicitly from principles that are assumed to be operative in psychophysical judgement. It is therefore important to stress at the outset certain basic differences between the two types of judgement.

In order to be able to make precise predictions of the "psychological magnitudes" of stimuli from a knowledge of their physical intensities, it is obvious that we must have some ready measure of what these physical intensities are. In psychophysical judgement such a measure is provided by conventional scales of physical measurement. However, the "psychological magnitudes" of the stimuli, i.e. the "sensations" they produce, cannot be directly observed but only inferred from the *responses* which the subjects make. When these responses can be ordered in terms of some criterion, as when they are expressed in terms of the categories of an absolute judgement scale, it is reasonable to speak of a "response" or "judgemental" continuum in addition to the "psychological" and "physical" continua.

Although these three continua are conceptually distinct, in practice what most theories of absolute judgement in psychophysics attempt to account for is the relationship between the physical and judgemental continua. In doing so, they may or may not make certain assumptions about the relationship between the judgemental and psychological continua—assumptions about the perceptual mechanisms underlying the phenomenon of judgement. However, this is a book about judgement, not perception. For this reason, we shall not presume to examine such assumptions directly except in so far as they seem to imply predictions about how a stimulus will be *judged* as opposed to simply "felt" or "perceived".

In social judgement these distinctions are of somewhat less consequence. If we ask subjects to report how favourable or unfavourable they consider a particular statement to be towards, say, the social position of Negroes, the distinction between the psychological continuum (of "apparent" favourability) and the judgemental continuum (of "reported" favourability) becomes rather hard to draw. In addition, we simply do not have anything corresponding to a physical continuum in this situation. We cannot talk of the "actual" favourability of the statement. All we can do is compare the *responses* given to the statements by different individuals or by the same individual in different situations.

In psychophysical judgement, therefore, we can define the positions of stimuli along both the physical and the judgemental continua reasonably objectively, and in addition we are able to theorize about the nature of the corresponding psychological continuum. In social judgement all we really have to go on are the positions of the stimuli along the judgemental continuum. In view of these differences, is it valid to attempt to apply psychophysical principles to social judgement? We intend to argue that this is both valid and useful, even though such an approach may not provide us with a definition of *all* the principles we may have to take account of in order to explain the effects to be considered. It is valid just so long as we evaluate such principles purely in terms of their predictive and explanatory power as theories of *judgemental* behaviour. Where the comparison between social and psychophysical judgement can become mere analogy is if we take a model developed to account for the relationship between sensations and physical intensities (however appealing that account may be) and attempt to apply it to situations where the notion of a physical continuum may be inappropriate and that of a psychological (as opposed to a judgemental) continuum may be indeterminate.

Remaining for the moment, therefore, within the general framework of psychophysics, what kinds of factors appear to affect how we distribute our judgements of a series of stimuli over the different categories of an absolute judgement scale? What conditions determine, for instance, whether we judge a particular weight to be "heavy" or "light"?

As we have already pointed out, the term "absolute judgement" is something of a misnomer. Wever and Zener (1928) proposed the term originally to distinguish this method of judgement from the so-called method of "comparative judgement", in which the subject is typically presented with more than one stimulus at a time and is asked to report which of the stimuli presented is, for example, "heavier" or "lighter". However, even when the subject is required to express his judgements in absolute rather than comparative terms, it cannot be assumed that he does so without, in some sense, comparing each individual stimulus which he has to judge with the others in the series.

It can be easily demonstrated that absolute judgements of a stimulus are relative to the total stimulus series. Suppose we ask a subject to lift a series of weights, the lightest of which weighs 50 g and the heaviest 200 g, and to tell us for each of the weights whether it is "very light", "light", "medium", "heavy" or "very heavy". After a few runs through the series the subject is likely to judge the 50 g weight as "very light" and the 200 g weight as "very heavy", and to assign intermediate categories to intermediate weights. Suppose, now, that without telling the subject we replace the old stimulus series by a new series which ranges from 200 g to 500 g. For a few trials the subject is likely to judge all the weights as very heavy, but after some runs through the new series, he is likely to judge the 200 g weight as "very light" and the 500 g weight as "very heavy". Thus, the same 200 g weight will be judged as "very heavy" in the context of a stimulus series of lighter weights and as "very light" in the context of a stimulus series of heavier weights. This type of phenomenon, termed "contrast effect", is the commonest and most widespread effect of varying the context within which we present stimuli to the subject in an absolute judgement task.

Why should the stimulus context affect judgements of stimuli in such a drastic way? The various theories to be considered in this chapter provide different answers to this question. Helson's (1964) "adaptation-level" theory argues that contrast effects in absolute judgements are due to processes of sensory adaptation. The same room might appear warm to someone entering it after walking through a snow storm and cold to someone who had been sitting all day long beside a blazing fire. A torch may dazzle us if shone into our eyes in the dark but may hardly be noticed on a summer's day. Whether the room appears warm or cold, or the torch dim or bright, will depend on the context in which we experience them—in this case, the level of stimulation to which we have become adapted. According to Helson, it is due to this kind of sensory adaptation that the 200 g weight is judged "very heavy" in one context and "very light" in another. After the subject adapted to a series of much lighter weights in the first series, the 200 g weight *appeared to be* very heavy, while it *appeared to be* "very light" once he had adapted to the second series of much heavier weights.

A different approach which centres around the semantic relativity of verbal labels such as "light", "heavy" or "large", "small", is taken by other theorists like Volkmann (1951). Volkmann argues that if we use such adjectives as "large", "small", etc. we have to decide what class of objects we are supposed to be judging. We are not contradicting ourselves if we say that a large rat is a small animal: we are simply saying that compared to other rats it is large whilst compared to other animals it is small. In other words, we are employing different standards for different comparisons. Before we can use terms like "large" or "small", therefore, we must define them in a manner applicable to the type of objects we wish to describe and the standards we wish to employ. Thus, Volkmann would argue that the context effects on judgement of the 200 g weight we described earlier were not necessarily due to sensory adaptation but to "semantic adaptation". The subject did not necessarily *perceive* the 200 g weight as different in the two contexts. He only adapted the verbal labels he was asked to use to the different context in the second series.

The second question considered by the theories to be discussed here is how the stimulus context affects absolute judgement of individual stimuli. Surprisingly enough, despite the basic disagreement about the processes underlying absolute judgements, these theories are fairly similar in their quantitative predictions of how stimuli will in fact be judged in varying stimulus contexts.

Helson's adaptation-level theory

Perhaps the most influential of all theories of absolute judgement has been Helson's adaptation-level theory (Helson, 1947, 1948, 1959, 1964). Its appeal seems to derive from its apparent applicability to many diverse areas of psychology, on the one hand, and from its apparent ability to generate quantitative empirical predictions on the other. The central assumption of adaptation-level (or AL) theory is basically very simple: every stimulus is perceived, and hence judged, in relation to some psychological "zero" or "point of perceived neutrality" which represents the level of adaptation of the organism to the stimuli presented.

In stimulus terms, Helson assumes that this level of adaptation, or AL, is a pooled effect of all past and present stimulation along the stimulus dimension in question. In other words the perceiver is supposed to compute some kind of "average" of all the stimulus intensities to which he is exposed, and the distinctiveness, or apparent intensity, of each stimulus is assumed to be proportional to its distance from this "average" value. However, with every new exposure of a stimulus which is at all discrepant from this average, the average will change: the AL will be "pulled" in the direction of each new stimulus as it occurs. This will have the effect of making the new stimulus appear more neutral, or less intense. If we look for long enough at a torch that is shone into our eyes in the dark, it will cease to dazzle us: we will have become "adapted" to a higher level of illumination than before, and, as a result of this rise in our AL, the torch will appear less bright and the surrounding darkness even darker.

In judgemental terms, AL is defined as the stimulus intensity rated as "medium" or "neutral" on a judgement scale. Thus, in general, if the judgement scale has an even number of categories AL will correspond to the middle limen, and if there are an odd number of categories it will correspond to the centre of the middle category. This definition assumes that what the subject in an absolute judgement task does is to match the centre of his judgement scale to his "point of perceived neutrality". As this point changes, so will the values of the stimuli judged as neutral. The subject's task is thus assumed to be one of judging the distance of each stimulus from prevailing AL, and the problem of explaining how the context in which a stimulus is presented affects the way in which it is judged is thus reduced to the problem of defining the conditions that lead to changes in AL.

Since, however, AL is defined in terms of the intensities of stimulation to which the subject has been exposed, the conditions which lead to changes in AL and hence to changes in judgement are, by definition, differences in the stimulus intensities experienced by the subject. Thus, if one wants to explain why a given weight is judged as "heavy" when presented immediately after a series of lighter weights, and as "light" when presented immediately after a series of heavier weights, then this is because different stimulus intensities have contributed to the AL prevailing in either case.

Helson defines AL, therefore, as the weighted logarithmic mean of three classes of stimuli. These are, firstly, "focal stimuli", which are those stimuli to which the subject's attention is directed at the time of judgement; secondly, "background" or "contextual stimuli", which are those stimuli to which focal stimuli may be compared by the subject; and thirdly, "residual stimuli", which cover any other possible source of variation, particularly the effects of past experience relevant to the particular perceptual or judgemental task in question.

This three-fold classification need not be interpreted too rigidly. As Helson writes:

> The division of stimuli into three classes (focal, background, and residual) is largely a matter of convenience . . . What is focal at one moment may become background or residual at the next moment, and what is background at one time may become focal at another time. The particular class to which stimuli are referred is far less important than is the determination of the contribution made by stimuli to level, regardless of what they are called.
>
> 1964, p. 59

What is important is that AL is supposed to represent the pooled effect of *all* stimulus exposures along any given stimulus dimension, and not simply of the particular stimuli which the subject has to judge.

Typical of the effects which AL theory attempts to explain are those obtained in an experiment by Helson (1947) on lifted weights. To take but one typical result, where subjects had to judge the heaviness of a series of weights of 200, 250, 300, 350 and 400 g, the mean value of the weights judged as "medium" was 250 g. When a weight of 900 g was added to the series, the observed "medium" rose to 313 g, and when the same 900 g weight was employed as a standard or "anchor" stimulus, i.e. when it was presented to the subjects before each presentation of a variable stimulus but did not have to be judged by them, the observed "medium" rose still further to 338 g. Such results are consistent with the assumption that AL is "pulled" in the direction of each new stimulus as it is presented, even if some of the stimuli do not have to be judged.

Similarly, there is evidence that past experience of subjects, even outside the experimental situation, may influence judgements in the kind of way which AL theory predicts. Tresselt (1948) presented a series of 12 weights, ranging from 11 to 560 g, to a group of 36 professional weight-lifters and a group of 36 watchmakers who were required to give absolute judgements of the heaviness of each weight. Their judgements were then compared with those given by a group of 120 students used in a previous study (Tresselt and Volkmann, 1942). The mean judgements given by the watchmakers were "heavier" than those given by the weight-lifters, with those given by the students lying between the two. The weight-lifters' judgements differed significantly from those of the students ($p < 0.05$), whilst the difference between the judgements of the students and the watchmakers just failed to attain significance at the 5 per cent level. But as the experiment progressed, there was a slow approach towards uniformity between the two groups. These results are broadly consistent with AL theory if it is assumed that subjects' AL's at the outset of the experiment were partly a function of the kinds of weights they typically had experience of lifting as part of their everyday life. Thus the watchmakers, who presumably had more experience of very light weights, should start off with a lower AL, and thus give more "heavy" judgements than the weight-lifters. However, since their AL's should gradually be pulled in the direction of the centre of the series of weights presented during the experiment, which was identical for both groups, these differences should become less marked over time, which is in fact what occurred.

As its name implies, AL theory assumes that the kinds of processes which are responsible for effects of this sort are at least analogous to the phenomenon of sensory adaptation so clearly demonstrated in such fields as colour perception (e.g. Helson and Michels, 1948). Helson, however, clearly assumes AL theory to be rather more than an attempt to explain certain kinds of perceptual illusions:

> Measurements of mass, space, and time are relative to the speed of light in Einstein's theory of relativity. Behavioral phenomena are relative to the state of the organism. In postulating adaptation level as the referent with respect to which behavioral phenomena are relative, psychology possesses an even more thorough-going relativity than does present-day physics. In relativity theory it is assumed that the speed of light has an absolute value in all systems whereas the concept of adaptation level provides for a *moving* zero to which measurements of behavior are referable.
>
> 1964, p. 31

This claim appears no less courageous when we learn what kinds of "behavioural phenomena" the theory attempts to cover:

> The basic premise of this book is that an individual's attitudes, values, ways of structuring his experiences, judgments of physical, aesthetic, and symbolic objects, intellectual and emotional behavior, learning and interpersonal relations all represent modes of adaptation to environmental and organismic forces.
>
> 1964, p. 37

But if such a premise is to lead to an *explanation* of all these different phenomena, then it is just as important to stress what distinguishes, as well as what may be common to, these different "modes of adaptation". If this is not done, then it remains possible that such a generality may only have been achieved through terminological equivocation. Considering AL theory as a general psychological theory, it is somewhat questionable whether Helson's definition of the concept of adaptation provides a particularly robust defense against charges of this kind. Although he clearly recognizes that the notion of sensory adaptation may be somewhat limited in its applicability, he is rather less explicit about what should be put in its place (Helson, 1964, p. 58).

If we consider AL theory as a theory of absolute judgement, however, Helson appears to regard the contrast effects found in judgements of lifted weights etc. as something basically akin to the phenomenon of sensory adaptation:

> Theories which imply we are dealing here merely with shifts in judgment or verbal categories do not account for the sensory changes that accompany shifts in AL. With change in *sensory character* of the stimuli there must be a difference in physiological process. For this reason we have used the term "adaptation level" to stress the basic nature of the phenomena.
>
> 1964, p. 136

Helson thus attempts to provide a model of judgement which is both predictive and explanatory. At a predictive level, shifts in judgement are assumed to occur whenever there is a change in the weighted logarithmic mean of the stimuli to which the individual is exposed. At an explanatory level, shifts in judgement are presumed to reflect changes in the "sensory character" of the stimuli which arise from a kind of process which, though it may not be identical with that of sensory adaptation, is at any rate not easily distinguishable from it.

Volkmann's "rubber-band" model

A very different kind of approach is that which stresses the relativity of the adjectival terms, or verbal categories, with respect to which the subject judges the stimuli. Before one can use terms such as "large" or "small" or "light" or "heavy", one must form some idea or expectation of the kind of stimuli to which they are to be applied. Within broad limits, it is meaningless to describe something as "large" without comparing it, implicitly or explicitly, with something else than can be described as "small". In a situation where one knows what sort of objects one is judging, one can form an idea of their probable range and accordingly make such comparisons. The subject in an absolute judgement experiment often cannot (except by chance) apply the judgement scale in a consistent and appropriate way until he *learns* the range of the stimuli he has to judge. This remains true whether or not any process of adaptation may be going on at the same time.

It is reasonable to ask, therefore, whether shifts in judgement of the kind so far described cannot be sufficiently explained in terms of the inevitable relativity of the judgement scale itself, without invoking any notion of shifts in the "sensory character" of the stimuli. One person who thinks they can is Volkmann, who argues:

> Suppose that a given discriminable aspect has been located by a discriminating person. What is the next thing that determines the person's discriminatory responses? The answer is simple: it is the particular range of stimuli that is offered for discrimination.
>
> 1951, p. 276

According to Volkmann, the person's "discriminatory responses" (*responses* not *sensations*) may be seen to depend on the stimulus range in terms of two "fundamental relations". The first of these, which applies especially to cases where judgements are made in terms of only two categories, is "the dependence of the centre of an absolute scale upon the stimulus-centre". This does not require the AL theory assumption of a point of perceived neutrality, or say anything about the sensitivity of the organism to stimulation: such factors might affect how the "discriminable aspect" of a stimulus is "located", but not how it is then judged. It is merely a statement about how people will sort the stimuli presented to them into different categories of the judgement scale.

The second relation is the "dependence of the width of a category (or of a scale of categories) upon the stimulus-range". Volkman cites evidence that "over a wide range the width of absolute categories (or of the entire scale) varies in rectilinear fashion with the stimulus-range". It is this assumption that has led Volkmann's theory to be called the "rubber-band" model. The analogy was suggested by Volkmann to Postman and Miller to help them interpret the contrast effects they found in judgements of temporal stimulus durations:

> The subjective scale is a flexible elastic scale. Introduction of an anchor outside the original range causes the subjective scale to be extended, in a manner analogous to a rubber band, beyond the original scale but remaining anchored to the stimulus of

smallest magnitude. As a result the same number of judgment categories must cover a wider range of stimulus durations, so that the width of each of the stimulus categories increases, while the number of judgments in the lower categories goes up.

Postman and Miller, 1945, p. 52

In Postman and Miller's study, subjects were required to judge the durations of five stimulus tones, lasting 250, 375, 500, 750 and 1000 milliseconds, in terms of a five-point absolute scale. Nine subjects judged these tones under each of five conditions. In the control condition, a total of 100 judgements were made by each subject to the tones presented singly. This was followed by four experimental sessions of 100 judgements each, during which a standard or "anchor" stimulus preceded the presentation of each stimulus tone. There were four such anchor stimuli, one for each experimental session, lasting 1000, 1150, 1400 and 1500 milliseconds. Subjects were not required to judge these anchors, nor instructed (as had been the practice in previous studies) to treat the anchors as equivalent to the end category of their judgement scale, but were told simply to use "the standard for purposes of comparison". In all four anchor conditions, the stimulus tones were judged to be shorter than in the control condition, with the extent of this shift being proportionate to the distance of the anchor from the other five stimuli. The effects for the 1150, 1400 and 1500 millisecond anchors are thus consistent with Volkmann's idea that subjects expanded their judgement scales to incorporate these longer stimulus durations. However, the fact that slight contrast effects still occurred with the 1000 millisecond anchor raises problems for the rubber-band model (though not for AL theory), since introduction of this anchor did not involve an extension of the range of stimuli presented to the subjects.

Radically different though Helson's and Volkmann's approaches may be, there is considerable overlap in the predictions they make. Expansion of the stimulus range by the introduction of anchors also leads, in most situations, to a shift in the value of AL predicted by Helson's formula, and hence to an effect of contrast, i.e. a shift in the judged values of the stimuli away from the end at which the anchor is introduced. Simply demonstrating the occurrence of such contrast effects does not necessarily amount to proof of one of the models as opposed to the other. In comparing the models with each other, therefore, it is perhaps best to concentrate on the evidence relating to a limited number of specific questions. Of these, some of the most useful to ask are: How valid are the assumptions made by each model concerning the interval properties of the absolute judgement scale? Do contrast effects appear to result primarily from "perceptual" shifts in the sensory character of the stimuli or "semantic" shifts in the meanings of the verbal categories of the scale? Do subjects appear to "learn" what the features of the stimulus distribution are, or merely become "adapted" to them? And finally, what *are* the features of the stimulus distribution that in fact are responsible for judgemental changes?

Interval properties of the judgement scale

Although they make similar predictions at a general level, Helson and Volkmann differ considerably from one another in the degree of precision they aspire to in their formulations, and this difference is reflected in the assumptions they make concerning the interval properties of the judgement scale.

Volkmann is never entirely explicit about the assumptions he is making. He states that the range of stimulus values that will be included in any one category of the judgement scale will be proportionate to the overall range of stimulus values to be encompassed by the judgement scale as a whole. Since it is the *range* of stimulus values that is assumed to be important, rather than, say, the proportionate *frequencies* of stimuli within different parts of the range, this implies that the scale is assumed to have equal interval properties; in other words, judgements in terms of the scale are assumed to convey information not only about the ordinal positions of the stimuli, but also about the distances between them along the dimension in question. Volkmann appears to imply that, with perfect discrimination, the subject will use each category of the scale to mark off equal distances along the psychological continuum; in other words, that equal intervals along the judgemental continuum will correspond to equal intervals along the psychological continuum. He does not appear to commit himself, however, to any definite assumptions about the relationship between intervals on the psychological continuum and intervals on the physical continuum.

Helson, on the other hand, is far more explicit. Equal intervals on the judgemental continuum are assumed to correspond to equal intervals on the psychological continuum, whilst intervals on the psychological continuum are assumed to be logarithmically related to intervals on the physical continuum. This assumption of a logarithmic relationship between the physical and psychological continua (and hence between the physical and judgemental continua) amounts to an assumption that the Weber–Fechner law is valid to a reasonable degree of approxima- tion. This assumption is reflected in the definition of AL as a weighted *logarithmic* mean of the various classes of stimuli, and also enables Michels and Helson (1949) to attempt "a reformulation of the Fechner law in terms of adaptation-level applied to rating-scale data".

Stevens (1958), however, attacks Helson on account of both these assumptions. Central to Stevens' critique is the distinction which he draws between "prothetic" and "metathetic" continua. Prothetic or "quantitative" continua include such dimensions as apparent length, duration, heaviness, loudness and brightness. Metathetic, or "qualita- tive" continua, on the other hand, include the dimensions of pitch, position, inclination and proportion. Considering first of all how AL theory is applied to judgements of prothetic continua (e.g. lifted weights), Stevens argues that it is incorrect to assume a logarithmic relationship between the physical and psychological continua, as implied by the Weber–Fechner law (cf. Stevens, 1957). Increases in psychological magnitude are a power function, not a logarithmic function, of increases in physical magnitude; in other words, Stevens (1958) claims that "equal stimulus-ratios produce equal sensation-ratios" (p. 636).

Stevens argues, moreover, that equal intervals on the judgement scale do not necessarily represent equal differences in psychological magnitude in the case of prothetic continua. The width of the judgement scale categories will be affected by the ability of the subject to discriminate between different stimulus magnitudes over different regions of the physical continuum. Such discrimination is typically better at the low end rather than the high end of the physical continuum, with the result that the scale categories at the low end tend to be narrower than those at the high end. However, the discriminability of one stimulus magni- tude from another is *not*, Stevens argues, a simple linear function of the distance between them along the psychological continuum of apparent intensity. The curve relating judgement to physical magnitude, there- fore, does not simply reflect the relationship between psychological magnitude and physical magnitude, but also that between stimulus discriminability and physical magnitude. Stevens claims that the rea- sonable predictive success of Helson's model derives from the fact that he makes two incorrect assumptions that absolute judgement scales are equal-interval scales and that the Weber–Fechner law is true:

The theory of adaptation-level incorrectly assumes that the intervals on a category-scale are subjectively equal, but it is mainly because this assumption is wrong that the "quantified" theory is able to predict the outcome of category-judgments with fair success. It comes about in this way. Fechner's logarithmic law, which the theory assumes to be true, represents a function that is concave downward when plotted against the scale of subjective magnitude. The category-scale is also concave downward when so plotted. Hence the wrong assumption that Fechner's law holds leads to predictions that bear a superficial resemblance to the behavior of category-judgments.

Stevens, 1958, p. 641

In the case of metathetic or "qualitative" dimensions, Stevens argues that "discrimination or resolving power" is approximately constant over the scale, instead of being relative to magnitude as in the case of prothetic continua. Since, however, it is this relationship between discrimination and magnitude that is responsible for the success Helson has with prothetic continua, Stevens (1958, p. 643) predicts that "the quantitative theory of adaptation-level will generally fail when . . . metathetic continua are involved". Furthermore, for continua of this kind "there is apparently no simple law relating psychological magnitude to stimulus" (p. 646). In other words, neither Fechner's logarithmic law nor Stevens' power law applies to all continua of this class. For such qualitative continua, therefore, Helson's theory is unlikely to provide accurate quantitative predictions except in special cases.

Helson's defence against these charges is to dispute the distinction between prothetic and metathetic continua (Helson, 1964, p. 173ff.). In any event, it could be questioned whether Helson lays as great a store by accuracy of quantitative prediction as might appear. If we concentrate simply on his definition of AL as a weighted logarithmic mean of three classes of stimuli, it is apparent that, for this definition to provide any precise quantitative prediction, the weightings assigned to each of the three classes must also be defined with an equivalent measure of precision. Typically, however, they are determined *ad hoc* for the particular stimulus distribution presented. Combined with the fact that Helson anyway does not regard the division of stimuli into classes as particularly rigid, or stable over time, it is clear that his formula can lead to extremely flexible predictions. This same lack of commitment to any really precise formulation applies even to his use of the log mean as the most appropriate measure:

All in all . . . the log mean has been found an easy and convenient base with which to start. Other definitions, such as the power mean (Behar & Bevan, 1961) and the median (Parducci, Calfee, Marshall & Davidson, 1960) are also compatible with adaptation-level and may be useful in certain cases.

Helson, 1964, p. 61

However, Helson fails to specify how these alternative formulations are compatible with his own, nor why they should only be useful "in certain cases".

In conclusion, therefore, one of the superficially most persuasive features of AL theory—its apparent ability to generate precise quantitative predictions concerning judgemental phenomena—turns out on closer inspection to be somewhat illusory. There appear to be no hard and fast criteria for determining the degree of rigour with which the quantitative theory of AL is intended to apply to any given situation, and even where an attempt *is* made to apply it rigorously, the moderate predictive success which it then obtains is, at least according to Stevens, an artifact of two separate incorrect assumptions incorporated in the model.

Volkmann's model makes fewer assumptions of a quantitative nature and therefore is open to fewer criticisms. It is perhaps a matter of opinion whether Helson should be more commended for his greater courage in attempting a quantitative formulation of his model than Volkmann for his greater caution in desisting from such an attempt. The point is only that one should not reject Volkmann's approach in favour of Helson's simply because the latter *claims* to be the more quantitative.

"Perceptual" versus "semantic" shifts

Perhaps the most obvious difference between Helson's and Volkmann's models is the emphasis which Volkmann places on changes in the verbal categories of the judgement scale compared with the emphasis which Helson places on changes in "sensory character". It is also one of the most difficult problems to resolve experimentally. Basically, the dilemma is as follows: Volkmann assumes that shifts in judgement reflect changes in the relationship between the physical and judgemental continua, that is between the physical and judged magnitudes of the stimuli, but not necessarily any changes in their psychological magnitudes, i.e. in the relationship between the physical and psychological continua. Helson, on the other hand, assumes that changes in judgement reflect changes in the relationship between the physical and psychological continua, that is between the actual and apparent magnitudes of the stimuli, but not necessarily in the relationship between the psychological and judge-

mental continua, i.e. in how a stimulus of a given apparent or psychological magnitude will be judged. However, the judgement task rarely
provides any measure of the psychological magnitudes of the stimuli
other than the reports given by the subjects in terms of the judgement
scale itself. The precise nature of the relationship between the psychological and judgemental continua is thus an extremely awkward one to
test empirically.

At least with some types of stimuli, however, subjects may make
introspective reports that imply that a perceptual change of some kind
has definitely taken place. Helson mentions the case of a subject presented with a series of weights ranging from 200 to 400 g both with and
without a 900 g "anchor". This subject reported that the observations
were much less fatiguing with the 900 g anchor than with the single-
stimuli method because he now found the weights so much lighter,
although actually the total weight lifted with the 900 g standard was
6000 g per series as against 1500 g with the single-stimuli method (1964,
p. 136). Although, from a strictly logical point of view, such comments
are still only *reports* of subjective experience, just as the judgements which
the subject makes in terms of the rating scale are reports, it would be
extremely pedantic to maintain in such cases that *no* perceptual change
had taken place. Two points, however, should be borne in mind. Firstly,
the fact that perceptual changes occur does not necessarily entail that
they are the result of an adaptation process. It is by no means inconceivable that for some kinds of stimuli such changes might only occur where
subjects are required to relate various stimuli to each other explicitly, as
in an absolute judgement task. Secondly, to demonstrate the occurrence
of perceptual changes in certain instances does not by itself establish
that such changes are either necessary or sufficient conditions for judgemental shifts in general. None the less, a limited number of studies have
addressed themselves specifically to the task of determining the role of
perceptual as opposed to semantic shifts.

A possible approach to this question might be to see if subliminal
stimuli interpolated between presentations of supraliminal stimuli have
any effect on judgement. This was the method adopted by Black and
Bevan (1960), who claim that subliminal stimulation had the effect of
lowering subjects' AL for weak electric shocks. Two groups of subjects
received a series of 100 supraliminal shocks lasting 200 milliseconds,
spaced at 20-second intervals. In the experimental group, subjects also
received subliminal shocks at 50 per cent of their own thresholds at the

midpoint of the intervals between consecutive supraliminal shocks, whilst in the control group only supraliminal shocks were presented. GSR measures appear to confirm that the interpolated stimuli for the experimental group were in fact below threshold (although the equipment broke down before the experiment was completed). Subjects were required to judge the intensity of the shocks in terms of a seven-point scale from "very strong" to "very weak", being told that they could add additional categories to either end of the scale if they wished. The judgements given by the experimental group were significantly (p <0·05) "stronger" than those of the control group. Black and Bevan argue that this was due to the fact that subjects in the experimental group had a lower AL for shocks than those in the control group, on the assumption that AL represents the pooled effect of *all* stimuli, both subliminal and supraliminal, to which the subjects were exposed.

Such results are clearly difficult to account for in terms of a model such as Volkmann's. It is quite implausible to argue that subjects in the experimental group "defined" the "weak" end of their judgement scale to incorporate stimuli which they did not even detect. The changes observed are undoubtedly perceptual and not merely semantic. This does not mean, however, that they are necessarily the result of a process of adaptation of the kind proposed by Helson. What appears to have happened is that the subliminal stimuli presented to the experimental group had a sensitizing effect, with a result that the subjects' absolute thresholds (as traditionally measured) to subsequent stimuli were effectively lowered. Somewhat comparable results with visual stimuli are reported by Baumgardt and Smith (1965), who found that a target stimulus was detected more easily when presented against a subliminal background than when presented alone. Although Black and Bevan interpret their results in terms of contrast, Baumgardt and Smith favour a summation principle (the "quanta addition" hypothesis).

A somewhat more straightforward way of comparing the roles of "perceptual" and "semantic" factors is to see whether "semantic" factors, such as the particular type of judgement scale used, substantially affect the type of judgemental shifts one obtains. Two studies which attempt to isolate such factors are those of Campbell *et al.* (1958) and Krantz and Campbell (1961). These studies both rest upon the assumption that it should be possible to distinguish "identity distortions or illusions" from "semantic redefinitions". As Campbell *et al.* put it:

. . . by employing a judgmental language that was (a) absolute, in the sense of referring to a situationally invariant aspect of the stimulus, (b) extra-experimentally anchored, so that it would not appear to be an arbitrary and transient linguistic convention for laboratory purposes only, and (c) unlimited, extensive, or extendible in terms of the number of categories. Such a language is provided by the measurement categories of science and everyday life, in terms of *ounces, inches,* . . . etc.

1958, p. 221

In the Campbell *et al.* (1958) experiment, subjects were required to judge the pitch of tones, using the piano keyboard as an "absolute, extensive, and extra-experimentally anchored" judgemental language. Contrast effects still occurred with changes in context, though not, as Campbell *et al.* point out, precisely in accordance with the predictions of AL theory, since recent stimuli had more influence on subsequent judgements than remote ones.

This kind of approach was taken a stage further by Krantz and Campbell (1961). Here the stimuli used were 13 white lines projected onto a screen and varying from 6·1 in. to 35·8 in. in length. Half the subjects started by judging a series consisting of the seven shortest lines only. The composition of the series was then gradually changed until it consisted finally of only the seven longest lines. For the other half of the subjects the order of presentation was reversed, so that they started with the seven longest lines and finished with the seven shortest. For all subjects, therefore, the middle stimulus appeared in all phases of the experiment, and it was subjects' judgements of this stimulus that constituted the main dependent variable.

In addition to this order manipulation, half the subjects were required to estimate the length of the lines in inches, whilst the other half responded in terms of an unrestricted rating scale centred at an "average" rating of 100. (Other variables considered were the amount of "pre-shift training", i.e. the number of trials with the initial seven stimuli before the composition of the series changed, and stimulus discriminability, manipulated by means of the illumination of the lines on the screen. The four manipulations constituted a $2 \times 2 \times 2 \times 2$ design.)

As predicted, the middle stimulus was judged as longer when presented in the context of the shortest, as opposed to the longest, seven stimuli. But these differences were far more marked when judgements were made in terms of the rating scale than in terms of "inches" estimates. Similarly, the amount of pre-shift training appeared to have some effect on ratings, but not on "inches" estimates. Stimulus discriminability had no effect.

Krantz and Campbell conclude that the significant context effects observed for the "inches" estimates "represent the operation of a single perceptual contrast process". The rating-scale data also "contains a second process of defining perceptual equivalents for novel judgemental terms", which "operates in an adaptation-level fashion". In other words, they view the shifts in the "inches" estimates as corresponding to purely "perceptual" shifts, and the judgemental changes in the "ratings" condition as corresponding to "perceptual" *plus* "semantic" shifts.

This distinction, however, may not be quite as clear-cut as they imply. To estimate the length of a line in inches is not the same thing as measuring it with a ruler, and inaccuracies of estimation, even if systematic, cannot be automatically assumed to arise from perceptual distortions rather than from an imperfect memory of what a line of, say, 12in. long "looks like". It is therefore not enough for the subject to know *that* a particular judgemental language is extra-experimentally anchored; he must also know *how* it is anchored. Whatever the nature of the judgemental language in terms of which he makes his responses, the subject must still "define perceptual equivalents" for the judgemental terms. In Krantz and Campbell's "ratings" condition, the subject is given a "novel" response language and thus a free choice as to how he should define the judgemental terms. He will nevertheless attempt to define them in a way appropriate to the distribution of the stimuli presented to him. In their "inches" condition, on the other hand, the perceptual equivalents for the judgemental terms are conventionally defined. The subject's task is thus one of trying to define the judgemental terms in a way that is as close as possible to their conventional usage. However, since he still has to use these terms in order to discriminate between the stimuli with which he is presented, the way he defines them may still be partly a function of the expectations or hypotheses which he forms, before and during the experiment, concerning the range and distribution of stimuli that are likely to be presented to him.

It is perhaps somewhat questionable, therefore, whether Krantz and Campbell succeed in demonstrating conclusively the occurrence of *purely* "perceptual" as opposed to "semantic" shifts. A similar uncertainty surrounds the interpretation of Harvey and Campbell's (1963) findings of context effects with weight estimates in terms of ounces, and Helson and Kozaki's (1968) results with estimates of visual number. This is by no means to deny the existence of perceptual contrast as a real phenomenon, at least for some classes of stimuli, but merely to point out that the very nature of the absolute judgement experiment makes it difficult to completely isolate such "perceptual" shifts, whatever the "semantic" properties of the judgement scale may be.

Whilst one may be sympathetic, therefore, with Helson's view that, at least for some types of stimuli, one cannot be dealing "merely with shifts in judgement or verbal categories", it is evident that some kind of re-definitional process appears to play a crucial (and perhaps the major) role in determining judgemental shifts in many situations. Helson's model contains no indication of how such a process might operate.

The role of subjects' expectations

If one leaves aside the question of whether the results reported by Krantz and Campbell (1961) represent "perceptual" or "semantic" shifts, the effect of their order manipulation may be regarded as a typical example of how changes in stimulus context, even within the same experimental session, can lead to changes in judgement. In general, if a series of stimuli is presented in order of increasing magnitude, the individual stimuli will tend, on average, to be judged as larger than they would be if the same series were presented in order of decreasing magnitude. This may be interpreted as consistent with AL theory, since "for any stimulus value in the ascending series, the mean of all the stimuli which preceded it is lower than the mean of the stimuli which would have preceded it if the series had been presented in descending order" (Parducci, 1959, p. 240). In other words, a greater number of stimuli will be above prevailing AL in the ascending than in the descending series.

Another way of looking at the same results is to regard them as the effect of a fairly mild form of deception. The subject comes to the experiment without usually any very firm ideas about what kinds of stimuli he is going to have to judge. The experimenter then presents him, during the initial trials, with a distribution of stimulus values that is deliberately unrepresentative of the kinds of stimulus values that he will have to judge in the later trials of the experiments. In other words, the experimenter creates false expectations on the part of the subject concerning the distribution of stimuli to which the judgement scale is to be applied. Considered in this way, the observed effects may be interpreted as indicating that subjects will judge individual stimuli in relation to what they

B

expect rather than simply in relation to what they have *experienced*, even though generally what they expect will be a function of what they have experienced. Tresselt's (1948) results, which we have already mentioned, may perhaps be interpreted thus: the different past experiences of the weight-lifters and watchmakers may have led to differences in their expectations about the kinds of weights they would be asked to judge, rather than any strictly sensory differences.

But suppose we drop the deception and tell the subjects beforehand what kind of stimuli they are going to be presented with. A common-sense interpretation would suggest that subjects in such a condition would be less likely to show shifts in judgement than subjects who had no such information. This prediction was confirmed in the first of three experiments reported by Parducci (1954) in which subjects were required to judge the distance between two 3-in. vertical lines printed beside each other on a card. These distances varied in $\frac{1}{2}$-in. steps from $\frac{1}{2}$ to 5 in. Subjects to whom the distribution of these distances had been described showed less susceptibility to the influence of a non-random presentation order than did subjects who were given no information about what range of distances to expect. These results are not easily reconciled with Helson's theory in that both groups of subjects had been presented with identical distributions of stimuli, and therefore should have had equivalent AL's and thus have given the same judgement as each other.

Two further studies, by Parducci (1956) and Parducci and Hohle (1957), also demonstrate the crucial role played by subjects' own expectations. In the first of these, subjects were required to judge the size of a series of square cards in terms of a five-category scale. They were either presented first with a narrow range of stimuli which expanded during the course of the experiment, or first with a wider range from which the larger stimuli were later dropped. Thus in both cases the subjects had to readjust their scales during the course of the experiment. It was found that subjects showed far greater shifts following expansion than following restriction of the stimulus range, and that this finding held also for judgement of the pitch of tones. The effects of two additional manipulations suggest that these shifts were more marked when it was made more obvious to the subjects that the stimulus distribution had changed. Restriction of the range by removal of the largest stimuli caused greater shifts when the original stimulus distribution was negatively rather than positively skewed, i.e. when it contained a relatively high, rather than a relatively low, proportion of the larger stimuli which were later excluded. Also, if restriction of the stimulus distribution was accompanied by a change in the colour of the cards, so that all the cards presented in the restricted series were of a different colour from all those presented in the original series, the amount of shift was increased.

Why should the shifts in judgement have been less marked following restriction rather than expansion of the stimulus range? A possible reason might have been that subjects did not modify their scales to such an extent following restriction of the range because they expected the missing stimuli to recur during the later trials of the experiment. To test this interpretation, Parducci and Hohle (1957) presented subjects with a series of nine circles of different diameters to be judged in terms of a five-category scale according to size. The stimuli were presented on pages of a booklet. During the course of the experiment, the stimulus distribution shifted to a restricted series consisting of the five smallest circles only. Between presentation of the original and the restricted series, subjects were given different amounts of information concerning the composition of the restricted series. There were four different types of information given. In the control condition, subjects were given no information. In the other conditions, subjects were told that some circles might appear to be omitted in the subsequent pages of the booklet, but that either these circles would appear again on later pages, or that they would appear again in some booklets but not in others (subjects not being told what kind of booklet they personally had), or, finally, that the missing circles would not reappear. In addition, the skewness of the original series was varied, half the subjects receiving a positively skewed distribution of stimuli, and half a negatively skewed distribution.

In accordance with Parducci's (1956) results it was found that groups who had received a positively skewed original series showed less shift than those who had received a negatively skewed one. In addition, greater shifts occurred where subjects were told that the series would or might change than when they were told that it would not change, or when they were given no information. This was far stronger when the original series had been negatively skewed, suggesting that such information was only effective when the shift was easily discriminated.

At a general level, therefore, these results confirm the common-sense prediction that, if subjects are told what type of changes to expect in the stimuli presented to them, or if it is made obvious to them when such changes occur, they will be more likely to readjust their scales accordingly than if the changes take them unawares. The judgements which a subject makes are therefore as much a function of his expectations about the future as of his experience in the recent past. However, it is difficult to see how such expectations of *future* stimulation could enter into any quantitative prediction of AL, which Helson defines as the pooled effect only of past and present stimulation. Adaptation, at least in the sense in which Helson uses the term, is not the same as anticipation, and it is clearly the latter concept which offers the more reasonable explanation of these results. Volkmann's approach, on the other hand, can incorporate such findings without much difficulty. Since the subject is assumed by Volkmann to be able to *decide* how to define his scale of judgement, then he is as capable of making this decision on the basis of future expectations as on the basis of past experience. At the same time, the finding that restriction of the stimulus range leads to less shift in judgement than does expansion of the range demonstrates an interesting fact about the anchoring properties of extreme stimuli. The individual's subjective scale may be a "flexible elastic scale", but it is made of a kind of "elastic" that stretches more easily than it contracts. Introduction of stimuli outside the original range will lead to more or less immediate expansion of the scale. Where subjects are presented first with the wider series, however, they will continue to use an extended scale for some time even after the extreme stimuli have been removed.

Features of the stimulus distribution that determine shifts in judgement: Parducci's range-frequency model

A difficulty one faces when attempting to choose between Helson's and Volkmann's explanations of contrast effects is that, in many studies, the way in which experimenters have manipulated differences in AL has been to introduce anchor stimuli at various distances beyond the end of the stimulus series. Thus, the higher the anchor above the end of the series, the higher is the subject's AL and thus, in terms of AL theory, the lower his judgements; or, alternatively, the higher the anchor, the higher is the upper end of the range of stimuli presented to the subject, and thus, in terms of the "rubber-band" model, the lower his judgements. Variation in AL is thus confounded, in such studies, with variation in stimulus range.

Where they are not confounded, however, as, for instance, where the proportionate frequencies of individual stimuli within a series are altered while the stimulus range remains constant, AL theory appears, at first sight, to score heavily over the "rubber-band" model. It is surprising that Volkmann did not pay more attention to this problem, since Johnson (1944) had already shown, with judgements of lifted weights, that the limen of a two-category scale ("light" or "heavy") was far higher for a negatively than for a positively skewed distribution of weights within the same stimulus range. These results are consistent with AL theory, but not with the "rubber-band" model, which, strictly speaking, would have predicted no difference between the limens for the two distributions.

However, to determine which parameters of the stimulus distribution are responsible for changes in judgement, it is not sufficient merely to observe what happens when the end-points of the stimulus range are held constant and the theoretical AL varied. One must also see what happens when the theoretical AL is held constant and other parameters are varied independently.

Helson's definition of AL as the (logarithmic) mean of presented stimuli was based, as we have seen, on his view of judgemental adaptation as a kind of pooling or averaging process. But the mean is only one of a number of possible measures of the centre of a stimulus distribution. Variation in the centre of the stimulus distribution can lead to variation in the centre of the individual's response scale, but this does not necessarily entail that it is the *mean* of the stimulus distribution that constitutes the best predictor of such changes in judgement.

Among other possible parameters are the *midpoint* of the range (i.e. the half-way point between the two end stimuli) and the *median* stimulus value. If both or either of these latter two measures could provide adequate predictions of changes in judgement, then certain implications would follow for a view of how the individual adjusts his scale of judgement to the particular distribution of stimuli presented to him. As Parducci (1963) points out:

> If the categories of judgment were assigned to fixed proportions of the range, symmetrical about the middle category, the adaptation level, or middle category of the scale of judgment, would center on the *midpoint* between the two stimulus extremes.
>
> p. 3

This would suggest a view of judgement essentially compatible with Volkmann's approach. However, if the median were shown to be important, then this would carry somewhat different implications. As Parducci goes on to say:

Another possibility is that different descriptive terms, categories of judgment, or portions of the response dimension, are used with fixed relative frequencies . . . In the simplest case, the two halves of the scale might be used with exactly equal frequency . . . The adaptation level would be the *median* of the stimulus values.

p. 4

This would imply an ordinal principle of judgement—a possibility that both Helson and Volkmann failed to explore. Johnson's (1944) results indicate that changes in judgement still occur when the range, and hence the midpoint, is held constant and the intermediate stimulus frequencies, and hence the mean and median, are varied. On the other hand, when the median is held constant, shifts in judgement still occur as a function of changes in the midpoint of the stimulus range (Parducci *et al.*, 1960; Parducci and Marshall, 1961a, 1961b). Neither the median nor the midpoint by itself, therefore, provides a sufficient basis for the prediction of shifts in judgement. In studies such as Johnson's, variation in the median is confounded with variation in the mean. It is therefore necessary to see what happens when the median is varied independently of the mean.

Parducci (1963) therefore presented subjects with a number of stimulus distributions which were constructed in such a way that the mean, midpoint and median of the distributions could all be varied independently or in combination with each other. Helson's theory would predict shifts in judgement only as a function of changes in the mean. Volkmann's theory would predict such shifts only as a function of changes in the midpoint. Parducci's results, however, are unequivocal. Using three different types of stimuli—lifted weights, numbers of dots in visually presented patterns, and squares of different sizes—he found that, with the mean held constant, independent variation either of the midpoint, or of the median, or of both the midpoint and the median in combination, produced highly significant shifts of judgement in the predicted direction. On the other hand, when the median and midpoint were both held constant, and the mean (and hence the AL as predicted by Helson) was varied, he found no significant shifts in the direction predicted by AL theory.

Further evidence also supports the conclusion that absolute judgements may be influenced by ordinal relationships between the stimuli being judged.

Since Parducci constructed his stimulus distributions as far as possible by using the same stimulus values in the different series, but varying their relative frequencies of occurrence, he was able to calculate the mean judgements given to any particular stimulus value in the different conditions. When the mean judgements of the stimuli in any given pair of conditions are plotted against each other, the resulting relationship tends to be curvilinear. However, if subjects had used their scales purely as interval scales, as assumed by both Helson and Volkmann, the relationship should have been linear. Instead, the form of the curvilinearity suggests that subjects were attempting to use the categories of the scale with the same relative frequencies, rather than simply to mark off equal-appearing intervals. This interpretation is further supported by the fact that the curvilinearity was even more pronounced when subjects had a record of the frequencies with which they were using particular response categories.

To explain these results, Parducci proposes what he terms a "range-frequency compromise" which assumes that the way in which subjects adjust their scales to the distribution of stimuli presented to them consists in a compromise between two basic tendencies of judgement: ". . . (a) to divide the range of stimuli into proportionate subranges, each category of judgment covering a fixed proportion of the range; and (b) to use the categories of judgment with proportionate frequencies, each category being used for a fixed proportion of the total number of judgements." (1963, p. 4.) The centre, or middle limen, of the judgement scale in any given instance, therefore, may be predicted from a weighted combination of the midpoint and median of the stimulus distribution.

The first of these two tendencies, the proportionate range principle, is essentially similar to Volkmann's "rubber-band" model. Like Volkmann, Parducci suggests that the subjects subdivide the stimulus range into as many segments as there are categories available. However, while Volkmann assumes that these segments are of equal size, Parducci makes no such assumption, but talks instead in terms of "*proportionate* subranges".

The second tendency, the proportionate frequency principle, is a novel feature of Parducci's model. Again, he states that the categories of the scale will tend to be used with *proportionate* rather than equal frequencies. However, although these proportions may vary with different sets of categories, in practice these variations have been so slight that in many cases he now assumes that the categories will be used for equal proportions of the total number of judgements.

In its earlier form the range-frequency model was concerned mainly with the middle limen of the response scale. If, as Helson and Volkmann assume, absolute judgement scales function as equal interval scales, then the judgement given to any one stimulus should be predictable from a knowledge of any single point on the scale, such as the middle limen, and of the width of any single scale category. Parducci, however, assumes that absolute judgement scales will be equal interval scales only under special circumstances, and for this reason has since extended his model to also predict the values of the category limens, that is, the boundaries between the various categories of the scale (Parducci, 1965). Again, his model meets with greater predictive success than Helson's or Volkmann's.

According to this interpretation, then, the mean of the stimulus distribution has no particular significance for predicting context effects in judgement, since *independent* variation of the mean has no effect. But where variation in the midpoint or median also involves variation in the mean, the mean will often lie fairly close to the centre of the judgement scale, and Helson's formula will thus meet with reasonable predictive success. This success, however, does not derive from the fact that judgemental adaptation represents the kind of averaging process postulated by Helson, but from the fact the mean is typically *equal* to both the midpoint and median for symmetrical distributions or *between* them for most skewed distributions. In other words, the mean is itself a kind of "compromise" between the midpoint and median in most of the studies which support Helson's theory. The judgement given to any particular stimulus in the series, moreover, will not be a simple linear function of its distance from the middle limen or AL, but will be determined by how the subject divides up the stimulus range and by the frequency with which he uses the various categories of the scale.

Of the three models considered in this chapter, therefore, Parducci's is the most successful in predicting how subjects will adjust their scales of judgement to the particular stimulus distribution with which they are presented. Although his prime concern seems to be merely with predicting, as opposed to explaining, judgemental behaviour, the principles which he invokes to do so suggest a view of judgement which has far more in common with Volkmann's approach than with Helson's. Whereas Helson seems happy to ascribe most, if not all, shifts in judgement to changes in the "state of the organism", both Volkmann and Parducci ascribe them essentially to an activity of the "discriminating person" who is faced with the task of sorting a series of stimuli into a number of categories.

The latter orientation, perhaps, has fewer of the trappings of a "grand theory" about it than AL theory. When applied to specific situations, however, it is by far the more economical in its assumptions and accurate in its predictions. The proportionate frequency principle allows one to predict the judged values of individual stimuli in a series in terms which do not depend critically on the validity of either Fechner's logarithmic law or Stevens' power law as descriptions of the relationship between physical intensity and psychological magnitude along the stimulus dimension employed. One does not have to affirm or deny the occurrence of true perceptual contrast in any specific instance, nor is any problem raised by the fact that subjects' judgements are influenced by their expectations concerning the stimuli with which they are to be presented.

Parducci's model thus corrects for the main shortcoming of the "rubber-band" model—its inability to account for the effects of inter-mediate stimuli—whilst reaffirming Volkmann's basic idea that extreme stimuli play a crucial role in defining the individual's frame of reference. It remains to be seen what conditions determine the relative importance in any specific instance of the range and frequency principles, that is the relative weightings of the midpoint and median as predictors of the centre of the judgement scale. None the less, the model is defined in a way that allows it to be generalized to situations where AL theory could only be extended by analogy.

3
Stimulus Distinctiveness and Stimulus Relevance

In the last chapter we concluded that probably the most reasonable way of looking at contrast effects in psychophysical judgement is to assume that subjects will tend to use the categories of their scale, as far as possible, with approximately equal frequencies, and to "anchor" the end categories of the scale to the extremes of the stimulus range. If this view is correct, one may then ask what it is that makes the stimulus extremes so important, and under what conditions this importance is enhanced or diminished.

One of the major arguments which Volkmann puts forward to justify his emphasis on the role of extreme stimuli is the fact that they are typically better discriminated than stimuli nearer the centre of the series. When a subject is in the process of working out how to adjust his scale to the particular stimuli with which he is presented, there is often considerable variability in his judgements of the stimuli between the two extremes, although the judged values of the extreme stimuli may remain relatively stable. In other words, Volkmann says:

> . . . it is primarily the *end-stimuli* that control the oscillations of the judgment scale. The center of the stimulus-range has no special functional significance whatever . . . We should not make the mistake of thinking that the operation of an absolute scale requires some implicit or averaged value equivalent in its effect to a standard stimulus. Indeed . . . the judgments are most variable (and consequently most likely to be in error) on the middle stimuli, exactly where an implicit standard might be located. Apparently it is not there.
>
> 1951, p. 283

According to Volkmann, then, each stimulus is judged in terms of its distance from the extremes and not from the centre of the series, since it is the extremes that constitute the more stable basis for comparison. This argument has been elaborated on by Eriksen and Hake (1957), who suggest that the subject in an absolute judgement experiment will tend to select some of the stimuli presented to him as standards against which to judge the other stimuli. Every time a stimulus is presented, he attempts to recall one of these "subjective standards" and to compare it with the stimulus he has to judge. They write:

> Essentially he transforms the task into a comparative judgment using the recalled value of the selected standard as the comparison stimulus. If it is assumed that subjects select the end stimuli to use as their subjective standards, the observed anchor effects [i.e. the relatively small number of errors made in judgements of the stimuli near the ends of the series] are the expected outcome. The frequent attempt to recall the value of the end stimuli should increase the accuracy of recognition of these stimuli when they do occur. Also the recognition accuracy of the other stimuli in the series should be directly related to the similarity of the standard and the comparison stimulus.
>
> p. 133

But there is at least one other way to account for the greater recognition accuracy of stimuli near the ends of the stimulus range. This is that recognition accuracy depends on the distinctiveness of a given stimulus —the extent to which it "stands out" from the other stimuli in the series. This is the view taken by Murdock (1960), who proposes that, with a series of stimuli which vary in magnitude, the distinctiveness of each stimulus depends on the difference between its magnitude and the magnitudes of all the other stimuli in the series. He states:

> Thus, with four stimuli, whose magnitudes were 2, 4, 6, and 8 units, the difference between the first stimulus and each of the other three would be 2, 4 and 6 respectively. The total distinctiveness would be the sum of these, or 12. Similarly, the distinctiveness of the second, third and fourth stimuli would be 8, 8 and 12 respectively. The total for the four stimuli would be 30%, 20%, 20% and 30% respectively. This, then, is basically the suggested procedure for quantifying the distinctiveness of stimuli.
>
> p. 17

Since Murdock assumed that the variability of absolute judgements is primarily a function of stimulus distinctiveness, he tested his measure of distinctiveness, $D\%$, by predicting the accuracy with which stimuli presented for absolute judgement can be identified. The more distinctive a stimulus is, the easier it should be to discriminate. "Therefore, if $D\%$ is valid it should predict performance in absolute judgement. So if for a given stimulus $D = 13\%$, then 13% of all correct identifications should occur to that particular stimulus." (1960, p. 18.) The results from a number of experiments he reports support these predictions.

Murdock calculates his measure of distinctiveness on the basis of differences in the psychological magnitudes, not the physical magnitudes, of the stimuli. In order to do this, he assumes a logarithmic relationship between the physical and psychological continua. Since Helson also assumes a logarithmic relationship, Murdock's predictions are essentially compatible with AL theory. In any series, the stimulus that will have the lowest value of $D\%$, i.e. the least distinctive stimulus, will be the one closest to the average of the psychological magnitudes of all the stimuli in the series. Since, however, the psychological magnitude of a stimulus is defined by Murdock as the logarithm of its physical magnitude, this "psychological average" will be equivalent to the logarithmic mean of the physical magnitudes of the stimuli; in other words, AL. This is consistent with Helson's assumption that stimuli near AL "either fail to elicit any response from the organism or bring forth responses that are indifferent, neutral, doubtful, equal or the like, depending on the context of stimulation" (1964, p. 128). Thus the further away a stimulus is from AL, the more distinctive it should be.

Thus we have two hypotheses to account for the fact that the variability of absolute judgements is higher for stimuli near the middle than the ends of a stimulus series. The first, Eriksen and Hake's "subjective standard" hypothesis, attributes better recognition of the end-stimuli to an activity which the subject undertakes in order to perform the judgement task more efficiently (which ties in with Volkmann's assumptions). Murdock's hypothesis, on the other hand, attributes this better recognition to the fact that the end-stimuli are more "distinctive" than the middle stimuli (which ties in with AL theory). For bipolar stimulus dimensions it is impossible to distinguish between these two points of view, at any rate at a general level. The stimuli which Eriksen and Hake predict that the subject will use as subjective standards will also be those which Murdock defines as being the most distinctive.

However, not all stimulus dimensions need necessarily be considered as bipolar. Colour hues, for example, may be thought of as an endless or circular continuum. As Eriksen and Hake point out: "By using a series of hues that vary from red through green, blue, and back to red again by varying through the purples, one can obtain a stimulus series that has no obvious breaks and no end points." (1957, p. 133.) They therefore selected 20 hues which were equally spaced on the Munsell system to form a circular continuum of this kind, and presented the series to two groups of subjects. Both groups were instructed to use the numbers 1 to

20 to identify the 20 colours, but differed in the response numbers attached to each stimulus. For one group, the extreme response numbers, 1 and 20, were in the red region of the continuum, whilst, for the other group, they were in the blue-green region. Eriksen and Hake predicted that "in the absence of obvious stimulus values to select as subjective standards, Ss would select their stimulus anchors in terms of the ends of the number series assigned them as responses" (p. 135). Thus, discrimination should be improved in and around the red region for the first group and the blue-green region for the second group.

Following a practice session in which they learned to use the response system, subjects each made a total of 20 judgements of each stimulus. Both groups showed the "anchor effects", or differences in discrimination, which Eriksen and Hake predicted, although these effects were somewhat confounded by differences in the discriminability of the hues as such. For one group, judgemental accuracy was highest for the colours which were assigned the responses 1 and 20. For the other group, the anchor effects were rather less marked but none the less quite apparent. The distributions of correct responses over the different colours were significantly different between the two groups. However, compared with the differences in judgemental accuracy between extreme and middle stimuli on ordinary bipolar dimensions, the improvement in the discriminability of the stimuli supposedly taken as subjective standards was relatively small. This suggests that, for ordinary stimulus dimensions, the distinctiveness of the end stimuli cannot be completely accounted for by the subjective standard hypothesis. Nevertheless, the finding that when an endless stimulus series is used subjects will make fewer errors in identifying stimuli to which they have been instructed to assign extreme *responses* can hardly be explained in terms of AL theory.

"Assimilation-contrast" in psychophysical judgement

Some findings which are difficult to reconcile with the "subjective standard" hypothesis—or almost any other theory for that matter—are the results of a study by Sherif *et al.* (1958). This study deserves particular attention in that it is supposed to validate the assumptions upon which they base their theory of social judgement, which we shall be considering later. Sherif *et al.* used a procedure in which an anchor stimulus (of constant magnitude for any given condition) was presented before each of the stimuli which the subjects had to judge. The subjects'

choice of which stimulus they should use as a standard was thus effectively made for them. The stimuli were six weights ranging from 55 to 141 g,
which the subjects had to judge in terms of a six-point scale. In the first
session, the series of weights was presented singly without any interpolated
anchor stimulus. Subjects were then given the following instructions:

> The stimuli will now be presented in pairs instead of singly. The first member of
> each pair will tell you what you are to call '6', the second you are to judge, as before,
> on the scale of 1 to 6. Tell me your judgment after the second member of each pair,
> even though at first you may not have an adequate basis for judgment.
>
> 1958, p. 151

There then followed nine sessions, in each of which a different anchor
stimulus was introduced. These ranged from 141 g to 347 g. It appears
that these were introduced in ascending order of magnitude for all
subjects, and that the effects of the value of the anchor were thus confounded with those of presentation order. Fortunately, this serious
methodological shortcoming does not appear to have biased the results,
since Parducci and Marshall (1962) obtained basically similar results
although they introduced the anchors in a random order. Sherif *et al.*
took as their dependent measure the mean of each subject's judgements
of the stimulus series in each of the experimental sessions. Compared
with the mean judgements obtained in the "no anchor" (i.e. the first)
condition, the mean judgements for eight of the nine anchor conditions
were shifted towards the "light" end of the scale; in other words, a
typical contrast effect was obtained. The exception was the condition in
which the weight of the anchor was 141 g, i.e. equal to the heaviest of the
series stimuli. In this condition, the mean judgements were "heavier"
than those in the "no anchor" condition, so that they showed a shift
towards and not away from the end at which the anchor stimulus was
introduced. Sherif *et al.* term this effect "assimilation". Two further
experiments showed some evidence for comparable assimilation effects
when anchors were introduced at the light extreme of the series. The
number of subjects used was six in the main experiment, and four and
three in the two subsequent experiments. Sherif *et al.* take these results as
supporting the following hypothesis:

> When an anchor is introduced at the end or slightly removed from the end of the
> series, there will be a displacement of the scale of judgment toward the anchor and
> assimilation of the new reference point in the series. When, however, the reference
> point is too remote there will be displacement in the opposite direction.
>
> 1958, p. 150

The contrast effects which they found in eight of the nine anchor conditions are typical of all experiments involving introduction of an anchor stimulus beyond the range of a stimulus series, such as, for example, the study by Postman and Miller (1945) described in Chapter 2. Expansion of the stimulus range requires expansion of the scale to incorporate the new stimulus, so judgements of the other stimuli are displaced towards the opposite end of the scale. The results of Sherif *et al.* are even less remarkable for these conditions, since, unlike Postman and Miller, they explicitly *instructed* their subjects to use the anchor to define the top category of their scale.

The "assimilation" effect found in the 141 g anchor condition is decidedly atypical of the kinds of context effects we have considered until now, and would seem incompatible with any of the three main theories of such effects: AL theory, the "rubber-band" model, and the range-frequency model. Nevertheless Parducci and Marshall (1962) have attempted to reconcile it with previous research by suggesting that it might be due to a central tendency effect. The term "central tendency effect" is used to describe the finding that when a standard is compared with a series of stimuli, the standard will be overestimated in recall if its value is markedly below the mean value of the other stimuli and underestimated if it is markedly above their mean value. Parducci and Marshall argue that since Sherif *et al.* always presented their weights in pairs and also told their subjects to use the anchor to define the top category, the subjects treated the task as one of comparative judgement, using the anchor as standard. In AL theory terms, this would mean that subjects would judge the stimuli not in terms of their distances from the series AL, but in terms of their distances from the point of subjective equality (PSE) of the anchor. However, because of the central tendency effect, the PSE or, in other words, the remembered value of the anchor should be underestimated, that is, seen as nearer to the mean of the other stimuli than it really is. This implies that the heaviest of the series stimuli should be seen as heavier than (the PSE of) the anchor, in the condition where the anchor is equal in weight to the heaviest of the series stimuli. "The anchoring conditions employed by Sherif *et al.* (1958) thus lower the value of the stimulus to which the 'heaviest' category is applied, and the entire scale of judgment is shifted down." (Parducci and Marshall, 1962, p. 427.) If this is correct, it explains the "assimilation" effect found by Sherif *et al.* in their 141 g anchor condition.

The occurrence of assimilation rather than contrast is thus seen by Parducci and Marshall (1962) as dependent on the subjects treating the task as one of comparative rather than absolute judgement, as a result of which the anchor stimulus no longer functions simply as just another stimulus but as a standard for comparison. Such an explanation, however, is not without problems of its own. The main difficulty consists in specifying the conditions under which the subject will come to treat the anchor in this way. Parducci and Marshall originally thought that it might have something to do with the particular instructions Sherif *et al.* gave to their subjects to use the anchor to define the top category of the scale. "Without verbal anchoring, the presentation of the 141-gm. weight . . . should produce contrast rather than assimilation." (Parducci and Marshall, 1962, p. 432.)

Parducci and Marshall therefore attempted a replication of the study Sherif *et al.*, varying the experimental instructions. With specific instructions to use the anchor as a standard, and also when judgements were made in terms of a comparative judgement scale, significant assimilation effects were obtained with the 141 g anchor. No assimilation effects were found for the 55 g anchor (equal to the lightest of the series stimuli), but this is interpreted as due to the operation of a negative time-order error. However, when the 141 g anchor was presented on alternate trials without any specific anchoring instructions, assimilation still occurred. To explain this last result, Parducci and Marshall invoke the notion of "self-anchoring". According to this notion subjects implicitly use the anchor as a standard for comparison, labelling it subjectively with the number of the category to which they would assign it, even without explicit instructions to do so. If they are correct, this would seem to apply to a large number of experimental situations. When the anchor is some distance beyond the end of the series, then the consequent expansion of the scale should result in contrast. When the anchor is equal to the extreme of the stimulus series, then, *if and when* a central tendency effect is operating, assimilation may result.

Although Parducci and Marshall view their study as an attempt to explain assimilation effects within a general AL theory approach, their results (like most of Parducci's other work) are more easily reconciled with Volkmann's general position than with Helson's. AL theory has difficulty in specifying when subjects will treat the anchor in this way, rather than simply judging each stimulus in terms of its distance from AL. Volkmann, on the other hand, would assume that subjects would *anyway* adopt the anchor as their standard, rather than the centre or AL of the stimulus series. The notion of "self-anchoring", in other words, is already implied in Volkmann's model, and also in Eriksen and Hake's (1957) "subjective standard" hypothesis.

The results of Sherif *et al.* (1958) and Parducci and Marshall (1962), however, still raise one difficulty for a "subjective standard" interpretation. It could be argued that, if Eriksen and Hake are right in assuming that subjects will anyway treat the extremes of the stimulus range as standards, then there should be no difference between the judgements given in the 141 g anchor condition and in the "no anchor" condition of either study. Or it could even be argued that there should have been differences in the opposite direction to those which in fact they found. In the "no anchor" condition, the 141 g stimulus occurred far less frequently than in the 141 g anchor condition, when it preceded each of the stimuli presented for judgement. The average time interval between presentation of the 141 g weight and any given stimulus in the series should thus have been longer in the "no anchor" than in the 141 g anchor condition. If the 141 g weight functioned as a standard in both conditions, therefore, it should have been even more affected by the central tendency in the "no anchor" condition.

Against this it could be argued that subjects in the 141 g anchor condition judged each stimulus only against a heavy "standard" stimulus, whereas in the "no anchor" condition Eriksen and Hake (1957) would predict that they would have used both the heavy and light extremes as "subjective standards". Thus, any effect on subjects' overall mean judgement of the stimulus series resulting from underestimation of the standard at the heavy end due to central tendency would, in the "no anchor" condition, be cancelled out by overestimation of the standard at the light end. If anchors were introduced at both the heavy and the light end of the scale simultaneously, therefore, no assimilation to either one extreme should occur. Volkmann in fact appears to have used exactly this kind of procedure in order to reduce the variability of subjects' judgements:

> If it is in fact the end-stimuli that control the principle properties of the absolute scale, it should be possible to intensify their effect. This we can do by presenting an auxiliary stimulus equal to the bottom judged stimulus, and by telling the subject that this stimulus is to represent the bottom category of his scale . . . The top category is anchored in a similar way, and we may call the whole procedure *end-anchoring*.
>
> 1951, p. 283

When this procedure is followed, "the width of the various absolute categories becomes drastically reduced: that is to say, the discrimination becomes finer".

It would seem, then, that assimilation, i.e. a shift in subjects' judgements of the series as a whole towards the anchor, may occur under conditions where (a) introduction of an anchor does not involve any noticeable extension of the stimulus range, (b) only one extreme of the series is adopted as a "subjective standard" by the judges, and (c) the stimulus dimension is one where a central tendency affect can be assumed to influence the remembered magnitude of any such "subjective standard".

In other conditions, it appears that subjects may adopt both extremes of the stimulus series as "subjective standards" with which to define the end categories of their scale. This effect may be enhanced by increasing the frequency with which these extreme stimuli are presented.

Classification and stimulus relevance

The work on subjective standards indicates that, in a general sense, judges may attach greater importance to certain stimuli in a series rather than others when adjusting their scale to the distribution of stimuli with which they are presented. The corollary of this is that, in more extreme circumstances, some stimuli may be treated as unimportant or irrelevant for the purposes of judgement. If this is so, then before we can determine the *effect* of any given stimulus, we must determine whether or not it will be seen as *relevant* by the subject. So far we have confined our attention to situations where the stimuli presented for judgement differ from one another in terms of a single attribute only. In the various experiments on lifted weights, for example, the stimuli used have differed *only* in weight, and not in shape or colour or any other attribute. They have all belonged obviously to the same class of objects; they have been identical in all aspects except the one in terms of which they have had to be discriminated.

But even if these other aspects had not been controlled, would it have made any difference? AL theory seems to imply that it would not. According to AL theory, the features of the stimuli that are relevant to how they are judged are merely those that contribute to AL, namely the magnitudes of the stimuli along the actual dimension being judged. Since the AL for any given stimulus dimension is assumed to represent the sensitivity of the organism to stimulation along that dimension, and since shifts in AL are assumed to represent changes in such sensitivity, the way in which any given stimulus is judged should be a function simply of the number of categories in the response scale and its own distance from AL. Any additional differences between the stimuli along dimensions other than the one being judged, therefore, should have no effect. If, for example, we have to judge the departure from squareness of a series of rectangles, then our judgements should not be influenced by, say, any differences in colour between the different stimuli, since such extraneous variation should have no effect on our AL for the particular dimension we are judging.

It should be pointed out that this is not the position which Helson himself adopts; but it is the position which seems to follow from the principles on which his theory is supposed to be based. Helson himself, however, makes the following point:

Stimuli are judged with respect to internal norms representing the pooled effects of present and past stimulation *in specified universes of discourse* [our italics]. Thus within classes (houses, dogs, men, automobiles) some members are large, some are medium, and some are small; and what is large in one class may be small compared with members of other classes.

1964, p. 126

Thus Helson would readily admit that, if we lift two objects of the same physical weight, we may judge one as light and one as heavy, if, for instance, one is an ash-tray and the other is a pipe. Helson would argue that we have different AL's for pipes and for ash-trays, since they belong to different classes of objects. The problem is seeing how this position can be reconciled with the view that our AL for judging weights, be they pipes of ash-trays, should represent our physiological sensitivity to weight *as such*. Furthermore, it immediately renders Tresselt's (1948) results inconsistent with AL theory. Any theory that assumes that judgements may be affected by such processes of stimulus classification *and* assumes that changes in judgement can be fully accounted for by changes in the sensitivity of the organism to stimulation, must also explain the relationship between sensitivity and such classification processes. Helson's (1964, p. 126) argument that a fountain-pen has only to weigh 4 oz to seem heavy, while a baseball bat has to weigh 40 oz "because in judging the pen only finger and hand muscles are involved, while in judging the bat these muscles plus those of the arms, shoulders, back and legs are involved", at least has its points of originality. (It implies, for instance, that if we had to pick a pen up off the floor it would seem lighter than if we picked it up off the table.) It seems to preclude, however, the possibility of any classification processes operating when the same muscular and/or sensory mechanisms are involved for both classes of stimuli. It cannot, for instance, explain findings such as those of Bevan and Pritchard (1963) with judgements of shape, who report that an anchor stimulus which significantly affected judgements of the stimulus series when it was the same colour as the other stimuli (black) had no effect at all when it was a different colour (grey). This is not a problem of which receptors become adapted; it is a problem of which stimuli are seen as relevant to the task of judgement and which are not.

The first systematic attempt to determine the role of stimulus relevance in judgement was that of Brown (1953), who took up a point mentioned by Johnson (1944), who observed that subjects in a lifted weights experiment might often move a chair or lift a book during rest periods between experimental sessions without this having any observable effect on their judgements of the stimulus weights in the actual task itself. Brown, therefore, attempted to see how far the influence of an anchor stimulus on judgements of lifted weights was a function of the distance of the anchor from the stimulus series, the similarity of the anchor to the other stimuli, and the instructions that accompanied the presentation of the anchor. The series stimuli were six cylindrical weights ranging from 80 to 144·17 g which subjects had to judge in terms of a five-point absolute scale. Subjects first underwent a control session in which the stimuli were presented without any anchor stimulus. They were then presented with the same weights, but with an anchor interpolated after every four stimulus weights. In half the conditions ("judged anchor" conditions), subjects were instructed to judge the anchor in the same way as the other stimuli. In the other ("unjudged anchor") conditions, subjects had to lift the anchor but not judge it. The weight of the anchor was either 144·17 g, 205·27 g or 292·23 g. For half the subjects (those in the "similar anchor" conditions) the anchor was also a cylindrical weight, identical in appearance to the other weights. For the others (those in the "dissimilar anchor" conditions), the anchor was in fact the tray on which the stimulus weights were passed to the subject, though identical in weight to the "similar anchors".

In the "dissimilar judged anchor" conditions, subjects were instructed as follows:

After judging the fourth object, please lift the tray and judge it just as you did the other objects.

In the "dissimilar unjudged anchor" conditions, however, subjects were told:

After the fourth object, please lift the tray by the knob and put it on the card where the objects were placed in order to make it easier for me to remove and re-present the tray to you with four more objects.

The instructions for the "similar unjudged anchor" conditions were far simpler, subjects merely being told "don't judge" as they lifted each anchor. These manipulations resulted in 12 conditions, with six subjects in each, comprising a $3 \times 2 \times 2$ factorial design.

Brown hypothesized that the amount of shift produced by the anchors would be greatest for the "similar judged anchors", next greatest for the "similar unjudged anchors", then for "dissimilar judged anchors" and least for the "dissimilar unjudged anchors". The data confirmed these predictions, although the influence of the dissimilar anchors (the trays) seems to have been partly vitiated by a size–weight illusion. None the less, Brown was able to conclude: "The anchor, to be effective, must be perceived as a member of the same class of objects as the other weights ..." (1953, p. 210.)

Unfortunately, Brown did not perform a special analysis to compare the "dissimilar anchor" conditions with the "no anchor" condition. The graphs he presents suggest no differences between the "no anchor" and "dissimilar unjudged anchor" conditions, although there seems to have been a slight effect in the "dissimilar judged anchor" conditions. Apparently, when a stimulus has to be judged on the same scale as the other stimuli, it is more difficult for subjects to dismiss it as completely irrelevant, even if it looks very different from the others.

While Brown's (1953) experiment was only designed to investigate the question of whether or not an anchor has to be of "the same class of objects" as the other stimuli in order to affect judgement, Bevan and Pritchard (1963) attempted to see how far such effects were a function of the *kind* of similarity between the anchor and the other stimuli. They used a stimulus series consisting of a square (5·0 cm $\times$ 5·0 cm) and three rectangles (4·8 cm $\times$ 5·2 cm; 4·6 cm $\times$ 5·4 cm; 4·4 cm $\times$ 5·6 cm). All figures were made of black cardboard mounted on white cardboard. The stimuli were presented tachistoscopically at 10-second intervals for $\frac{1}{2}$ second each and were rated in terms of departure from squareness in terms of a seven-point scale, to which subjects were told that they could add further categories if they wished. In the first of their experiments, ratings of these stimuli in a "no anchor" condition were compared with ratings of the same stimuli after a rectangular anchor stimulus (4·0 cm × 6·0 cm) had been introduced. As in all subsequent anchor conditions, this stimulus was presented on every third trial and was rated in the same way as the other stimuli. The introduction of the rectangular anchor produced a significant contrast effect on the mean judgements of the other stimuli, which were rated as "squarer" in the "anchor" than in the "no anchor" condition.

After they had demonstrated in this way that an anchor which was similar in shape, size and colour to the series stimuli had a significant effect on judgement, Bevan and Pritchard (1963) introduced two new anchors that resembled the series stimuli in size and colour but differed in shape. These two anchors were a circle (5·0 cm diameter) and an ellipse (4·0 cm × 6·0 cm). Neither of these anchors produced any shift in judgement. These results led Bevan and Pritchard to a conclusion very similar to Brown's, namely:

> At least in the case of the dimension selected for study, the anchor-designate must be identified as a member of the same class of stimuli as the series member when the criterion is the dimension for which judgments are called. Relevance of the anchor-designate thus is defined by membership in the class of judged objects. When the critical dimension is departure from squareness, the anchor must have the basic property of phenomenally square objects, i.e. rectangularity.

> 1963, p. 59

In three further experiments reported in the same paper, Bevan and Pritchard (1963) went on to demonstrate that even similarity in the criterial attribute of shape may not be enough to make the anchor appear relevant and hence affect judgements of the other stimuli. They used three additional anchors which retained the same height-by-length ratio as the anchor which had proved so effective in the first experiment, but varied the size and colour. The first was a small rectangle, one quarter of the area of the original anchor; the second was a large rectangle, four times the area of the original; and the third was identical in size and shape to the original, but made of grey instead of black cardboard. In none of these three conditions did the mean judgement of the stimulus series differ significantly from that obtained in the "no anchor" condition, although the large rectangle produced a slight but significant ($p < 0.05$) difference in the slope of the judgemental function, as compared with the control condition. These results are particularly striking if one considers that the anchors were judged on the same scale as the series stimuli, and that the average rating each of these anchors obtained in terms of the scale did not differ significantly from the average rating of the anchor stimulus used in the first experiment.

Therefore Brown's (1953) and Bevan and Pritchard's (1963) studies both demonstrate that, for an anchor to be effective, it must be similar to the series stimuli not only in terms of the actual stimulus attribute being judged, but also in terms of most other attributes as well. In both these studies it was argued that, with increasing dissimilarity between the anchor and series stimuli, subjects should cease to regard the anchor as belonging to the same class of objects as the series stimuli and hence should no longer see it as relevant. If, however, the relevance of the anchor depends upon its perceived class-membership, rather than upon the degree of its similarity to the other stimuli as such, then this would seem to imply that relevance–irrelevance should perhaps be thought of more as a dichotomy than as two poles of a continuum. In its crudest form the argument would be that either the anchor is seen as a member of the same class of objects as the series stimuli or it is not; hence, either it is seen as relevant or it is seen as irrelevant. In practice, of course, things may be rather more complex. There may well be differences depending on whether the "dissimilar" anchor can be defined by inclusion as a member of a separate stimulus class, or merely defined by exclusion as *not* a member of the same class as the series stimuli. Furthermore, class boundaries may overlap or be uncertainly defined, and there may therefore be occasions when the anchor is seen as neither completely irrelevant nor perfectly relevant. None the less, the possibility of some kind of discontinuity cannot be completely ruled out.

If this assumption is correct, the effectiveness of an anchor should not decrease monotonically with decreasing similarity between itself and the series stimuli. Instead, there should be a critical point of dissimilarity up to which the anchor should exert more or less its full effect, but beyond which it should completely lose its influence. Brown's (1953) and Bevan and Pritchard's (1963) findings that dissimilar anchors produced no more than negligible effects would appear to provide some support for such an interpretation. Both studies, however, compared only similar and very dissimilar anchors, rather than varying the degree of similarity continuously from complete similarity to extreme dissimilarity.

A study by Pritchard and Bevan (1966) goes some way towards meeting this point. As in the Bevan and Pritchard (1963) study, subjects had to judge squares and rectangles in terms of departure from squareness. The stimulus series was identical to that used in the previous study. In addition they used nine anchor stimuli, all more rectangular than any of the series stimuli and all with identical height-by-length ratios. Whereas the area of the series stimuli was approximately 25 cm², however, the anchors varied in area from 6 cm² to 96 cm². A trend analysis conducted on the mean judgements of the series stimuli in the anchor conditions indicated that only the quadratic component was significant ($p < 0.001$). In other words, the results suggest a curvilinear relationship between the size of the anchor and its effectiveness, with the greatest shifts in judgement occurring for the anchor of the same area as the series stimuli. If one looks at the effects for the moderately and extremely dissimilar anchors, moreover, there are no conditions in which the mean judgement of the series stimuli are significantly different from *both* the mean judgements in the "no anchor" condition *and* the mean judgements in the "similar anchor" condition where the anchor was of the same area as the other stimuli. Where the anchors are very large or very small, the mean judgements do not differ significantly from those in the "no anchor" condition. Where the anchors are less dissimilar, the mean judgements are hardly any different from those obtained in the "similar" anchor condition. Thus these results are not inconsistent with the possibility that relevance–irrelevance may operate as a discontinuous rather than as a continuous variable, although the evidence on this particular point is by no means conclusive.

One point, however, is quite clear. Mere exposure to a given stimulus is not enough for that stimulus to affect how the subject will define the categories of his judgement scale, at least so long as no gross changes in sensory adaptation are involved. Instead, the stimulus must be seen by the subject as relevant to the other stimuli which he has to judge. We have argued that AL theory fails to deal with this problem satisfactorily. Obviously we have or can develop different standards or frames of reference for judging pipes, pens, bats and so on for as many distinct classes of objects as we please, but it is far from obvious how this can be reconciled with the assumptions underlying AL theory.

On the other hand, the two "range models", namely the rubber-band model and the range-frequency compromise, make no specific assumptions about what stimuli are or are not to be included within an individual's frame of reference at any point in time. Thus there is no basic incompatibility between these models and the finding that judgements are affected only by those stimuli which the individual regards as relevant. The very notion of "the end-points of the stimulus range" seems to imply boundaries and the exclusion of extraneous stimuli in a way that the notion of "the pooled effect of past and present stimulation" does not. One could easily, therefore, incorporate into the models principles that would allow us to determine exactly when a stimulus will be seen as relevant and when it will not. Unfortunately, the evidence so far tells us only that some principles are operating; it does not tell us exactly what these principles are.

4

The Effects of Incidental Stimulus Variation on Absolute Judgements

One of the major differences between the kind of stimuli typically presented to subjects in psychophysical experiments and the kind of objects we encounter in everyday life is that the former are made to differ from one another in terms of a single attribute only, such as weight, whereas the latter differ from one another usually in terms of a very large number of attributes such as colour, shape, texture, etc. For most of the questions with which psychophysics is concerned, this type of control is of course quite crucial. As early as 1860 we find Fechner (p. 97) mentioning that he had had to discard the results of one year's experimenting with lifted weights when he discovered that some stimuli of the same size and weight had been judged differently from one another because of differences in the positions of their centre of gravity. Obviously, if one is concerned with such questions as the relationship between differences in weight and differences in apparent heaviness, one must use stimuli which can only be discriminated from one another in terms of weight and no other physical characteristic.

In social judgement experiments, however, where we are concerned with such questions as how we categorize other people and the opinions which they express, it is impossible to construct anything comparable in the way of a series of stimuli varying along only one dimension. We may collect a set of statements which differ from one another in, say, the extent to which they support or oppose a given type of policy or viewpoint, but these same statements will almost certainly also differ from each other in terms of such aspects as the number of words they use, the degree of abstractness or concreteness of the ideas which they express, their acceptability or unacceptability to the person who has to judge them, and so on. Hence if we wish to make any valid comparison between social and psychophysical judgement, we cannot restrict our attention to those principles that account for how people judge stimuli which vary along only one dimension. We must see how people categorize stimuli which vary in terms of many attributes simultaneously.

Let us therefore draw a distinction between what may be termed the *focal* and the *peripheral* attributes of a stimulus. The focal attribute may be defined, quite simply, as that attribute which the subject is required to judge. All other attributes of the stimulus are peripheral. Thus, with Fechner's weights, the focal attribute of each stimulus is its weight; other attributes, such as its shape, temperature, centre of gravity, etc. are all peripheral. As Fechner discovered, incidental variation among the stimuli in terms of such peripheral attributes or dimensions may distort how the stimuli are judged along the focal dimension. But our concern is not with these distortions as such. In themselves they are, as far as we know, effects which are specific to the sensory domain investigated and are not necessarily generalizable to judgements of other kinds of stimuli. Instead we are interested in the kinds of effects which occur when *changes* in the focal attribute are accompanied by *changes* in a peripheral attribute, regardless of what precisely these attributes may be.

As we saw in the last chapter, studies on stimulus relevance show that one stimulus may be regarded by subjects as irrelevant to the other stimuli which they are judging, even when it is similar to them in terms of the focal attribute, if it is markedly different from the others in terms of its peripheral attributes. But suppose instead that *all* the stimuli presented for judgement differ from each other in terms of both focal and peripheral attributes, as in the case with most of the objects we have to distinguish between in everyday life. How, in such cases, are judgements of stimuli along the focal dimension affected by their relative positions along the peripheral dimensions?

In considering this question, it is useful to distinguish between cases where such incidental variation along a peripheral dimension is *correlated* with variation along the focal dimension, and cases where it is *uncorrelated*. For any given series of stimuli, incidental stimulus variation may be said to be *correlated* if there is a consistent and predictable relationship between differences in the stimulus values along the focal dimension and differences along the peripheral dimension. If, on the other hand, there is no consistent and predictable relationship between differences on the peripheral dimension and differences on the focal dimension, this would be a case of *uncorrelated* incidental stimulus variation. To take a simple example, cars differ from one another in terms of size, colour and price. The size and price of cars are two attributes which are reasonably well correlated with each other: bigger cars, on average, tend to be more expensive than smaller cars. If we hear that two people, Tom and Jim, have both bought cars, and Tom's car is bigger than Jim's, we will be more likely to be right than wrong if we predict Tom's to be the more expensive. On the other hand, since there is no stable and predictable relationship between the price of cars and their colour, nor between their colour and their size, if all we knew was that Tom's car was red and Jim's was blue, we could only guess which was the larger or more expensive.

It will be noticed that since this distinction depends only on whether or not the values of the stimuli on one dimension are correlated with their values on another dimension, it does not matter which dimension we make focal and which peripheral. It does not matter, in other words, whether we try and predict the price of cars on the basis of their size, or their size on the basis of their price, so long as either prediction is possible. Similarly, since this definition is concerned only with the *relationship* between different stimulus dimensions, it does not matter what the specific stimulus dimensions are, so long as each provides a possible basis for discriminating between the stimuli in question, whatever these may be. It is a distinction, therefore, which is applicable both to psychophysical and social judgement, both inside and outside the laboratory.

The evidence we shall discuss in this chapter is basically concerned with the kinds of judgemental effects that occur as the result of correlated as opposed to uncorrelated incidental stimulus variation. As with the other kinds of judgemental effects we have considered so far, most of the evidence comes from judgements of stimuli varying along physical dimensions such as size and weight. However, just as the notion of incidental stimulus variation applies to both social and psychophysical stimuli, so, as we intend to argue in later chapters, the principles that account for the effects of such variation may be profitably extended to the study of social judgement.

Accentuation theory

Whereas the models we described in Chapter 2 were all concerned with the judgemental effects that arise as a function of the relationships between stimuli on the focal dimension only, another approach which may be called "accentuation theory" is concerned specifically with the effects of incidental stimulus variation on judgement. The basic assumptions of this approach are set out in a paper by Tajfel (1959a), who argues that when a series of stimuli varies concurrently along two or more dimensions, this should affect the ability of subjects to discriminate between stimuli on the focal dimension. When stimulus differences along two dimensions are highly correlated, the difference between two stimuli on one dimension is a good predictor of the difference between those stimuli on the other dimension. Therefore the additional or "superimposed" differences on the peripheral dimension should increase the discriminability of the stimuli along the focal dimension. Tajfel proposes that this improvement in discrimination, which occurs when there is a correlation between focal and peripheral stimulus variation, should lead to an *accentuation of the judged differences* between the stimuli on the focal dimension. As a consequence of this accentuation, the stimuli at the lower end of the series should be underestimated and those at the upper end overestimated.

To take a hypothetical example, suppose we ask subjects to judge the lengths of one of two series of lines. The lengths of the lines in the two series, I and II, are identical, but, whereas all the lines in series I are drawn in the same ink, the lines in series II are drawn in inks of various shades, so that the longer the line, the lighter is its shade, thus constituting a condition of correlated peripheral stimulus variation. It would seem reasonably obvious that subjects judging series II have an easier task than those judging series I. As soon as they have realized that there is a stable and predictable relationship between length and shade, they have *two* cues on the basis of which to discriminate between the stimuli, whereas subjects judging series I have only *one* cue, that of length. According to Tajfel's model, the differences between consecutive line lengths in series II should therefore be judged as greater than the corresponding differences in series I. Furthermore, as compared with judgements of the corresponding lines in series I, the length of the shorter lines in series II should be underestimated and the length of the longer lines overestimated. If, however, we added a third series, where the lines also varied both in length and shade, but where length and shade were *uncorrelated*, then differences in shade would not be predictive of differences in length and so, according to Tajfel, no accentuation effects should occur.

Since such accentuation effects are considered to be a function of the *correlation* between stimulus differences on the focal and peripheral dimensions, it should not matter crucially what types of dimensions are used. In fact, Tajfel (1957) first formulated his model as an attempt to account for the effects of value on judgements of physical magnitude, in particular judgements of the size of coins. Tajfel (1957) argued that since coins vary concurrently in both value and size, more valuable coins being generally larger than less valuable ones, an accentuation theory approach could explain the results of a number of studies (e.g. Bruner and Goodman, 1947; Bruner and Rodrigues, 1957) which found that subjects overestimated the size of coins—especially larger ones. At the same time, he was able to explain why value did *not* affect judgements of physical magnitude in a number of studies employing stimuli whose values were uncorrelated with their physical magnitudes. We shall return to this application of Tajfel's theory later.

So far we have only considered situations where variation along the peripheral dimension has been continuous, that is where the number of stimulus gradations on the peripheral dimension has been equal to the number of stimulus gradations on the focal dimension. Coins of different sizes, for example, are also of different values. Such continuous variation, however, is by no means a prerequisite for the occurrence of accentuation effects. Accentuation theory can also be applied to cases where the number of gradations on the focal dimension exceeds the number of gradations on the peripheral dimension, i.e. where the various stimuli may be thought of as falling into distinct *classes* on the basis of some peripheral attribute. In such cases, the peripheral stimulus variation may be said to constitute a *classification* superimposed on the stimulus series. As with other cases of incidental stimulus variation, superimposed classifications can be either correlated or uncorrelated. An example of a correlated classification would be one where a series of lines to be judged in terms of length varied also in colour, so that the longer half of the series were all drawn in red and the shorter half in blue. An uncorrelated classification would be one where the lines were either red or blue, but where there was no difference between the average lengths of the red and blue lines.

In his discussion of the effects of superimposed classifications, Tajfel

(1959a) restricts himself to the case of dichotomous classifications, but his predictions should apply equally well to situations with more than two classes. Against the crucial distinction is that between correlated and uncorrelated incidental stimulus variation. Specifically, he suggests:

> When a classification in terms of an attribute other than the physical dimension which is being judged is superimposed on a series of stimuli in such a way that one part of the physical series tends to fall consistently into one class, and the other into the other class, judgements of physical magnitude of the stimuli falling into the distinct classes will show a shift in the direction determined by the class membership of the stimuli, when compared with judgements of a series identical with respect to this physical dimension, on which such a classification is not superimposed. When a classification in terms of an attribute other than the physical dimension which is being judged is superimposed on a series of stimuli, and the changes in the physical magnitudes of the stimuli bear no consistent relationship to the assignment of the stimuli to the distinct classes, this classification will have no effect on the judged relationships in the physical dimension between the stimuli of the series.
>
> pp. 20–21

It is interesting to note that, as stated above, Tajfel's (1959a) hypothesis predicts merely that, when a correlated classification is superimposed on a stimulus series, this will lead to an increase in the judged differences *between* the two classes of stimuli, or, as Tajfel puts it, to an accentuation of *interclass* differences. No specific predictions follow from this hypothesis regarding the differences between the stimuli *within* each class, i.e. the *intraclass* differences.

To make these predictions clearer, let us suppose that subjects have to judge one of two series of eight weights. The two series are identical in terms of weight, but in one of the series the four heaviest weights are all painted red and the four lightest all painted blue, whereas in the other series, although four weights are red and four are blue, there is no relationship between their colour and their weight. If we now consider the mean judgements for each of the stimuli in both of the series, Tajfel's (1959a) hypothesis implies that the judged differences between stimuli 1 and 2, 2 and 3, 3 and 4, and those between 5 and 6, 6 and 7, and 7 and 8 should be the same whether the superimposed classification is correlated or uncorrelated. The presence of the correlated classification should alter only the judged difference between stimuli 4 and 5, that is those at the class boundaries. This interval should be seen as greater in the first series than in the second, whilst the other intervals remain unaffected. In *relative* terms, therefore, the difference between the stimuli at the class boundaries should be exaggerated in comparison to the other differences.

More recently Tajfel and Wilkes (1963) predicted that the presence of a correlated superimposed classification should lead both to an accentuation of *interclass* differences, and to a reduction of *intraclass* differences. Thus, in our example above, not only should the differences between stimuli 4 and 5 be accentuated, but the differences between all the other pairs of adjacent stimuli should be reduced in the series where the colour of the stimuli was consistently related to their weight as compared with the other randomly classified series. In other words, whereas in the earlier statement of the theory Tajfel (1959a) predicts only that stimuli which are *different* in terms of some peripheral attribute are judged as more different in terms of the focal attribute (if focal and peripheral differences are correlated), Tajfel and Wilkes (1963) predict also that stimuli which are *similar* in terms of such a peripheral attribute will be judged as more similar.

The strength of the effects resulting from correlated incidental stimulus variation may depend upon a number of factors. With stimuli that vary concurrently on two dimensions, the extent to which judgements of the stimuli in terms of one attribute are influenced by differences between the stimuli in terms of the other attribute might be predicted to be partly a function of the ease with which the stimuli could be discriminated on each dimension. For stimuli varying along only one dimension, the major factor determining the discriminability of the stimuli is the distance between them on the focal dimension of judgement. For stimuli varying concurrently on two dimensions, the discriminability of the stimuli on the peripheral dimension might be assumed in some sense to supplement the discriminability of the stimuli on the focal dimension if the two dimensions are correlated. It is reasonable to suppose, therefore, that accentuation effects should occur only when the stimuli are at least as discriminable on the peripheral dimension as they are on the focal dimension. If discriminations on the focal dimension can be made with much greater ease than discriminations on the peripheral dimension, the additional cues provided by correlated peripheral variation might not be particularly helpful to subjects making judgements of the focal stimulus attribute. Within these limits, however, the following should be true:

1. With constant discriminability of the stimuli on the peripheral dimension, accentuation effects should increase as the discriminability

of the stimuli on the focal dimension decreases. The same incidental stimulus variation should lead to stronger accentuation effects when superimposed on a series of stimuli with low focal discriminability than when superimposed on a stimulus series with high focal discriminability. With low focal discriminability, the correlated incidental variation should be treated by subjects as a more important cue than when focal discriminability is high. However, this should only be true up to the point where focal discriminability is so low that subjects can no longer see the relationship between focal and peripheral variation.

2. With constant discriminability of the stimuli on the focal dimension, accentuation effects should increase as the discriminability of the stimuli on the peripheral dimension increases.

This last prediction has important consequences for social judgement situations, where what we may wish to call the "peripheral dimension" may not be any single "objective" attribute of the stimuli as such, but may depend on subjects' own evaluative reactions to the objects of judgement—reactions which may vary in their distinctiveness from individual to individual.

The effects of superimposed classifications

The most convincing support for Tajfel's theory comes from studies concerned with the effects of superimposed classifications on judgements of physical magnitude. When a correlated classification is superimposed on a physical series, "the class identification of a stimulus provides a supplementary source of information about the relationship of its magnitude to the magnitude of the other stimuli, whether identified as belonging to the same class or to a different class" (Tajfel and Wilkes, 1963, p. 103). Thus the presence of such a classification should lead to firstly an exaggeration of the judged differences between stimuli falling into different classes (accentuation of interclass differences) and secondly a minimization of the judged differences among the stimuli within any single class (reduction of intraclass differences).

To test these hypotheses, Tajfel and Wilkes (1963) had subjects estimate (in centimetres) the lengths of eight lines ranging in 5 per cent increments from 16·2 cm to 22·9 cm. The main experimental manipulation was concerned with the effects of different superimposed classifications on these estimates. In the experimental condition a classification was superimposed in such a way that there was a stable and

c

predictable relationship between the lengths of the lines and their class membership. This was achieved by having each of the shorter four lines labelled with a large A drawn above its centre, whilst each of the four longer lines was labelled with a large B. (For half of the subjects in the experimental group the labelling was reversed, i.e. the short lines were labelled B and the long lines A.) To test whether the presence of these labels would have any effect on subjects' estimates in the absence of any correlation between the labels and the line lengths, one control group was presented with a randomly classified series in which the lines were again labelled either A or B, but where this labelling bore no relationship to the length of the lines. Each of the lines was labelled A in half the presentations and B in the other half. A second control group judged the lines without any labels.

The main results indicated a sharp increase in the interclass differences for the experimental group as compared with the two control groups. This was tested by means of an analysis of variance performed on the judged differences between stimuli 4 and 5, i.e. the stimuli at the boundaries of the two classes in the experimental series. This indicated that these differences were significantly larger in the experimental group than in the control groups, whereas the two control groups did not differ significantly. An analysis of the intraclass differences suggested a tendency for the stimuli within each class to be judged as more similar in the experimental group than in the control groups, but this failed to reach significance. Tajfel and Wilkes (1963) thus succeeded in demonstrating the accentuation of interclass differences, but failed to show any unequivocal evidence of a reduction of intraclass differences.

Two experiments, by Marchand (1970) and Lilli (1970), essentially corroborate these results. Marchand had subjects estimate the lengths of the base lines of eight squares under correlated and random (uncorrelated) classification conditions. She found that when the four smaller squares fell into one class and the four larger squares into another class, an accentuation of interclass differences occurred as compared with when the squares were randomly classified. She did not specifically test for a reduction of intraclass differences in the correlated classification condition, but her data show no evidence of such a tendency. Similar results were reported by Lilli (1970) who conducted several studies using as stimuli either the Tajfel and Wilkes (1963) lines, or schematic drawings of faces from which subjects had to estimate the height of the foreheads. Again, significant increases in interclass differences were reported, but no decrease in intraclass differences. Lilli's (1970) experiment is especially interesting because he also manipulated the consistency of the relationship between the classification and the focal stimulus magnitudes. Whereas the Tajfel and Wilkes (1963) and Marchand (1970) studies employed classifications with either perfect or zero correlations with the focal magnitudes, Lilli also used classifications with intermediate degrees of correlation. He found that as the degree of correlation between the classification and the focal stimulus magnitudes was decreased, the magnitude of the interclass accentuation effects diminished very rapidly. This last result is not all that surprising in view of the stimulus materials used. With unambiguous stimuli such as those he employed, any inconsistency in the relationship between the classification and the focal stimulus magnitudes would be likely to be detected immediately by the subjects, who might, as a result, immediately come to doubt the predictive properties of the classification. With more ambiguous stimuli, once the classification has been learned, subjects might be more likely to overlook inconsistencies, with the result that any increase in the inconsistency of the classification should lead to a more gradual decrease in the size of the accentuation effects.

The results of the experiments by Lilli (1970), Marchand (1970) and Tajfel and Wilkes (1963) thus provide qualified support for Tajfel's hypotheses. Whilst his predictions regarding the accentuation of interclass differences are supported in all three studies, his predictions regarding the decrease of intraclass differences receive only very tentative support in the Tajfel and Wilkes (1963) experiment, and no support at all in Lilli's (1970) and Marchand's (1970) experiments. Thus, while the presence of a correlated classification superimposed on a series of stimuli may lead to stimuli which are different in terms of the peripheral attribute being judged as more different in terms of the focal attribute, stimuli which are similar in terms of the peripheral attribute are not necessarily judged as more similar in terms of the focal attribute.

Although none of these studies, therefore, substantiates the prediction of a reduction of intraclass differences, some tentative support for this prediction comes from a study of the effects of stereotyping on person perception. Stereotyping in this context may be defined as the "action of assigning attributes to a person solely on the basis of the class or category to which he belongs" (Secord and Backman, 1964, p. 67). In the majority of studies on stereotyping, subjects have generally been required to make judgements of the personality etc. of other individuals on the basis of extremely minimal information. Typical of such studies are those in which subjects are required to make such judgements from photographs of people who are identifiable as belonging to particular ethnic groups (e.g. Secord, 1959; Secord *et al.*, 1956). Under such conditions of minimal information, there is typically a failure, at least among more prejudiced subjects, to distinguish between different stimulus persons belonging to a stereotyped group.

A somewhat more interesting question is whether such processes are still effective when subjects are actually confronted with the people they have to judge. If stereotyping is viewed within the framework of accentuation theory, it should apply to such situations also. If two stimulus persons are identified as belonging to different ethnic groups, and these groups are assumed to differ in terms of some personality characteristic by the subjects, then knowledge of the ethnic identity of the stimulus persons should be equivalent in its effect to a correlated superimposed classification on how they are rated on that personality characteristic. If, however, they have to be rated on a personality characteristic with regard to which the two groups are not assumed to differ, then knowledge of their ethnic identity should be equivalent in its effect to an uncorrelated superimposed classification, and should thus have no effect on subjects' judgements. It should be noted, of course, that such classifications, whether their basis be ethnic or any- thing else, do not need to be *actually* correlated with the personality trait in question for accentuation effects to occur. All that is necessary is that subjects should *believe* there is a difference in terms of the character- istic they are judging. Ethnic identity can therefore function as a correlated classification in the case of certain characteristics, which form part of the stereotype of either group, and also as an uncorrelated classification in the case of characteristics which do not form part of the stereotype.

Tajfel *et al.* (1964), therefore, attempted to see whether people belonging to the same ethnic group would be judged as more similar to each other on dimensions which formed part of the stereotype of their group than on dimensions which did not form part of the stereotype. Subjects in this experiment had to rate two Indians and two Canadians on a number of bipolar rating scales. Each of the four stimulus persons was rated by the subjects immediately after he had been interviewed in front of them for approximately eight minutes. The authors predicted that the two Indians would be rated as more similar to each other on traits which formed part of the Indian stereotype than on traits which were unrelated to the stereotype. Similarly, the two Canadians were predicted to be seen as more similar to each other in terms of traits which formed part of the Canadian stereotype than on unrelated traits. Separate analyses conducted on the ratings given to the Indians and Canadians confirmed these predictions. Tajfel *et al.* (1964) conclude that their findings present evidence for a "minimization of the differences between members of an ethnic group on traits which subjectively characterize that group" (p. 199).

A possible criticism of this experiment is that the design does not allow one to eliminate the alternative possibility that the people being judged were *in fact* more similar as far as the relevant traits were concerned—in other words, that the stereotypes were accurate at least for the particular people being judged. To adopt this explanation, however, one would not only have to assume that the people were more similar in terms of the relevant traits, but that subjects were able to detect this similarity during an eight-minute interview in which the interviewees were asked mainly about what kinds of books or films they liked. The interpretation of these findings which Tajfel *et al.* offer in terms of a minimization of intraclass differences would clearly seem to be the more plausible. If they are correct, however, this raises the question of why no such minimization was found in the experiments using estimates of line length (Tajfel and Wilkes, 1963; Lilli, 1970; Marchand, 1970). There are so many differences between the two situations that any answer to this question must necessarily be extremely tentative. The extreme indeterminacy of the positions of each of the four stimulus persons on the various dimensions, combined with a highly discriminable classification, may have contributed to the reduction of intraclass differences which Tajfel *et al.* (1964) found. This would imply that one might expect a reduction of intraclass differences only under conditions of low focal and high peripheral discriminability, but that one might still expect an accentuation of interclass differences under conditions where the proportion of peripheral to focal discriminability was too low for a reduction of intraclass differences to occur.

The effects of value on judgements of physical magnitude

One of the best documented areas of research concerned with the

effects of incidental stimulus variation is that concerned with the judgement of physical objects which carry some kind of "value" or emotional
significance for the people who judge them. In terms of the distinction
we have adopted in this chapter, the problem is one of how variation
in the peripheral attribute of value may influence subjects' judgements
along the focal dimension of physical magnitude. But before discussing
how accentuation theory may be applied to this question a brief review
of some of the relevant research might be helpful.

Most of the early work in this area was concerned with testing a
number of hypotheses first formulated by Bruner and Goodman (1947),
who proposed that the size of a valued object should be overestimated in
relation to the size of a value-neutral object of identical physical dimensions; and that this overestimation should be greater, the greater the
difference in value between the two objects. To test these hypotheses,
they compared size judgements of coins with size judgements of cardboard discs of the same diameter. The 10-year-old children who served
as subjects were instructed to adjust the size of a circular spot of light so
that its area appeared equal to that of a disc or coin which they were
given to hold in their hands. They made this adjustment by turning a
knob on a box which controlled the area of a light spot projected from
behind a ground-glass screen. In this way, the experimental group
estimated the size of coins of various denominations (1 ¢, 5 ¢, 10 ¢,
25 ¢ and 50 ¢), while the control group estimated the size of grey cardboard discs of identical diameter to the coins. The results showed that
the children tended to overestimate the size of the coins as compared
with the cardboard discs, and that this overestimation was more marked
in the case of the higher as opposed to the lower value coins.

Carter and Schooler (1949) replicated the Bruner and Goodman
(1947) study with some minor alterations in procedure. They used a
somewhat modified apparatus to produce the circular light spot and
they asked their control group to judge valueless metal discs as well as
cardboard discs. A comparison of the coin judgements with the judgements of the metal and cardboard discs showed that the 25 ¢ and 50 ¢
coins were significantly overestimated relative to the corresponding
cardboard discs, but only the 50 ¢ coin was significantly overestimated
relative to the corresponding metal disc. A replication of this study by
Bruner and Rodrigues (1953), using only 1 ¢, 5 ¢ and 25 ¢ coins, found
that all three coins were overestimated relative to the cardboard discs,
though not significantly so in the case of the 1 ¢ coin. No overestima-

tion occurred, however, relative to the corresponding metal discs.

A possible conclusion one might draw from these results is that the actual value of the coins was unimportant, and that the observed effects were simply due to some factor which made metal discs appear to be of greater size than cardboard discs. Nevertheless, this conclusion, which Bruner and Rodrigues seem to favour, would not explain the over-estimation found by Carter and Schooler (1949) with the 50 ¢ coin which was not included in the Bruner and Rodrigues (1953) study. It is possible that the differences found with the 50 ¢ coin were still not due to differences in value, but to differences in, for instance, the surface texture of the coin as opposed to the metal disc. This argument, how-ever, could not explain the results of a more recent study by Holzkamp and Perlwitz (1966), who used the same stimulus for both experimental and control groups. Their stimulus was a circular disc glued to the back of a ground-glass screen which was illuminated from behind by a strong light, so that what the subjects saw was a dark circle against a bright background. In the experimental group subjects were told that the shadow was caused by a 5 mark coin (the largest German coin), whilst the control group were told it was caused by a cardboard disc. Subjects made their estimates by adjusting a circular spot of light, as in the Bruner and Goodman (1947) study, so that it appeared equal in size to the shadow on the screen. The estimates given by the experimental group were significantly larger than those given by the control group.

Since Holzkamp and Perlwitz (1966) used a stimulus which differed *only* in its assumed value in each condition, an explanation of the over-estimation effects found in the previous studies *only* in terms of hypo-thesized differences in the apparent size of metal as opposed to card-board objects would seem implausible. Instead of arguing that coins are overestimated relative to cardboard discs because they are made of metal, a more reasonable conclusion might be that metal discs are overestimated because they look like coins whereas cardboard discs do not.

Another set of findings supports the conclusion that the overesti-mation effects found with coins may in fact be due to their value, rather than to some other extraneous factor. As we mentioned earlier, one of Bruner and Goodman's (1947) hypotheses was that objects of greater value should be overestimated more than objects of lesser value, as compared with value-neutral objects of the same size. One way to test this hypothesis is to see whether coins of high value are overestimated more than coins of low value. However, the problem with this is that more valuable coins tend also to be larger. If they are overestimated more than the less valuable coins therefore, this could be due to the size difference and not to the difference in value. One way out of this difficulty might be to use a foreign coin, and to tell one group of subjects that it was of very low value and another group of subjects that it was of very high value. A different method, which Bruner and Goodman (1947) employed, is to make use of differences among the subjects in the value they place upon a given coin. Obviously, a coin of any given denomination could be assumed to represent a greater subjective value for a beggar than a millionaire. Bruner and Goodman (1947) therefore divided up the children in their experimental group into a "rich" and a "poor" group according to the economic backgrounds of their families. As expected, the "poor" group gave larger estimates than the "rich" group. Carter and Schooler (1949) found a similar tendency, but this only attained significance for the 1 ¢ coin. A more successful study was that by Ashley et al. (1951), who induced their subjects under hypnosis to believe that they were either very rich or very poor. This method had the advantage that each subject could be used as his own control, with the judgements he made during his hypnotically induced "rich" state being compared with those he made during his induced "poor" state. They found that subjects made significantly larger estimates of coin sizes when induced to believe they were poor than when induced to believe they were rich. Similar results were also found by Holzkamp (1965), who essentially replicated the Bruner and Goodman (1947) study, the only difference being that the same children had to judge both the coins and the cardboard discs. Comparing "rich" and "poor" children with respect to the differences between their judgements of the coins and of the corresponding cardboard discs, he found that "poor" children overestimated the coin sizes to a relatively greater extent than the "rich" children.

The effects of value on judgements of physical magnitude have not only been demonstrated with coins but also with various other valued objects. Bruner and Postman (1948) found overestimation of discs bearing "emotionally relevant" symbols, i.e. a dollar sign and a swastika (the effects for the former being more marked and consistent), as compared with discs bearing "neutral" symbols. Subsequent studies by Klein et al. (1951) and Solley and Lee (1955) failed to replicate these results for discs bearing a swastika. Lambert et al. (1949) found overestimation of the size of poker chips which could be exchanged for candy. Their subjects (3- to 5-year-old nursery children) judged the poker chips before and after a reward period during which they could exchange the chips for candy. The judged size of the chips was larger after the reward period than before. There then followed an extinction period in which the chips could no longer be exchanged, at the end of which the size estimates of the chips were no longer different from those given before the reward period.

The studies which we have mentioned represent only a small sample of the research concerned with the effects of value on judgements of physical magnitude, but they seem sufficient to demonstrate that such effects cannot all be dismissed as artifactual. At the same time, there are so many instances where judgements of physical magnitude are not affected by value that one cannot just accept Bruner and Goodman's (1947) simple hypothesis that the physical magnitudes of valued objects will be overestimated in relation to that of value-neutral objects. It seems rather that value may lead to overestimation in some cases but not in others. The important question, therefore, is how to predict when such effects will occur and when they will not.

An accentuation theory account of the effects of value on judgements of physical magnitude

One of the major theoretical analyses of the effects of value on judgements of physical magnitude is that proposed by Tajfel (1957). Tajfel takes as his starting point an analysis performed by Bruner and Rodrigues (1953) on their own results and those of Carter and Schooler (1949). In both these experiments there was little or no evidence of overestimation when size estimates of coins were compared with those of metal discs of the same diameter. Bruner and Rodrigues (1953), however, pointed out that, despite their failure to find significant overestimation of coins relative to metal discs, in both studies judgements of the coins were more "distorted" than judgements of metal or cardboard discs. In the Carter and Schooler (1949) study, Bruner and Rodrigues concluded:

Judgements of coins showed an average distortion ranging from 5 per cent underestimation for the penny to 10 per cent overestimation for the half-dollar. There is a difference here of 15 per cent (diameter) in apparent size between the coin of lowest value and that of highest value used in the Carter & Schooler experiments. For aluminium discs, the corresponding figures are 1 per cent underestimation for the penny size

C*

and 5 per cent overestimation for the half-dollar size—6 percentage points. For the cardboard discs, the separation is 4 per cent underestimation for the penny size and 4 per cent overestimation for the half-dollar size, a separation of 8 percentage points. Thus, while the tendency toward such distortion is present in both coins and discs, it appears to be more marked for the former than for the latter.

1953, p. 17

In their own study they found, with coins, an average distortion ranging from 1·47 per cent overestimation for the penny to 16·34 per cent overestimation for the 25 ¢ coin (quarter)—approximately 15 percentage points. For metal discs, the corresponding figures were 5·04 per cent overestimation for the penny size disc and 13·58 overestimation for the quarter size disc, a difference of approximately 8·5 percentage points. The estimates of the penny size cardboard disc showed 1·67 per cent underestimation and those of the quarter size cardboard disc 5·03 overestimation, a separation of approximately 7 percentage points. These differences in the "average range of distortions" between coins on the one hand and metal or cardboard discs on the other are statistically significant in Bruner and Rodrigues' (1953) own data. This analysis clearly shows, therefore, that the differences between the judged sizes of coins of different denominations are greater than those between metal or cardboard discs of the same diameter as the coins. In other words, the judged differences between the elements of a series of coins are *accentuated* relative to the judged differences between a corresponding series of metal or cardboard discs.

Tajfel (1957) suggests that this accentuation of differences is due to the fact that the elements of a series of coins vary concurrently along two dimensions—size and value—whereas the elements of a series of cardboard or metal discs vary along only one dimension, that of size. The effects found with coins are thus a special case of the more general principle that, where differences along a peripheral dimension (in this case, value) are correlated with differences along the focal dimension (in this case, size), this will lead to an accentuation of the judged differences between the stimuli on the focal dimension. The effects of value are thus not assumed, *a priori*, to be any different in kind from those of other superimposed cues.

If we accept this line of argument, however, there still remains one problem. In our earlier discussion of accentuation effects we were only concerned with accentuation of absolute judgements, that is, with accentuation effects which occur when one stimulus is judged against the background of the series of which it is a part. The coin studies, on the other hand, essentially employed a kind of comparative judgement procedure. Subjects had to compare the size of a circular light spot with the coin they were judging, and adjust the size of the spot so that it appeared equal to that of the coin. However, as Tajfel argues:

> In view of the evidence concerning the effects that all elements of a series, past and present, have on the quantitative judgments of its individual members (e.g. Helson, 1948; Johnson, 1955) it may reasonably be assumed that the judgments of magnitude given by the subjects in the . . . overestimation experiments were not only determined by the perceived relationship, at the time of judgment, between a stimulus of the value series and a standard; they must have been affected as well by the background of perceived relationships between this particular stimulus and all other stimuli of the same series.
>
> 1957, p. 69

Tajfel's (1957) application of accentuation theory to the coin studies thus provides an extremely succinct account of a previously confused area. Accentuation of the judged differences between the consecutive members of a series of coins, relative to the judged differences between the consecutive members of a series of neutral discs, implies that the judged extension of the valued series should be larger than that of the neutral series. For example, the difference between the judged diameter of the penny and half-dollar in the Carter and Schooler (1949) study is 15·4 mm, whereas the corresponding difference for the cardboard discs is 13·9 mm. If such accentuation effects are strong enough to lead to a sizeable extension of the judgements of the valued series, judgements of certain stimuli in the valued stimuli are likely to differ significantly from judgements of the corresponding neutral stimuli. The most likely candidates to show such an effect are the stimuli near or at the extremes of the valued series. Towards the end of the series, consecutive accentuation effects should have added up sufficiently to lead to a reliable displacement of the end stimuli of the valued series as compared with the corresponding stimuli in the neutral series. The most convincing support for Tajfel's explanation of the results of the coin studies would have been a finding of reliable underestimation of the smallest coins as well as reliable overestimation of the largest coins. In the studies discussed, however, such underestimation effects are far less marked and consistent than the overestimation effects found with the larger coins.

Although Tajfel himself seems to assume that such displacements should occur symmetrically towards both extremes of the series, this does not appear to be a necessary implication of the principles on which his model is based. It is quite consistent with the assumptions of accentuation theory that one end of the valued series should stay put while the other end is extended. Since all that accentuation theory assumes is that the apparent differences between members of the valued series are accentuated relative to the corresponding differences in the neutral series, it cannot predict whether the larger coins will be overestimated or the smaller coins underestimated or whether both will occur simultaneously. What the coin studies show quite clearly is that judgements of smaller coins are less liable to distortion than judgements of larger coins. This is not altogether surprising in view of the fact that the possible range of responses open to the subject are more clearly limited at the lower than at the upper end of the series. The lower extreme, in other words, is more securely "anchored" than the upper extreme of the coin series. It seems, therefore, essential to distinguish between effects that relate to differences in the extension, dispersion or "polarization" of an individual's judgements of a series of stimuli, and displacements of the average or centre of his judgements of the series as a whole. Whereas the former kind of differences are accountable for in terms of accentuation theory, the latter are more likely to be related to the principles outlined in Chapter 2. Both kinds of effects would seem to be operating in the case of the coin studies.

Another aspect of these studies may also be accounted for in accentuation theory terms. It has been argued (Holzkamp, 1965) that Tajfel's model cannot explain the finding that "poor" subjects show more marked overestimation effects than "rich" subjects when judging coin sizes (Bruner and Goodman, 1947; Ashley *et al.*, 1951). This criticism is unjustified. Although Tajfel does not discuss the problem specifically in his 1957 paper, these results are quite consistent with his more explicit discussion of the underlying principles (1959a); here he states that where a superimposed classification "is of inherent value or of emotional relevance to the subject" the resulting accentuation effects "will be more pronounced" (p. 21). It is reasonable to assume that, if the peripheral stimulus variation is more "salient" or subjectively important for some subjects than for others, then those subjects for whom it is more salient should be more influenced by it when they come to judge the positions of the stimuli along the focal dimension. The finding that "poor" subjects show more overestimation than "rich" subjects is interpreted by Bruner and Goodman (1947) and Ashley *et al.* (1951) as being due to the fact that the subjective value of the coins was greater for the "poor" than for the "rich" subjects. If this assumption is correct, it implies that the value of the coins was a more "salient" peripheral attribute for the "poor" subjects than for the "rich" subjects, and should therefore have had greater effect on their judgement of size.

   Tajfel's (1957) discussion, however, is not restricted to the coin studies. As we mentioned earlier, a number of studies showed over-estimation of valued objects other than coins, whilst others failed to show such effects. To account for these seemingly contradictory results, Tajfel adopts a distinction which is basically the same as that between correlated and uncorrelated peripheral variation. In terms of this distinction, he distinguishes two groups of experiments:

> In one group, changes in the magnitude of the stimuli under investigation are relevant to the changes in value. The experiments on coins provide an example here: in general, the larger the coin, the greater its value. The experiment of Dukes & Bevan (1952), in which judgments of weights of jars filled with sand were compared with judgments of weights of jars filled with candy, would also be "relevant" in this sense: heavier jars would presumably contain more candy, and thus have greater "value". On the other hand, several experiments have been reported in which changes in value have in no apparent way been related to changes in the physical dimension which the subjects were requested to judge.
>
> 1957, pp. 192–193

Examples of this "irrelevant" group are the studies by Lambert *et al.* (1949), Lysak and Gilchrist (1955), Bruner and Postman (1948), Klein *et al.* (1951) and Solley and Lee (1955).

   In the Lambert *et al.* (1949) experiment, subjects had to judge the size of poker chips which could be exchanged for candy; but since all chips were of the same size their size was irrelevant to their "value". In the Lysak and Gilchrist (1955) study, the size of dollar bills of various denominations was compared with the size of other rectangles; again, since all dollar bills are the same size, their size is irrelevant to their value. In the studies by Bruner and Postman (1948), Klein *et al.* (1951) and Solley and Lee (1955), discs bearing swastikas were compared in size to discs bearing neutral symbols; again, large swastika discs would not appear any more "emotionally significant" than small swastika discs. Tajfel (1957) argues that since, in this "irrelevant" group, the "value" of any given stimulus was not a cue to its size, the question of any accentuation of the judged differences among the members of the valued series, such as occurs in the "relevant" group of experiments, would not arise. As he puts it, no "intraserial" effects should occur for the "irrelevant" group. He argues, however, that even in this group the value of an object may still lead to an accentuation of physical differences between a valued and a neutral object (i.e. to an "inter-serial" effect). The difference in value between the two objects would constitute an additional distinctive feature, superimposed on any physical difference between them, which subjects might be unable to completely disregard. Nevertheless, as Tajfel points out, this would not necessarily lead to overestimation rather than underestimation, and therefore no consistent overestimation effects should be predicted for the "irrelevant" group.

Tajfel's (1957) notion of "interserial" as opposed to "intraserial" effects does not seem to follow in any very clear or coherent way from the rest of his argument. It is particularly confusing in cases where a valued object is compared with a neutral object of the same size. Here there would be no "physical difference" between the objects to be accentuated, whatever the differences between them on the peripheral dimension of value. Tajfel's argument with regard to such cases may perhaps be best paraphrased as follows: that, in the "irrelevant" group, subjects presented with two stimuli which differ in terms of a peripheral attribute (value) will treat the stimuli as though they were different in terms of other attributes also, including the focal attribute (size), even where there is no difference in terms of the focal attribute and where there is no a priori reason to assume that the two stimuli, if they did differ in terms of the focal attribute, would differ in one direction rather than another. Stimuli which differ in value may thus also be judged to differ in size, but this should not lead to consistent tendencies over different individuals for the valued object to be overestimated rather than under-estimated, unless value and size are considered by the subjects to be correlated for the particular types of stimuli in question. The prediction which this leads to, therefore, is that valued objects should not be con-sistently overestimated or underestimated relative to neutral objects in the "irrelevant" group of studies. This is the same as what would be predicted by a simpler application of accentuation theory, ignoring Tajfel's distinction between "interserial" and "intraserial" effects: un-correlated peripheral stimulus variation should have no effect on judge-ments of the focal stimulus attribute. It is therefore not altogether surprising that Tajfel does not pursue this distinction in his later papers.

The distinction drawn by Tajfel and Wilkes (1963) between "interclass" and "intraclass" differences, it must be emphasized, is something completely unrelated. Both the accentuation of interclass differences and the reduction of intraclass differences are examples of effects relating to the differences between members of the same stimulus series. In other words, they are both types of "intraserial" effects.

As we have seen already, the prediction (however derived) that *no* overestimation effects should occur in the "irrelevant" group of studies is inconsistent with at least some of the findings reported. But before we discuss the inconsistencies, let us consider the consistent findings. Lysak and Gilchrist (1955) found that the sizes of dollar bills were not reliably overestimated as compared with rectangles. Only Bruner and Postman (1948) found overestimation of discs bearing a swastika; Klein *et al.* (1951) and Solley and Lee (1955) could not replicate this finding. A disc bearing a dollar sign was overestimated in the Bruner and Postman (1948), the Solley and Lee (1955), and one of the Klein *et al.* (1951) experiments, but this may have been due to its vicarious resemblance to a coin. Most damaging to Tajfel's explanation is Lambert *et al.*'s (1949) finding of overestimation of poker chips after they had been associated with rewards. Here Tajfel (1957) argues that the overestimation may have been due to the fact that the number of chips each child earned determined the candy he received. Each chip was exchangeable for one candy. For children of the age group used, the relationship "more chips = more rewards" may have been equivalent to the relationship "bigger chips = more rewards". If this interpretation of the results of Lambert *et al.* (1949) is correct, no overestimation effects should occur if the number of chips each child earned bore no fixed relationship to the amount of candy he received. To test this hypothesis, Tajfel and Winter (1963) replicated the Lambert *et al.* (1949) experiment but added one further experimental group where the chips were associated with varying amounts of candy (between 1 and 5 candies per chip). While Lambert *et al.*'s (1949) findings of overestimation were replicated in the condition where there was a one-to-one relationship between number of chips and amount of candy, no overestimation was found for the group where the relationship was variable. Other consistent and inconsistent results of experiments in the "irrelevant" group are discussed by Tajfel in his 1957 article, to which the reader is referred for further details. In general, Tajfel's predictions would appear to meet with reasonable success in both groups of studies, though the number of contradictory findings is somewhat larger in the "irrelevant" group.

Holzkamp's theory of the effects of value on judgements of physical magnitude

Tajfel's accentuation theory account of the effects of value on judgements of physical magnitude has recently been challenged by Holzkamp and his co-workers (Holzkamp, 1965; Holzkamp and Perlwitz, 1966; Holzkamp and Keiler, 1967; Holzkamp *et al.* 1968). Holzkamp claims that the results of these studies unambiguously support his own theory and refute Tajfel's. Unlike Tajfel's theory, which is a general psychophysical model dealing with variation in value only as a special case of incidental stimulus variation, Holzkamp restricts his model to the explanation of the effects of value. Basic to Holzkamp's theory are three assumptions. The first assumption is about the relationship between value and size in our environment, the second about our learning of this relationship and the third about the effects of this learning on our perceptual judgements of valued objects.

Holzkamp assumes that a stable and predictable relationship exists in our environment between the size of objects and their value. For any given class of objects, larger objects are usually of higher value—either positive or negative—than smaller objects. Large diamonds are more valuable than small diamonds and large wounds are more dangerous than small wounds. We *learn* therefore that "better" things are generally larger than "less good" things, and that "worse" things are generally larger than "less bad" things. Holzkamp argues that this learned relationship plays an important role in judgements of the size of valued objects. The long-standing association between size and value leads us to approach valued objects with the expectation that they will be larger than objects of lesser value: we adopt a "perceptual hypothesis" that valued objects will be larger than neutral ones.

When a subject is required to judge the size of a valued object, therefore, the response he gives will represent a compromise between this "perceptual hypothesis" and the "perceptual information"—the sensory input from the object itself. When the size of a coin is compared to the size of a neutral disc (or a circular light patch) of equal diameter, there is, according to Holzkamp, a cognitive imbalance between the "perceptual hypothesis" and the "perceptual information". According to the perceptual *hypothesis*, the coin is the "big thing" whereas the metal disc is the "small thing". According to the perceptual *information*, the coin and the metal disc are the same size. When the subject is instructed to select, from a series of metal discs, the one which is equal in size to the coin, this cognitive imbalance prevents him from selecting the disc which is of equal physical size. If he selected a disc of equal size, the "small thing" (small according to the perceptual hypothesis) would be as big as the "big thing". To resolve this cognitive imbalance, he will judge the disc of equal size as being smaller than the coin and will therefore select a larger disc as the one which is equal to the coin. This compromise between the perceptual hypothesis and the perceptual information thus produces the overestimation of the size of the coin.

Since the overestimation of valued objects is due to our learning of a certain relationship between value and size, it should be possible to reverse this process in the laboratory. Holzkamp suggests that if subjects learned in an experiment that, for a certain class of objects, increases in size were accompanied by decreases in value, the size of valued objects of this class should be underestimated. Since this learning would supposedly run counter to our everyday experience, the effects on judgements should not be very stable and should be extinguished soon after the end of the experimental session.

Holzkamp's emphasis on the supposed relationship between value and *size*, as opposed to accentuation theory's emphasis on the relationship between peripheral and focal dimensions in general, raises the question of whether Holzkamp's model predicts that value will affect judgements of physical attributes in general, or only judgements of size. Holzkamp's answer is that he predicts that value should affect judgements of only those physical attributes which have been learned to change concurrently with value. He thus introduces a distinction which is similar to our distinction between correlated and uncorrelated incidental stimulus variation, or Tajfel's distinction between the "relevant" and "irrelevant" groups of experiments. There is, however, one important difference between Holzkamp's distinction and that of Tajfel. Tajfel assumes that value will affect judgements of physical magnitudes only if, *for a given class of objects*, changes in value have in the past been correlated with changes in the physical dimension being judged. Coin size estimates will show accentuation effects, since larger *coins* are usually of higher value than smaller *coins*. However, since the size of swastikas bears no relationship to their "value", no accentuation effects should occur for such stimuli. Holzkamp, on the other hand, seems to assume that once it has been learned that value changes and changes on some physical dimension are correlated, value will affect all judgements on that dimension *for all classes of objects*. In other words, since we have learned that objects of high positive or negative value are larger than more neutral objects, this expectation or hypothesis will influence our judgements of the size of *all* valued objects, regardless of whether the relationship holds for the particular class of objects being judged. Therefore, discs bearing swastikas should be overestimated as compared with discs bearing neutral symbols, even though the size of a swastika is irrelevant to its value.

These last assumptions seem to be quite inconsistent with Holzkamp's other statement that value will lead to underestimation of certain objects if subjects have learned, during an experiment, that, for the particular class of objects they are judging, size decreases with increasing value. If, as a result of what is assumed to be a process of life-long learning, subjects develop the expectation that *all* highly valued objects will be larger than neutral objects, how could one hope to reverse this process during an experiment? Holzkamp never discusses this point specifically, but he would probably argue that subjects will tend to generalize the relationship "the greater the value the larger the object" to all classes of objects unless they have direct evidence that a different relationship exists for the class of objects they are judging. If they learn explicitly that, for a given class of objects, size decreases with increasing value, their judgements of objects of this class should be affected only by this newly learned relationship.

The most problematic part of Holzkamp's theory is certainly his assumption that highly valued objects are usually larger than objects of lesser value. Part of the difficulty is that when he talks of increases in value as being related to increases in size he is talking about value *intensity* irrespective of whether this value is positive or negative. If one finds an instance of where stimuli decrease in positive value as they increase in size, this would be inconsistent with Holzkamp's theory if it is assumed that the smallest stimuli are intensely positive and the largest stimuli are neutral, but consistent with his theory if it is assumed that the smallest stimuli are neutral and the largest stimuli are intensely negative. In other words, Holzkamp effectively assumes the existence of an absolute zero or neutral point on the value continuum. Whether any set of findings are taken to support or contradict his theory, therefore, will depend on where one considers this neutral point to be for the particular stimuli in question. However, even if one found an instance where objects of higher value intensity were smaller than their more neutral counterparts, this by itself would not amount to a falsification of Holzkamp's assumption. Holzkamp's theory does not demand that the proposed relationship between size and value should hold for *all* stimuli, but only for the *majority* of stimuli which form our environment. Any empirical test of this assumption would therefore seem to require some kind of "representative survey" of all objects in our environment. Even if we make the questionable supposition that the number of object classes in our environment is both finite and determinate, this would seem to be a task of herculean proportions.

None the less, some findings by Naatz (1970) appear to lend support to Holzkamp's assumption. Subjects in this study were required to compose a list of names of ten objects; these could be any concrete perceptual objects other than people. Half the subjects were required to list objects which they liked and half objects which they disliked. Naatz then selected one object from each subject's list, choosing only objects which could be variable in size, and attempting, as far as possible, to select different objects for each subject. Each subject then had to rate his liking of the object selected from his list three times on a ten-point bipolar scale ranging from extreme disliking (-5) to extreme liking ($+5$). For one rating the object was described as a "big" object, for another as "medium sized" and finally as "small". For example, if the object "diamond" had been selected from a given subject's list, the subject would have to rate his liking for the three concepts "big diamond", "medium-sized diamond" and "small diamond". (The order in which these categories were rated was rotated across subjects.) Naatz predicted that the subjects who rated objects of positive value would like the objects more when described as big rather than small, whilst the subjects who rated objects of negative value should dislike them more when they were big rather than small. As can be seen in Table 4.1 these predictions were well supported.

It is very difficult to assess the validity of Naatz's (1970) results. It is by no means clear whether his findings in fact reflect the relationship between size and value which exist in our environment for the particular object classes which were chosen from the subjects' lists, or whether they are just the result of an "experimenter effect". Asking the subjects to rate the same object three times, each time with a different qualifier,

TABLE 4.1

Liking mean ratings of big, medium-sized and small objects by positive and negative value groups (Naatz, 1970)

Size of object	Positive value	Negative value
Small	+2·82	−2·40
Medium sized	+3·72	−3·57
Big	+4·09	−4·54

might have led them to suppose that they were expected to give different ratings on each occasion, and to use the supposed size of the object as a basis for their judgement of liking. Moreover, even if we discount the possibility of an "experimenter effect", it is still impossible to determine how "representative" were the classes of objects which the subjects were required to judge.

It may none the less be true that subjects adopt a "perceptual hypothesis" concerning the relationship between size and value even if they have no valid basis for doing so. We must therefore consider how far Holzkamp's predictions are consistent with the results which he himself reports and also with the older studies already considered. To take the older studies first, it would seem that Holzkamp advances exactly the same predictions as Bruner and Goodman (1947) did more than 20 years ago. Like them, he predicts that the size of valued objects will be overestimated relative to the size of neutral objects, and that the overestimation will be more marked the greater the value of the object. One has to ask how Holzkamp could take up a position which even Bruner has long abandoned on account of the findings of the Carter and Schooler (1949) and Bruner and Rodrigues (1953) studies. Holzkamp's answer is that Bruner relinquished his position too easily. As he points out, Bruner and Rodrigues' (1953) finding, that the mean ("intraserial") differences between members of a series of coins were significantly accentuated relative to the corresponding differences in a neutral series, is quite consistent with Bruner and Goodman's (1947) hypotheses. If one assumes that the magnitude of any overestimation effect is proportionate to the value of the object, coins of higher value should be overestimated more than coins of lower value and so the "average range of distortions" should be greater for coins than for neutral discs. This is quite true. However, the reason why Bruner abandoned his old position was not the finding of such *accentuation* effects, but the failure to find significant overestimation of any of the coins relative to the corresponding metal discs, for which Holzkamp cannot offer any satisfactory explanation.

Support for Holzkamp's theory comes from those studies in what Tajfel calls the "irrelevant" group which still found overestimation of valued objects. Bruner and Postman's (1948) finding of overestimation for a disc bearing a swastika, is inconsistent with Tajfel's theory but consistent with Holzkamp's. As the reader will remember, Klein *et al.* (1951) and Solley and Lee (1955) both failed to replicate this finding. Lambert *et al.*'s (1949) finding of overestimation of poker chips fits easily into Holzkamp's theory but not into Tajfel's, but the explanation of this result which Tajfel and Winter (1963) proposed does not seem unreasonable. Holzkamp suggests, however, that Tajfel and Winter's (1963) failure to find overestimation of the chips when each chip was rewarded with a variable amount of candy may have been due to the fact that the children, who for no apparent reason sometimes received four or five candies per chip, and at other times only one or two, might have interpreted the small rewards as some kind of punishment. Reward and punishment would thus cancel each other out and the chips would be basically as neutral as if they had never been rewarded. Even if one does not go as far as this, one must agree that the chances of attaching "value" to the chips would have been somewhat lower than in the condition with a one-to-one relationship between number of chips and number of candies. It is nevertheless worth noting that Holzkamp's argument implies that the subjective neutral point on the value continuum for any class of objects may not be absolute, but relative to the particular range of values received. As we mentioned earlier, to admit the possibility of any such relativity would seem to raise problems concerning the verifiability of Holzkamp's assumption about the distribution of value and size in our environment.

Holzkamp admits that most of the older studies in Tajfel's "irrelevant" group have methodological shortcomings which leave their results open to alternative explanations. Although he attempts to refute the alternative explanations which Tajfel proposes, there is no more evidence for his refutations than for Tajfel's explanations. Holzkamp and Keiler (1967) therefore conducted an experiment which was designed to avoid the methodological pitfalls of earlier studies and establish unambiguously whether or not value would lead to overestimation even when the size of the objects judged was irrelevant to their value. The study was conducted at several schools in West Berlin using 10- to 13-year-old children as subjects. The stimuli were small white plastic rods, rectangular in shape and all of the same physical dimensions. For the experimental subjects either positive or negative value was attached to the rods, while no value was attached to them for the control group. Holzkamp and Keiler predicted that when either positive or negative value was attached to the rods their length would be overestimated.

Judgements of the length of the rods were given using a light box similar to that used by Bruner and Goodman (1947), except that, instead of a circular light spot, it projected a rectangular light patch of the same width as the plastic rod but of adjustable length. Subjects made their judgements with one of the rods displayed next to the light box. For the two experimental groups, value was attached to the rods by having the children's teachers hand the rods out during their regular teaching periods, either as a reward for good behaviour (positive value condition) or as a punishment for bad behaviour (negative value condition). The children were told that at the end of a two- or three-week period the child with the greatest number of rods (positive value condition) or with the smallest number (negative value condition) in each class could choose a prize. A list of the prizes which could be chosen was handed out to the children at the beginning of the experiment. The experiment lasted in all for seven weeks. It started with a period of three weeks during which value was attached to the rods. This value period was followed by a two-week extinction period during which the rods were merely used to lay out geometrical figures or for other "neutral" purposes. This extinction period was followed by another value period lasting two weeks. For half of the experimental group, positive value was attached to the rods, during the first period and negative value during the second. For the other half, the negative value period preceded the positive one. Each subject had to estimate the length of the rods at four different times: before the first value period (E_1), after the first value period (E_2), after the extinction period (E_3) and after the second value period (E_4). The control group were required to give four estimates of the length of the rods at equivalent time intervals to the experimental group. For these subjects, however, the rods were used throughout for "neutral" purposes, as in the extinction period for the experimental group.

Holzkamp and Keiler predicted that, compared to the control group, the experimental subjects should overestimate the length of the rods after the first value period (E_2), regardless of whether this had been a positive or negative value condition. The extinction period should lead to a decrease in overestimation (at E_3), but the amount of over-estimation should increase again after the second value period (E_4). These predictions were confirmed for each of the two experimental groups separately. Except for the difference between E_1 and E_2 for the experimental group with positive value established first, all the mean differences between consecutive estimates $(E_2-E_1, E_3-E_2, E_4-E_3)$ were significantly larger for the experimental than for the control subjects.

The procedure and design of this study seems to avoid all the problems of the earlier experiments. By attaching value to the stimulus presented for judgement during the course of the experiment rather than using stimuli of intrinsic value, Holzkamp and Keiler were able to ensure that the stimuli presented to experimental and control subjects were identical in all aspects save that of value. By using rectangular rods rather than discs, they avoided the problems which would have been raised by stimuli that bore any resemblance to coins or bank notes. Because they used 10- to 13-year-old children as subjects rather than 2- to 5-year-old children, as in the Lambert *et al.* (1949) study, their findings cannot be interpreted as due to the fact that their subjects had not yet developed the concept of preservation of quantity. The results of this study, therefore, quite unambiguously support Holzkamp's theory but are inconsistent with Tajfel's predictions.

Another major difference between Holzkamp's and Tajfel's predictions, which Holzkamp investigated in a second experiment (Holzkamp *et al.* 1968), is concerned with whether the *direction* of the value-size correlation should affect how stimuli are judged. According to Tajfel, correlated peripheral variation along the value dimension should lead to increased discriminability and hence to an accentuation of judged differences along the focal dimension of size. The magnitude of this effect should depend on the "personal relevance" to the subject of the peripheral variation, and on the *degree* of correlation between the peripheral and focal dimensions; but it should *not* depend on the direction, or sign, of this correlation. In other words, it should make no difference whether the more valued stimuli are larger or smaller than the more neutral ones, so long as the degree of the correlation remains the same. If, for example, a foreign country were to adopt British coinage as its currency, but use the ½p coin as the coin of highest value and the 50p coin as the coin of least value, the same accentuation effects should still occur if judgements of these coins were compared to those of neutral discs.

According to Holzkamp, however, the direction of the value-size correlation is very important. Overestimation of valued objects occurs because we have learned that "better" things are usually "bigger" than "less good" things. If we lived in this imaginary country where the largest coins had the smallest value we would have learned that "better" things were usually "smaller" than "less good" things, and so should underestimate the sizes of valued objects. To test this prediction, Holzkamp *et al.* (1968) conducted a further study on children from West Berlin schools. The stimuli were rectangular rods of six different lengths. In the control group, subjects were given several sets of these rods, being told that the rods were of no personal significance to them, but that they should keep them until a certain date when they should be given back to the teacher. The experimental subjects, who attended a different school, were told by their teachers that, for a trial period of a few weeks, they would be given rods of various lengths instead of numerical grades. Grades at German schools vary between 1 and 6 with 1 being the best possible and 6 the worst possible grade. The children were told that the 25 mm rod would correspond to grade 1, the 30 mm rod to grade 2, and so on in 5 mm intervals up to the 50 mm rod which would correspond to grade 6. They were each told to keep the rods they received and hand them back to the teacher at the end of the trial period, when their overall grade would be determined by the length of rods they returned. Thus a stimulus series was created in which increases in value were correlated with decreases in size.

In comparing the estimates of the rod lengths given by control and experimental subjects at the end of the trial period, Holzkamp *et al.* (1968) considered only judgements of the rods which symbolized grades 1 to 3. In accordance with their predictions, it was found that the experimental subjects underestimated the rods in comparison to the control group. The rationale behind this restriction in the analysis was that only rods associated with positively valued grades should be underestimated since only the judgements of the positively valued rods should be affected by the learned relationship that "better rods are shorter than less good rods". As rating scale judgements indicated, the subjects considered only grades 1 to 3 as good grades; grades 5 and 6 were considered bad, whilst 4 occupied a neutral position. However, as Ertel and Stubbe (1970) recently pointed out, since grades 5 and 6 were thought of as distinctly negative, the experimental subjects should not only have learned the relationship "better rods are shorter than less good rods", but also "worse rods are longer than less bad rods". Length and "value intensity" should thus have been negatively correlated at the short end and positively correlated at the long end. This second relationship should have led to an overestimation of rods 5 and 6 in the experimental group. Although Holzkamp *et al.* (1968) present no data for the estimates of rods 4, 5 and 6, Naatz and Hümmelink (1971) have recently re-analysed their data, and report that rods 4 and 5 were underestimated by the experimental as compared with the control subjects, whilst rod 6 showed no effect in either direction. These results appear to contradict Holzkamp's theory.

It is ironical to note that the results which would have been predicted from Holzkamp's theory would have been more consistent with Tajfel's theory than the actual results which Holzkamp *et al.* (1968) obtained. Tajfel's theory would predict that since the size of the rods was correlated with their value, the judged differences between the rods should have been accentuated, with the result that the shorter rods should be underestimated and the longer rods overestimated by the experimental as opposed to the control subjects. The failure of Holzkamp *et al.* (1968) to find overestimation of the longer rods is thus inconsistent with Tajfel's assumption that such accentuation effects should operate symmetrically at either end of the stimulus series.

Taken by themselves, these results are only moderately damaging to Tafjel's theory; but taken in the context of all the other results of experiments in the "relevant" group, they make one wonder whether the direction of the value-size correlation is really unimportant. Is it really just a coincidence that Holzkamp *et al.* (1968), after creating a valued series with a negative value-size correlation, found underestimation for 5 out of the 6 rods in their series, whilst the elements of valued series with positive value-size correlations (e.g. coins) have generally been overestimated? In view of the numerous inconsistencies in the findings of the coin studies, we cannot exclude the possibility of a coincidence, but it would nevertheless be interesting to repeat the Holzkamp *et al.* (1968) experiment with a second experimental group added. For this group, good grades would be associated with long rods and bad grades with short rods. If, as Tajfel suggests, the direction of the value-size correlation is unimportant, the two experimental groups should not differ in their estimates. If, however, the new group showed *both* accentuation of judged differences between the rods *and* over-estimation of the rods as a whole, then this would suggest that Tajfel is incorrect in assuming that the direction of the value-size correlation is unimportant.

It is therefore worth reiterating the point we made earlier, that it is not a necessary requirement of accentuation theory as here formulated that accentuation or polarization effects should operate symmetrically at either extreme of the response continuum. One subject's set of ratings may differ from another's both in terms of their dispersion or extremity, and also in terms of the centre or average rating of the series as a whole. (According to Torgerson (1958), this corresponds, in general terms, to a distinction between the "unit" and "origin" of an individual's reference scale.) Accentuation theory is properly concerned only with differences in the first of these two parameters. Neither the theoretical principles nor the empirical findings which we have outlined in this chapter suggest that the direction of the value-size correlation should affect the extent of polarization of the subject's judgements. Neverthe-less, it is quite conceivable that the direction of the correlation may have an effect on the centre of the subject's reference scale, that is, on whether the stimuli as a whole tend to be over- or underestimated. When the two effects are superimposed, the result should show an asymmetrical extension of the subject's range of judgements relative to judgements made in the absence of a value correlation, such as was observed in the coin studies and in the Holzkamp *et al.* (1968) experi-ment.

Results which provide some indirect support for this interpretation come from a study by Tajfel (1959b). Subjects were presented with a series of ten weights which they had to judge in terms of heaviness on a seven-point scale. The lightest weight was 200 g and there was an increment of 10 per cent from one stimulus to the next. Each subject underwent two experimental sessions separated by an interval of 24 hours. Each session consisted of two parts. In the first part, subjects were required to lift the series of weights but were not required to judge them. In the second part, which followed after a rest period of a few minutes, subjects were required to judge the stimuli as they lifted them. The first part consisted of 12 randomized presentations of the whole stimulus series. In the second part, 11 such randomized orders were used. There were four experimental conditions. In *Experiment 1,* "value was associated with the heavy end of the series". This was achieved by giving the subjects a "bonus" worth 3d towards the price of a book token each time one of the two heaviest stimuli was presented in the first part of one of the two experimental sessions. All subjects in this group underwent one session during the first part of which they were given bonuses ("value" session), and one session in which no bonuses were given ("neutral" session). For half the subjects the value session was on the first day and the neutral session on the second day, whereas for the other half the order of sessions was reversed. No bonuses were given during the second parts of either session, when subjects were giving their judgements. In *Experiment 2*, the procedure was identical, except that the bonuses were presented with the two lightest, instead of the two heaviest stimuli. *Experiment 3* followed the same procedure, except that the bonuses were paired randomly with each of the stimulus weights. *Experiment 4* was a replication of Experiments 1 and 2, except that the bonuses (paper tokens) were valueless.

The main results show a greater accentuation of differences between the various stimuli for judgements made during the value sessions of Experiments 1 and 2 than during the neutral sessions of the two experiments. In Experiments 2 and 4, however, there was no difference between the sessions in which bonuses were and were not given to the subjects. The association of value with either extreme thus produced an increase in the judged separation of both extremes, and of adjacent stimuli at either extreme. This effect was shown to be highly significant by a number of analyses. If we assume that the effect of this somewhat unusual procedure can be considered more or less equivalent to that of superimposing a *continuum* of value on the weight continuum, so as to produce conditions of correlated peripheral variation in the value sessions of Experiments 1 and 2, these results are consistent with an accentuation theory approach.

When the mean judgements of each of the stimuli for the value and neutral sessions of the first two experiments are compared, the extension of the judged range appears symmetrical. In other words, there is no evidence of the pattern suggested by the coin studies and the Holzkamp *et al.* (1968) experiment which led us to suppose that a positive correlation between value and physical magnitude might produce over-estimation, and a negative correlation, underestimation. Put another way, the accentuation effects produced by the value association do not appear to be accompanied by any effect of assimilation of the judged magnitudes towards the more positively valued end of the scale.

Closer inspection of the data which Tajfel presents, however, suggests that such assimilation to the valued end may indeed have occurred after all. The reason why this effect is not apparent in a comparison of the value and neutral sessions of either of the first two experiments, considered in isolation, seems to be due to the fact that Tajfel combines the scores of *all* subjects in each experiment when calculating the mean ratings for each stimulus in the value and neutral sessions. However, half the subjects whose scores were used to make up the means for the neutral session had undergone a value session the day before. It is not implausible that the possible carry-over effect of the value session for these subjects may have been sufficient to disguise any "assimilation" effect within any single experiment, though not necessarily when comparing the results of different experiments.

Support for this interpretation comes from the fact that the mean ratings of the individual stimuli in both the value and neutral sessions of Experiment 1 are higher than those of Experiment 2. Similarly, comparisons of both the value and neutral sessions of Experiments 1 and 2 with the neutral sessions of the last two experiments show clear evidence of such assimilation. Table 4.2 shows the number of stimulus

TABLE 4.2

Number of stimuli showing average shifts in the direction of assimilation to, or contrast from, the valued end of the series in various comparisons between condition (Tajfel, 1959b)

Comparison	Number assimilated	Number contrasted
1V versus 2V	10	0
1V versus 3N	9	1
1V versus 4N	6	4
2V versus 3N	10	0
2V versus 4N	9	1
1N versus 2N	10	0
1N versus 3N	7	2
1N versus 4N	7	2
2N versus 3N	9	0
2N versus 4N	9	1

Note: 1, 2, 3 and 4 refer to Experiment numbers.
V = value session.
N = neutral session.

weights which, in terms of the means which Tajfel (1959b) presents, show shifts which are in a direction which is either consistent or inconsistent with the hypothesis of an effect of assimilation towards the more valued end of the series for each of the ten such comparisons between conditions.

Further evidence for an assimilation effect is given by Tajfel's analysis of the mean ratings of the series as a whole made by each subject in each of the experimental conditions, taking into account only their ratings in the first session. When tested by Mann–Whitney U-tests, the only significant differences found were those between the (first day) value sessions in Experiments 1 and 2 (the mean judgements given by all subjects in Experiment 1 were "heavier" than those for subjects in Experiment 2), and those between the (first day) value session in Experiment 2 and the (first day) neutral sessions of all four experiments ("lighter" judgements being given in the value session of Experiment 2). Both these differences achieved significance at the 5 per cent level.

Although such results are suggestive rather than conclusive, they do imply a tendency which is not explained by Tajfel's accentuation theory account of the effects of value on judgements of physical magnitude. In accordance with accentuation theory, either positive or negative correlation between the value of objects and the physical magnitude will lead to an accentuation of judged differences between elements of the stimulus series. In addition a positive correlation between value and size seems, if anything, to produce overestimation, whereas a negative correlation seems, if anything, to produce underestimation; in other words, there is a tendency for the judged magnitudes of the stimuli to be assimilated towards the more valued end of the scale.

This last effect is quite consistent with Holzkamp's predictions. His notion that subjects adopt a "perceptual hypothesis" may provide at least part of the answer to the question of why such effects occur, although for such an explanation to be fully convincing one would need to know rather more about how such "hypotheses" are acquired. Alternatively, assimilation of judgements towards the valued extreme may reflect one instance of the general phenomenon of positivity bias, reflecting a possible tendency for subjects to give more "positive" than "negative" responses (see Chapter 7). Another very real possibility is that assimilation of judgements towards the valued extreme may be connected to the type of assimilation effects we discussed in Chapter 3 (Sherif et al., 1958; Parducci and Marshall, 1962) and may reflect the fact that subjects are using the more valued stimuli as "subjective standards".

These are questions, regrettably, which we must leave unanswered. But whatever the solution, the *unilateral* shifts in judgement which variations in value produce do not explain away the *extension* of the range of judgements which occurs at the same time. This, we have argued, is better accounted for by the more general judgemental principles of accentuation theory.

5

Theories of Social Judgement

The principles of judgement that most adequately account for the performance of subjects in a psychophysical judgement task can, it has been argued, be applied to a great variety of different types of stimuli with, generally, no more than minor modifications of detail. It is of relatively minor importance whether the stimuli used are lifted weights, colours, numbers, or displays of dots. What is important is how the subject construes the requirements of the judgement task. There would seem to be no obvious reason, therefore, why the same principles could not also be used to explain the judgement of stimuli such as attitude statements, outcomes of an interaction, etc. We shall therefore proceed upon the working hypothesis that such context effects as have been found or can be demonstrated in the area of social judgement will be explicable in terms of such principles as, for example, the range frequency compromise and the influence of incidental stimulus variations.

There is nothing new in claiming social and psychophysical judgement to be related to each other. Most of the investigators we shall mention have drawn upon the comparison to a greater or lesser extent. However, as will be seen, the real question is no longer whether such a comparison is possible, but how useful it is in explaining the effects observed. It will be argued that such a comparison can be extremely useful, but only in so far as it is realized that, just as in psychophysical judgement, no single principle is likely to be able to explain all the effects observed.

There is one important respect in which evaluative judgements of stimuli such as attitude statements differ from psychophysical judgement. In social judgements there is no "absolute" or "physical" measure that we can use of the position of any particular item or set of items along a given continuum. There is no way, therefore, in which we can relate the "psychological continuum" in terms of which the subject judges a series of stimuli to any underlying "physical continuum". We cannot make a comparison between any objective scale of measurement and the subjective scale used by any individual. All we can do is compare the subjective scales of different individuals or groups of individuals with each other. When we say that an individual or group of individuals "displaces" a given item in a particular direction along the dimension of judgement, this is merely a shorthand way of saying that the judgement of that item given by that individual or group differs, in a particular way, from the judgement of the same items given by the same individual or group under different conditions or by a different individual or group under the same condition.

Originally interest in the question of the judgement of attitude statements was not motivated by an interest in demonstrating that principles of judgement derived from the study of psychophysical judgement were also applicable to evaluative judgements of complex stimuli such as attitude statements. Instead, interest in the question derived from its relevance to techniques of attitude scale construction, in particular to Thurstone's method of equal-appearing intervals.

The method of equal-appearing intervals was introduced in 1929 by Thurstone and Chave as a method for constructing attitude scales assumed to have the properties of equal interval scales. When applied in its original form, each of the subjects is given an envelope containing between 100 and 130 paper slips. On each of these slips a statement is printed expressing a certain degree of favourability or unfavourability towards the attitude object of interest (e.g. Church, Negroes, etc.). The subjects are asked to sort the statements into eleven piles according to the degree of favourability or unfavourability expressed. Typically, pile "one" contains statements that seem to express the most unfavourable feelings about the psychological object, pile "two" the items next most unfavourable, and so on up to pile "eleven", in which the most favourable statements are placed. The subjects are warned to disregard their own opinion and to judge the items as objectively as possible. The mean or median category to which each statement is assigned by the different judges is then taken as a measure of the favourability of the attitude which it expresses. This measure is termed the "scale value" of the statement. Instead of the "sorting method" originally suggested by Thurstone and Chave, most of the more recent studies have used a "rating method". With the rating method, all the statements are printed in a booklet rather than on separate paper slips. An eleven-point rating scale is printed below each statement and the subject is requested to mark his rating of the given statement on the scale. The rating method is preferable to the sorting method when judgements are performed in group experiments rather than individually.

Thurstone and Chave (1929) believed that the judging of the statements would be done similarly by those judges who had favourable and those who had unfavourable attitudes towards the psychological object under consideration. They stated that "if the scale value is to be regarded as valid, the scale values of the statements should not be affected by the opinion of the people who help to construct it" (1929, p. 92). Although Thurstone and Chave did not test this assumption themselves, they suggested the following experimental design which became a paradigm for most of the early experimental research conducted in the area of social judgement.

The experimental test for this assumption consists merely in constructing two scales for the same issue with the same set of statements. One of the two scales will be constructed on the return from several hundred readers of militaristic sympathies and the other will be constructed with the same statements on the return from several hundred pacifists. If the scale values are practically the same in the two scales, the validity of the method will be pretty well established.

1929, pp. 92–93

The effects of judges' attitudes on ratings of attitude statements

The first person to test Thurstone's assumption empirically was Hinckley (1932). He had statements, expressing attitudes towards Negroes, categorized by two groups of white judges, one with anti-Negro attitudes and the other with pro-Negro attitudes, and by a group of Negro judges. Hinckley found that the average scale values for pro-Negro whites was highly correlated $(r=0.98)$ with those of the anti-Negro white group. The scale values for the Negro judges were also closely correlated with those for the anti-Negro white judges $(r=0.93)$. On the basis of these results, Hinckley concluded that "the scale which we have constructed for measuring attitudes towards the social position of the Negro is not influenced in its measuring function by the subjects used in the construction (1932, p. 203). Essentially the same result was found by Beyle (1932) who constructed scales to measure attitudes towards candidates in government elections, by Ferguson (1935) using attitudes towards war, by Pintner and Forlano (1937) using attitudes towards patriotism

D

and by Eysenck and Crown (1949) using attitudes towards Jews. All these studies found correlations higher than 0·90 between the scale values based on the ratings of different groups of judges, and so concluded that the measuring properties of scales constructed by the method of equal-appearing intervals were unaffected by the attitudes of judges.

As a result of this apparently overwhelming evidence, Thurstone's assumption became a well-accepted "fact" in the field of attitude measurement, although at the same time in other areas of social psychology a great deal of evidence was accumulating which would have been difficult to reconcile with this assumption, had a reconciliation been attempted. In a field study of evaluations of skin colour by Negro youths (Johnson, 1941, cited by Hovland and Sherif, 1952), a tendency was found for Negro subjects' estimates of their own skin colour to be somewhat lighter than they appeared to the tester. The same kind of effect was shown in a subsequent laboratory study by Marks (1943), who found a tendency for Negro subjects to estimate their own skin colour to be nearer to light brown (at that time perceived as the most desirable) than they really were. Those subjects with the darkest skin colour rated a larger proportion of other individuals as lighter than average, whereas lighter-skinned subjects rated a larger number of individuals as dark.

Similar effects were observed on a different continuum by Hinckley and Rethlingshafer (1951), who asked white college students of varying heights to estimate the height of an average American male. The mean estimate made by the tall men was compared with that made by the short men. A significant difference between the two groups was found, with the tall men making the higher estimate. The same subjects were also asked to judge a number of different heights ranging from five to seven feet in terms of a verbal scale ranging from "very very short" to "very very tall". It was found that "the short men consistently overestimated the heights as compared to the judgements of the tall men" (1951, p. 251).

These findings as well as the pioneer studies by Levine *et al.* (1942), and Schafer and Murphy (1943) seemed to support the then well-accepted theory ("The New Look") that perception is affected by the perceiver's needs, values, and attitudes. Thurstone's assumption, on the other hand, directly contradicted it. As Ager and Dawes (1965, p. 533) put it later: "Rating of favorability of attitude is a subdomain of perception of attitude. And if perception is influenced by the attitude of the perceiver, it would be odd if a narrow subdomain of perception were not."

The Thurstone assumption was no longer thought of merely as a question of scaling methodology, but as a question of judgement and perception. The situation has been excellently summed up by Hovland and Sherif:

> Thus we have the paradox that some leading texts in social psychology say in the chapter on perception and judgment that judgments are greatly affected by the individual's attitudes and motives while in the chapter on scaling methods they state that judgments of the meaning of items are unaffected by the positions of the judges who do the sorting.

1952, p. 23

It was this paradox that led Hovland and Sherif (1952) to re-examine the evidence concerning the effects of judges' attitudes on their ratings. They argued that it was unreasonable to expect any noticeable differences in judgement between different groups of judges unless one used judges who differed widely in attitude. The failure of previous studies to find an effect of judges' attitudes may therefore have been due to their failure to include subjects holding sufficiently extreme positions at either end of the attitude continuum. This criticism is certainly justified with respect to some of the studies. Ferguson (1935) and Pintner and Forlano (1937), for example, admit that they were unable to secure subjects of widely differing attitudes towards the issues investigated. On the other hand, this criticism does not seem at first sight to apply to the study by Hinckley (1932), whose original sample of judges appears to have included groups who represented both extremes of the attitude continuum. Hovland and Sherif, however, suggested that Hinckley may have unwittingly excluded most of his more extreme subjects by use of a "carelessness criterion" originally proposed by Thurstone and Chave (1929). According to this criterion, all subjects who placed more than a certain proportion of statements (about 30 per cent of the total series) into one of the eleven piles were automatically eliminated from consideration, on the assumption that they had been careless in their placement of the items. Hovland and Sherif, for reasons we shall shortly discuss, hypothesized a tendency for judges with more extreme attitudes to displace their judgements of statements with which they disagreed towards the end of the scale opposite to their own position, which would result in a piling up of judgements in the extreme categories for these judges. If this were so, then the "carelessness criterion" would have the effect of excluding a disproportionate number of the more extreme subjects and thus of narrowing down the range of attitudes represented among those retained in the analysis.

In order to test these assumptions, Hovland and Sherif replicated Hinckley's (1932) study without using the "carelessness criterion". Although theirs is one of the "classic" studies in social psychology, its merits lie more in its originality than in refinements of methodology. The data are presented in a way which makes an independent assessment of the interpretations offered very difficult: most of the conclusions seem to have been based on an analysis of the scale values of only eleven out of the 114 statements considered to be equally "appropriate" for the Negro and the white population. The only analysis in which all the data were used is one of the frequencies with which the statements were assigned to the different categories. We will therefore base our interpretation on an analysis of these distributions.

Hovland and Sherif (1952) used the same set of 114 statements expressing attitudes towards the Negro that had been used by Hinckley (1932). These statements were rated by four groups of subjects assumed to be in ordinal but not equidistant positions along the favourable–unfavourable continuum. The group consisted of Negro subjects, pro-Negro white subjects, "average" white subjects, and anti-Negro white

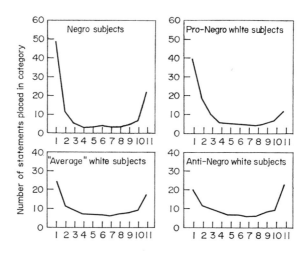

Fig. 5.1. Number of statements placed in each of eleven categories by each group of judges. (Adapted with permission from C. I. Hovland and M. Sherif, 1952.)

subjects. Figure 5.1 presents the frequency distribution of the number of statements placed into each of the eleven categories by each group of judges. It is obvious that compared to the "average" white subjects the Negro subjects and the pro-Negro white subjects placed a disproportionately high number of statements into category 1, the most unfavourable category. In other words, the judges with extreme pro-Negro attitudes "lumped together" statements at the end of the scale which they rejected, rating more statements as extremely unfavourable towards Negroes than did the average white subjects. However, Hovland and Sherif (1952) had expected that the anti-Negro subjects would show the opposite tendency, that is, that they would judge a greater number of statements as favourable than would the average white subjects. Contrary to their expectation, there was no indication of such an effect. This last result appears somewhat less surprising if one reads Hovland and Sherif's (1952, p. 827) description of the average white subjects. The average white subjects were students "from a number of different colleges throughout the South", most of them from "an area in southeastern Oklahoma popularly known as 'Little Dixie'. In general, students attending these schools are from a lower socio-economic level than those attending the state university. The educational level of this area is relatively low." From this description, it seems extremely likely that the majority of these students held anti-Negro attitudes and that, therefore, only a minor difference existed between the average white subjects' and the anti-Negro subjects' attitudes towards Negroes.

A clearer indication of the form of these effects is given by Zavalloni and Cook's (1965) replication of the Hovland and Sherif study. They carried out two sub-studies in which judgements were obtained from subjects for the complete set of 114 Hinckley items. In the first of these substudies, subjects were selected on the basis of their membership of groups in which it was reasonable to expect attitudes of a particular degree of favourableness or unfavourableness to predominate. These groups were:

Group I White students active in organizations working for integration.
Group II White students active in the same organization as Group I.
Group III Students taking an optional course in intergroup relations and assumed to have egalitarian attitudes without being actively concerned with questions of race relations.

Group IV   Students from right-wing political organizations.

Group V   "Pledges" of fraternities known to have led a campaign against the admission of Negroes to a border-state university.

Zavalloni and Cook made the assumption that the order above corresponded to how the groups could be ranked in terms of favourableness towards Negroes, but not that they were evenly spaced along the attitude continuum.

In the second substudy a large group of introductory psychology students filled out a questionnaire which was used to assess their attitudes on the issue. This questionnaire was administered after subjects had completed their rating of the 114 items. Ratings were then compared for those subjects who were classified on the basis of their questionnaire responses as falling within the most prejudiced, middle and least prejudiced quintiles.

For the judgement task all the subjects were given the same instructions as subjects in the Hovland and Sherif (1952) study. They had to sort the statements into eleven categories. Statements expressing the most unfavourable attitudes towards Negroes were to be sorted into category 1 and statements expressing the most favourable attitudes into category 11. To compare the results of the Zavalloni and Cook study with those of the Hovland and Sherif study, we computed the frequency with which statements had been assigned to the different categories by the criterion groups in the Zavalloni and Cook study. A comparison of these frequencies between the two studies indicated that Zavalloni and Cook's groups I, II, and III were similar to Hovland and Sherif's Negro and pro-Negro white subjects, whereas groups IV and V were similar to Hovland and Sherif's average white and anti-Negro subjects. This last finding tends to support our suspicion that Hovland and Sherif's average white subjects actually held fairly anti-Negro attitudes.

The major analysis of the Zavalloni and Cook study, however, was not based on the frequency with which items were assigned to the different categories but on the mean ratings of each of the statements. For this analysis, the items were divided into three subsets designated as unfavourable, intermediate and favourable. This division was performed on the basis of the mean scale values assigned to the 114 Hinckley items in an earlier study (Upshaw, 1962). The subset of unfavourable items was formed from the 58 statements which had received scale values of 4·99 or less in Upshaw's study. The intermediate subset contained the 23 statements with Upshaw scale values between 5·00 and 7·99, whereas the 33 statements with scale values of 8·00 and more were assigned to the favourable subset.

Table 5.1 presents the mean ratings given by the five criterion groups to the unfavourable, intermediate, and favourable statements. The differences between the mean ratings of the groups were highly significant for unfavourable and intermediate items, but not significant for the favourable statements. Group I, the Negro group, gives the lowest (most unfavourable) mean ratings for both unfavourable and intermediate items, and Group V the highest (most favourable). Mean ratings of the favourable items, however, do not follow this pattern. "Differences among the groups in the mean ratings of these items are small and irregular. To the extent that any trend can be distinguished, it is in the direction opposite to that predicted; that is, the more equalitarian subjects show some tendency to rate these items higher (more favourable) than the anti-Negro subjects." (Zavalloni and Cook, 1965, p. 46.) The mean rating of the subjects selected from a heterogeneous group on the basis of an attitude questionnaire show the same pattern as those of the criterion group.

TABLE 5.1

Mean ratings of unfavourable, intermediate, and favourable items by five different criterion groups (Zavalloni and Cook, 1965)

Group	Unfavourable items	Intermediate items	Favourable items
I	1·76	4·29	9·02
II	1·90	4·52	8·86
III	2·14	4·97	8·87
IV	2·48	5·37	8·48
V	2·84	6·05	8·77

Although the tendency for the "pro" judges to rate favourable statements more favourably than "anti" judges was not statistically significant in the Zavalloni and Cook study, it reached acceptable levels of significance in studies by Upshaw (1962) and Selltiz et al. (1965). Since Upshaw's study will be presented in detail in our discussion of Upshaw's variable-perspective model, we will describe here only the Selltiz et al. study. Selltiz et al. collected a new item pool of 106 statements which contained only 33 of the original Hinckley statements. With this new item pool they essentially replicated the Zavalloni and Cook study. They selected subjects according to their membership of four criterion groups. The first three of these groups corresponded to the first three groups used by Zavalloni and Cook. The fourth group corresponded to a combination of Zavalloni and Cook's groups IV and V. In order to check whether "some kinds of items are perceived differently in different parts of the country over and above individual differences in attitudes towards race relations" they attempted to secure subjects from each of three geographical areas in the United States: north-east, mid-west and border south. For purposes of analysis, they divided their items into five subsets designated as extremely unfavourable, moderately unfavourable, intermediate, moderately favourable, and extremely favourable on the basis of the scale values computed from the ratings of the total sample of subjects.

Table 5.2 presents the mean rating of the different classes of items by subjects in the different criterion groups in the north-east—results which were fairly typical of those obtained in the other areas also. The differences between the criterion groups were highly significant for all the item subsets. The extremely unfavourable, moderately unfavourable, and intermediate items were rated lower (less favourable) by the pro-Negro subjects than by the anti-Negro subjects (only the mean ratings of the moderately favourable items do not show any regular pattern at all, whereas the extremely favourable items were judged as more favourable by the pro-Negro subjects than by the anti-Negro subjects. Thus, the more favourable the judges' attitudes toward Negroes, the more extreme or polarized were their ratings of statements expressing attitudes on this issue.

TABLE 5.2

Mean ratings of different subsets of items by subjects in different criterion groups (north-east) (Selltiz *et al.*, 1965)

	Subsets				
Group	Extremely unfavourable	Moderately unfavourable	Intermediate	Moderately favourable	Extremely favourable
I	1·74	2·68	5·03	8·41	10·12
II	1·89	3·03	4·49	7·89	9·54
III	2·06	3·54	5·87	8·51	9·79
IV	2·47	4·09	6·09	8·00	9·17

As a check on the adequacy of the selection of subjects according to criterion groups, all subjects within each region had to fill out a Self-

Report Attitude Inventory, which was a Likert type of scale measuring attitudes towards Negroes. Possible scores on that inventory ranged from 0 (most prejudiced against Negroes) to 57 (least prejudiced against Negroes). Though the average scores of the different groups on this attitude measure supported Selltiz et al.'s assumption about the ordinal position of the groups, they also showed that, in terms of their absolute position, subjects in group IV (the most anti-Negro group) "would seem to be best described as moderately favourable in both the north-east and mid-west, and as intermediate or moderately unfavourable in the border south". However, the wide range of attitudinal positions represented among the subjects of group IV made it possible to identify subjects who held less favourable attitudes than the average member of group IV. Therefore, all subjects within each region, regardless of their criterion group status, were grouped on the basis of their scores on the attitude measure into a highly prejudiced, an intermediate, and a hardly prejudiced group. The most prejudiced group of the border south subjects, for example, had scores between 7 and 20; the scores of the intermediate group ranged between 35 and 46, and those of the least prejudiced group between 53 and 57. A comparison of the mean ratings of the five classes of items given by the subjects of the most prejudiced, the middle, and the least prejudiced quintiles of each geographical group showed the same pattern as that of the criterion group. These last findings are very important since they demonstrate that even if one secures anti-Negro judges with really extreme anti-Negro attitudes, one will still find that the pro-Negro judges give more polarized ratings than the anti-Negro judges.

It seems that a fairly consistent picture emerges from the four studies reviewed so far. In all four studies, ratings of attitude statements were found to vary as a function of the judges' attitudes. This invalidates Thurstone and Chave's (1929) assumption that the scale values of attitude statements are not affected by the attitude of the individuals by whom the statements are rated, at least as far as statements of attitudes towards Negroes are concerned. The precise form of the relationship between judges' attitudes on their ratings of attitude statements is slightly more ambiguous. While in all four studies more extreme ratings of the unfavourable statements were given by the pro-Negro than by the anti-Negro judges, results for the favourable statements were less consistent. In the Hovland and Sherif study, as far as can be told from the category frequencies, favourable statements seem to have been judged

D*

similarly by pro- and anti-Negro judges. In the Zavalloni and Cook study, judges with favourable attitudes towards Negroes showed a slight, though not statistically significant, tendency to rate the favourable statements as more favourable than did the anti-Negro judges. An inspection of the ungrouped data indicates that this tendency would have been much stronger had Zavalloni and Cook not grouped together the extremely favourable and moderately favourable statements in their analysis. Finally, in the Upshaw as well as in the Selltiz *et al.* study, favourable statements were rated more favourably by pro-Negro judges than by anti-Negro judges. Thus, in all four studies, the effect of judges' attitudes on rating seems to have varied as a function of the position of the statements on the attitude continuum. While judges with favourable attitudes (as compared with judges with unfavourable attitudes) displaced unfavourable statements towards the unfavourable end of the scale, they either did not displace the favourable statements (Hovland and Sherif, 1952), or, if they did, tended to displace them towards the favourable end of the scale (Upshaw, 1962; Selltiz *et al.*, 1965; Zavalloni and Cook, 1965).

There is one study by Ward (1966) which apparently failed to provide any evidence to show that the effect of judges' attitudes was dependent on the scale position of the statements. Ward reported that in his study favourable and unfavourable statements of attitudes towards Negroes were rated less favourably by pro-Negro judges than by anti-Negro judges. In other words, Ward did not find any evidence of a relationship between judges' attitudes and polarization of the kind found in previous studies. However, in a comment on Ward's study, Eiser (1971b) suggested that Ward's failure to find the typical pattern of polarization of ratings may have been due to the criteria according to which he eliminated from his analysis the responses of a large proportion of his subjects. Ward excluded 57 out of an original total of 261 pro-Negro subjects and 24 out of 55 anti-Negro subjects because they apparently confused the end-points of the rating scale. These subjects were eliminated on the basis of their responses to the first two items. The first of these items was an unfavourable item with a control group mean rating of 2·1 and the second a favourable item with a control group mean rating of 9·3. Subjects' questionnaires were discarded on the basis of the following criterion:

Those subjects who judged the first statement as negative (i.e. checked any interval between 1 and 5 and who also judged the second statement as positive (i.e. checked any interval between 7 and 11) were assumed to have understood directions. All other subjects were assumed to have misunderstood directions, and their questionnaires were discarded.

Ward, 1966, pp. 468–469

According to this criterion, a subject could have been excluded for confusing the end-points of the rating scale even if he rated the first item as less favourable than the second but failed to assign them to different halves of the scale. Also, any subject who rated either of the two items as 6 (midpoint of the scale) would have been excluded from the analysis. As Eiser concludes:

> We thus have a situation in which, first, proportionately about twice as many anti-Negro as pro-Negro subjects were eliminated by this criterion, and, second, there is a distinct possibility that a number of those eliminated may not, in fact, have confused the ends of the scale, but may merely have shown a tendency to use less extreme categories with greater frequency. When it is remembered that anti-Negro subjects typically give less extreme ratings than pro-Negro subjects, it is reasonable to conclude that relatively more anti-Negro than pro-Negro subjects who had *not* confused the ends of the scale might still have been excluded by Ward's criterion. If this were so, it would explain why Ward's results show no marked differences between the pro-Negro and the anti-Negro subjects in terms of the overall dispersion or polarization of their ratings . . . It appears quite probable, therefore, that the discrepancy between Ward's results and those of previous studies is at least partly artifactual.

1971b, pp. 82–83

All the studies we have discussed so far which reported an effect of judges' attitudes on their ratings have used statements of attitudes towards the Negro. We therefore have to ask whether there is any evidence that judges' attitudes towards issues other than the Negro question affect their ratings of relevant attitude statements. Furthermore, if attitude effects on ratings of statements have been demonstrated for other areas, has the relationship between judges' attitudes and their ratings been similar to that found with the Negro scale?

While the first question can be simply answered in the affirmative, the second is somewhat more problematic. There are studies using different attitude statements which found the same relationship between judges' attitudes and their ratings as has been found in the Negro studies. However, there are at least two studies which yielded somewhat different results.

A study with results which are in line with those discussed so far is the one by Eiser (1971a). We will discuss results of this study in detail later, and will be concerned here only with the findings regarding the effects of judges' attitudes. In this study, statements of attitudes towards drug-use were used as stimulus material and subjects were divided into two groups, depending on whether they held fairly "permissive" or fairly "restrictive" attitudes towards drug-use. It was found that the more permissive subjects gave significantly more polarized ratings of the item series than did the more restrictive subjects.

Another set of results which are fairly similar to the ones reported so far comes from two studies by Prothro (1955, 1957). He used 40 statements of the Grice–Remmers Generalized Attitude Scale (Grice, 1934). Each item of that scale contains a statement which could be applied to any national, racial, or religious group. In the later of these two studies Prothro made the items apply to Arabs and used Arab students as subjects. Since this study was conducted in Beirut at the time of the 1956 Suez crisis, the subjects can be assumed to have been highly involved. When the ratings given by these subjects were compared with those of the control group, who in the earlier study had rated the statements in their general form referring to no specific group, it was found that the favourable statements were rated more favourably when referring to Arabs than when referring to no specific group. Similarly, the unfavourable statements were rated more unfavourable when referring to Arabs than when referring to no specific group. Since the Arab students who served as judges could be described as "pro" judges when rating statements about Arabs and as neutral judges when rating statements referring to no specific group, the results seem to fit in nicely with the studies reported so far. Compared to the condition where judges had fairly neutral attitudes, judges in the condition where they had an extremely favourable attitude gave more polarized ratings. Unfortunately not all of the results of Prothro's (1955) earlier study quite fit this pattern. In the experimental condition of this study, the same statements had been made to apply to Jews instead of Arabs. The results obtained in the control condition show that the anti-Jewish Arab students rated 36 out of 40 statements as expressing a less favourable attitude when they referred to Jews than when they referred to no specific social group. Since the Arab students could be described as "anti" judges in the experimental condition of this study, we would have expected them to give less polarized ratings of the statements in the experimental condition than in the control condition if their rating behaviour was to parallel that shown by anti-Negro judges in the other studies mentioned. Prothro's (1955) earlier results seem therefore to be quite inconsistent with the results of most of the studies we have so far reported (Selltiz *et al.*, 1965; Upshaw, 1962; Zavalloni and Cook, 1965). However, Prothro's results are difficult to interpret since it is not at all certain that, as he apparently assumes, a condition where subjects rate statements referring to no specific group is the same as a situation where subjects rate statements applying to a social group towards which they have a neutral attitude. It is not even certain whether subjects rating such generalized items do not think of some social group to whom the items would apply. It could be, for example, that when rating the unfavourable statements they think of some social group towards whom they have unfavourable feelings, but think of some group whom they like when rating the favourable statements. To avoid this difficulty with the generalized items we compared directly the ratings of the items referring to Arabs with the ratings of the items referring to Jews. Since in both conditions Arab students served as judges they can be considered "pro" judges when the statements are made to refer to Arabs and "anti" judges when the statements are made to refer to Jews. A scatterplot of the ratings of the "pro" judges against the ratings of the "anti" judges indicates a tendency for the "pro" judges to give more polarized ratings. The same tendency becomes apparent in a comparison of the numbers of statements assigned to the most extreme categories when the statements were made to refer to Arabs and Jews respectively. When the 40 statements referred to Arabs (that is when the subjects could be considered "pro" judges), 12 statements were assigned to the most favourable category (scale value below 2·0) and 10 statements were assigned to the most unfavourable category (scale value above 10·0), as compared to 3 and 5 respectively when the statements referred to Jews (that is when the subjects could be considered "anti" judges). If analysed in this way, Prothro's results seem to be in line with the findings reported earlier. Nevertheless, one has to keep in mind that the design of Prothro's studies deviates from the classical social judgement paradigm. Instead of instructing judges with different attitudes to rate the same set of attitude statements, Prothro makes judges with similar attitudes rate different sets of attitude statements, or at least statements referring to different social groups. Any conclusion drawn from a comparison of Prothro's results with results of the social judgement studies which used the classical social judgement paradigm must therefore remain somewhat tentative.

There are two studies by Manis (1960, 1961) which show a relationship between judges' attitudes and their ratings which is clearly different from that found in the studies discussed so far. In both studies, Manis presented college students with a series of short communications about the fraternity system. The series contained an equal number of pro-fraternity, neutral, and anti-fraternity communications. The subjects were asked to rate the attitude expressed by each of the communications on a set of bipolar evaluative rating scales (semantic differentials). Manis found in both studies that judges with favourable or unfavourable attitudes towards the fraternity system rated the anti-fraternity messages as more "anti" and the pro-fraternity messages as more "pro" than did the judges with a neutral attitude towards fraternities. In other words, Manis found that, in accordance with the results of studies reported so far, "pro" judges gave more polarized ratings of favourable and un-favourable communications than did judges with neutral attitudes to-wards the fraternity system. However, Manis's "pro" and "anti" judges gave equally polarized ratings and both gave more polarized ratings than did the neutral judges. Although differences in the procedure of Manis's studies and the studies reported earlier may account for the differences in results, Manis's findings raise the possibility that the relationship between judges' attitudes and their ratings of attitude studies found in one attitude area may not necessarily hold for all attitude areas.

Thus, in the 40 years since Thurstone and Chave (1929) suggested that rating of attitude statements was not affected by the raters' atti-tudes, more than a dozen studies have been conducted to test this assumption (e.g. Beyle, 1932; Hinckley, 1932, 1963; Ferguson, 1935; Pintner and Forlano, 1937; Eysenck and Crown, 1949; Hovland and Sherif, 1952; Prothro, 1955, 1957; Manis, 1960, 1961; Upshaw, 1962; Selltiz *et al.*, 1965; Zavalloni and Cook, 1965; Ward, 1966; Eiser, 1971a). Since the majority of these studies (e.g. Hovland and Sherif, 1952; Prothro, 1955, 1957; Manis, 1960, 1961; Upshaw, 1962; Selltiz *et al.*, 1965; Zavalloni and Cook, 1965; Ward, 1966; Eiser, 1971a) found a difference in the ratings given by groups of judges who differed in their atti-tudes, it is now generally accepted that such ratings are affected by the attitudes of the individuals who are used as judges. The effect of judges' attitudes seems to be related to the scale position of the statements, with unfavourable statements being displaced in one direction and favour-able statements being either unaffected or displaced in the opposite direction. The typical finding of the studies using statements of attitudes towards Negroes is that the more favourable the judges' attitudes towards Negroes, the more polarized are their ratings. The results of Eiser's (1971a) study on attitudes towards drug-use and of Prothro's (1955, 1957) studies on attitudes towards Arabs and Jews, seem to point in a similar direction, although in the case of Prothro's studies procedural differences make a comparison difficult. Manis (1960, 1961), using statements of attitudes towards college fraternities, found that not only judges with favourable attitudes but also judges with unfavourable attitudes gave more polarized ratings than did neutral judges. Possible explanations of this difference in results between Manis's studies and the other studies will be discussed later.

The failure of some studies (e.g. Beyle, 1932; Hinckley, 1932, 1963; Ferguson, 1935; Pintner and Forlano, 1937; Eysenck and Crown, 1949) to find an effect due to judges' attitudes has been attributed by Hovland and Sherif (1952) to the failure of these studies to include judges with extreme attitudes either in their subject sample or their analysis. However, there is one further important difference between studies which contradicted the Thurstone and Chave assumption and those which did not. All of the studies which claim to have found no difference between ratings of different groups of judges seem to have merely computed the linear correlations between the different sets of ratings. Since the scale values computed from the ratings of different groups correlated highly with each other, they concluded that no difference existed between the two sets of scale values. More recently, however, Ager and Dawes (1965, p. 533) pointed out: " . . . a correlation is a bad measure of the similarity between ratings; . . . while correlation is relatively sensitive to agreement in rank ordering (of favorability) of attitude, it is relatively insensitive to perceived differences between attitudes similarly ranked." That this criticism is justified is indicated by the finding that in most studies, where an analysis of the mean scale values indicated a significant difference between the scales, the same set of scale values were nevertheless highly correlated. For example, in Upshaw's (1962) study the ratings given by "pro" and "anti" judges were very highly correlated, although the "pro" judges rated unfavourable statements more unfavourably and favourable statements more favourably than did the "anti" judges.

The effects of judges' personality on ratings of attitude statements

White and Harvey (1965) recently criticized research relating judges' attitudes to attitude rating for their complete disregard of personality variables which might mediate the observed relationship between attitude rating and raters' attitudes. They consider that since in none of these studies had the influence of personality been controlled for, some of the effects which were attributed to attitudinal differences may, in fact, have been due to personality influences. Specifically, they argue: " . . . the finding that with increased extremity and intensity of attitude goes the tendency for the individual to dichotomize his psychological scale and to pile up his judgments of the issue at the ends of the scale . . . would be predicted from at least three different personality theories, that of Adorno, Frenkel-Brunswick, Levinson and Sanford (1950), of Rokeach (1960), and of Harvey, Hunt and Schroder (1961)." (1965, pp. 334–335.) Variations on the dimensions of authoritarianism (Frenkel-Brunswick, 1949; Adorno et al., 1950), dogmatism (Rokeach, 1951, 1960) and concreteness–abstractness (Harvey et al., 1961) are assumed to be related to variations in cognitive complexity. Individuals high on authoritarianism and dogmatism, as well as more concrete individuals, are presumed to be less cognitively complex than individuals low on authoritarianism and dogmatism, and more abstract individuals. Individuals of higher cognitive complexity are presumed to employ more dimensions and make finer discriminations in perceiving and evaluating social stimuli than individuals of low cognitive complexity. Thus individuals of low cognitive complexity should be prone to use relatively undifferentiated and discontinuous internal standards. According to White and Harvey, the use of such standards should result in a greater use of extreme categories, that is, in greater polarization of judgements.

As we have seen in the previous section of this chapter, White and Harvey's statement that judges with more extreme and more intense attitudes should tend to give more polarized ratings than judges with less extreme or intense attitudes somewhat misrepresents the typical research findings in this area. It has been found only in the studies using attitudes towards college fraternities (Manis, 1960, 1961) that more extreme judges gave more polarized ratings than judges holding neutral positions. With ratings of statements about the use of drugs it has been found that only those extreme judges who held favourable attitudes gave more polarized ratings than neutral judges (Eiser, 1971a). Judges with extremely unfavourable attitudes actually gave less polarized ratings than the neutral judges. Similarly, with statements of attitudes towards the Negro, favourable judges gave more extreme ratings than neutral judges while judges with unfavourable attitudes tended to be least polarized in their ratings (Hovland and Sherif, 1952; Selltiz *et al.*, 1965; Upshaw, 1962; Zavalloni and Cook, 1965). The last finding is particularly damaging for White and Harvey's predictions with regard to the "Authoritarian Personality". Since the greater authoritarianism goes a tendency of prejudice towards minority groups, it is actually the anti-Negro subjects who should give the most polarized ratings and the pro-Negro subjects who should give the least polarized ratings. Furthermore, there is no reason to assume that the pro-Negro or pro-drug judges should be more dogmatic or more concrete than the anti-Negro or anti-drug judges. There seems to be little support, therefore, for White and Harvey's claim that the relationship observed between raters' *attitudes* and their attitude ratings can be largely attributed to personality rather than attitudinal variables.

There *is* evidence, however, for a relationship between polarization of attitude ratings and personality variables. White and Harvey's (1965) study is one of the most extensive investigations of the relationship between judges' personality and their rating of attitude statements. The major prediction tested in this study was: "Individuals higher in authoritarianism, dogmatism, and more abstract Ss tend to . . . concentrate their judgments disproportionately into both the more highly favorable and the more highly unfavorable extremes of the scale." (1965, p. 337.) They used statements of attitudes towards the Mormon or LDS (Latter Day Saints) Church. Subjects were University of Utah students who were members of the LDS Church. Thus, the attitude issue was an issue in which the subjects were highly involved. A highly involving issue was selected because "although the conditions under which personality factors exercise maximal influence are not absolutely clear, the evidence seems to favor the alternative that personality influences are triggered and accentuated by conditions of high ego-involvement" (White and Harvey, 1965, p. 336). All subjects had a highly favourable attitude towards the issue investigated. Subjects' authoritarianism, dogmatism, and concreteness–abstractness was assessed, respectively, by Form 40–45 of the California F Scale (Adorno *et al.*, 1950), Rokeach's (1960) Dogmatism (D) Scale and Harvey's (1964, 1965) "This I believe" (TIB) test. In a second session, subjects had to rate the attitudes expressed by the statements of Hardy's (1949) scale of opinions towards the LDS Church, and their agreement or disagreement with these statements.

On the basis of their responses to the personality test, subjects were divided into groups high or low on the three personality dimensions. Differences in attitude were controlled by matching the two groups on each personality dimension with regard to their attitude positions. Use of extreme categories was tested by comparing for each personality dimension the percentage of items placed into the extreme categories (Categories 1, 2, 10 and 11). As predicted, the more concrete subjects placed a greater percentage of items into the extreme categories than did the more abstract subjects. Contrary to predictions, neither authoritarianism nor dogmatism were found to be significantly related to category usage.

White and Harvey's (1965) hypothesis that in rating highly ego-involving attitude statements, judges of low cognitive complexity will give more polarized ratings than highly complex judges is further supported by findings reported in a recent paper by Warr and Coffman (1970, p. 119). In one of the studies reported in this paper, judges who ranged in their own attitude from moderately favourable to extremely favourable towards Negroes rated statements of attitudes towards Negroes. Judges' cognitive complexity was measured by the Paragraph Completion Test (Schroder et al., 1967). A two-way analysis of variance (Cognitive Complexity × Attitude) resulted in a significant interaction. Neither the attitude nor the complexity main effect reached significance. Polarization of ratings was greatest for judges with extreme attitudes and low cognitive complexity. Since extremity of attitudes and degree of ego-involvement are typically highly correlated, the Warr and Coffman findings seem to be fully consistent with White and Harvey's results. Thus, the evidence presented so far seems unambiguously to support the hypothesis that under conditions of high involvement, judges with low cognitive complexity give more polarized ratings than judges with high cognitive complexity, regardless of the attitude position held by the judges. However, the results of both studies could be also accounted for if it were assumed that the effect of judges' attitudes would be greater for judges of low cognitive complexity than for judges of high cognitive complexity. Since, relative to cognitively complex individuals, cognitively less complex individuals are assumed to have "a poorer capacity to 'act as if', to assume the role of the other" (Harvey, 1967, p. 206), they would presumably have greater difficulties when judging attitude statements in disregarding their own position on the attitude continuum. One would therefore expect that less complex judges, in rating attitude statements, would be more affected by their own attitude position than judges of higher cognitive complexity.

There is in fact an important difference between the two interpretations. White and Harvey see polarization as essentially unrelated to the attitude position of judges and as mainly determined by their degree of cognitive complexity. We see polarization as mainly determined by their attitude position. If the degree of cognitive complexity of judges has an effect it should mainly strengthen or weaken the dependence of attitude ratings on their attitudes.

There is one set of findings which does not seem to be consistent with either White and Harvey's (1965) interpretation or with our own. In a study by Larsen (1971), subjects rated sets of attitude statements relating to three attitude issues which ranged in involvement from highly involving to uninvolving. Subjects in this study were students at the Brigham Young University who were members of the Mormon Church. The three attitude issues used were Communism, the "liquor by the drink" issue, which was a local State issue on control of the sale of liquor, and television. Since the Mormon Church is opposed to Communism and to "liquor by the drink", the subjects were assumed to have strong negative attitudes towards both of these issues. However, subjects' ego-involvement in the "liquor by the drink" issue should be less strong than their involvement in the issue of Communism, since the Mormon Church has opposed the "liquor by the drink" issue much less strongly than Communism. Since the Mormon Church neither supports nor opposes television, the television issue was assumed to be the least involving of the three issues. Nothing was known about subjects' attitudes towards the television issue.

The experiment took place in two sessions. During the first session, subjects filled out the Dogmatism Scale (Rokeach, 1960) and Bieri's Cognitive Complexity Test (Bieri *et al.*, 1966). In the second session, they rated 121 statements on each attitudinal issue in terms of the attitude expressed towards each of the issues. As expected, subjects were found to be most involved in the Communism issue and least involved in the television issue. Larsen conducted two two-way analyses of variance (Complexity × Issues and Dogmatism × Issues) on the ratings. He found no significant relationship between cognitive complexity and the polarization of judges' ratings. Dogmatism, on the other hand, turned out to be significantly related to polarization of ratings of all three issues. Highly dogmatic judges gave more polarized ratings than undogmatic judges. The main effect for issues also reached significance. Ratings of statements about the television issue were least polarized, while ratings of the Communism statements were most polarized. This could be due to the difference in judges' involvement across the three issues, but it might simply mean that the set of television statements contained a smaller proportion of extreme statements than the set of "liquor by the drink" statements or the set of Communism statements. The Dogmatism × Issue interaction with an F-value of less than 1·0 did not reach significance. Thus, the difference between high and low dogmatism subjects in polarization of ratings did not vary significantly with the degree of judges' involvement. This is inconsistent with the expectation that the effect of personality factors should be stronger for judgements of highly involving stimuli than for judgements of uninvolving stimulus material.

The results of Larsen's study are in one way or another inconsistent with the results of both the White and Harvey (1965) and the Warr and Coffman (1970) study. Larsen's finding of a relationship between polarization of ratings and degree of dogmatism is somewhat puzzling in view of the fact that White and Harvey (1965), who used a very similar subject pool, did not find such a relationship. Larsen's failure to find a relationship between cognitive complexity and polarization of ratings, on the other hand, is less puzzling, despite the fact that in both the previous studies cognitive complexity and polarization of ratings have been found to be related. In each of the three studies different tests were used to measure cognitive complexity. An extensive study of the generality of cognitive complexity as a personality construct (Vannoy, 1965) found most of the tests of cognitive complexity to be virtually unrelated. For example, the correlation between subjects' scores on Bieri's Cognitive Complexity Test (Bieri et al., 1966) and Schroder's Paragraph Completion Test (Schroder et al., 1967) was practically zero (Vannoy, 1965).

Finally, Larsen's failure to find a significant Dogmatism × Issue interaction, although the issues varied in involvement, is inconsistent with the hypothesis that judges' personality affects ratings only under conditions of high ego-involvement. It is not inconsistent with our interpretation of the Warr and Coffman (1970) findings to assume that most of the judges held fairly extreme attitudes towards television. But in the absence of any information about judges' attitudes towards the television issue such a speculation is rather pointless.

It seems that the only conclusion we can draw from our discussion of the three studies which investigated the relationship between judges' personality and polarization of ratings is that there is evidence that *some* kind of a relationship exists. However, it is not at all clear precisely which personality factors are the crucial ones. The most reasonable assumption seems to be that polarization is related to some aspects of cognitive complexity with complex judges giving less polarized ratings than the cognitively simple judges. This difference between simple and complex judges in polarization of ratings may be due to the use of "more undifferentiated and more discontinuous internal standards" (White and Harvey, 1965, p. 335) by the cognitively simple judges. It could also equally well be accounted for in terms of differences between cognitively complex and cognitively simple judges in their ability to disregard their own attitude in rating attitude statements. For a differential test of these two interpretations a study would be needed which tested the effects of involvement, cognitive complexity, and judges' own position on attitude ratings. While the White and Harvey (1965) and Warr and Coffman (1970) interpretation would predict an involvement by cognitive complexity interaction but not an attitude by cognitive complexity interaction on polarization of judgement, the latter interpretation would suggest an attitude by cognitive complexity but not an involvement by cognitive complexity interaction.

However, even if White and Harvey's (1965) interpretation of the relationship between cognitive complexity and polarization were correct, we would still reject their suggestion that the majority of the findings of attitude rating studies could be attributed to differences in judges' cognitive complexity rather than to differences in judges' attitudes. The fact that in most studies polarization was not found to be linearly related to extremity of judges' attitudes seems difficult to reconcile with an interpretation of the results purely in terms of judges' cognitive complexity. Although it does not seem too implausible to assume that individuals holding an extreme position on an issue are cognitively less complex than individuals holding a more moderate position, there appear to be no grounds for supposing that, for instance, anti-Negro judges should be cognitively more complex than moderate or pro-Negro judges, or that anti-drug judges should be more complex than moderate or pro-drug judges.

The application of theories of psychophysical judgement to social judgement

By the time social psychologists became interested in the social judgement implications of the attitude rating task, a number of more or less sophisticated judgemental models had already been developed in the area of psychophysics (e.g. AL theory, the "rubber-band" model). As we have seen, these theories were formulated in such a manner that they could be extended to situations other than the purely psychophysical. It is therefore not surprising that more or less modified versions of these theories were applied to the area of social judgement. In the following sections we will discuss the applications of these psychophysical models to social judgement.

The application of adaptation-level theory to social judgement

Originally, AL theory was proposed by Helson to account for shifts in judgements of sensory stimuli, such as colours and weights, due to changes in the stimulus context. Helson demonstrated that the physical value of the stimulus at adaptation level is a function of such factors as the physical values of all stimuli being judged, of anchor or comparison stimuli, and of residual factors of past experience. However, since Helson claimed that processes of adaptation underly all human behaviour, AL theory should apply equally well to judgements of attitude statements.

In terms of the three classes of stimuli which according to Helson contribute to AL, a person's attitude can be conceived of as a residual factor of past experience. A person who has a favourable attitude towards some attitude object supposedly differs in his past experience with the object from a person who holds an unfavourable attitude. Specifically, it might be supposed that the kinds of viewpoints which the person with a favourable attitude has tended to hear expressed by other people in the past are likely to have been more favourable than those to which the person with unfavourable attitudes has been exposed. Therefore, the AL of a favourable subject should be nearer to the favourable end of the attitude continuum than that of a person with unfavourable attitudes. By AL theory all stimuli are judged according to their distance above or below the prevailing AL; hence the ratings of judges with favourable attitudes should differ from those of judges with unfavourable attitudes. As compared with unfavourable judges, favourable judges should rate the statements as expressing a less favourable attitude.

AL theory thus predicts the effects of judges' attitudes on ratings to be unrelated to the relative position of the attitude statement on the attitude continuum. If a group of judges displace attitude statements relative to some other group, all statements, favourable, neutral and unfavourable, should be displaced in the same direction. When, for example, statements of attitudes towards Negroes are rated by groups of judges ranging in their own attitudes from pro-Negro to anti-Negro, AL theory would predict each of the statements to be rated least favourably by the most anti-Negro subjects. As we pointed out earlier, this is not what has been typically observed in studies of the relationship between judges' attitudes and their ratings of attitude statements.

Of the studies we have discussed so far, there are only two which found a significant effect of judges' attitudes on ratings which was unrelated to the scale position of the attitude statements rated. One of these is Prothro's (1955) first study using the Grice–Remmers Generalized Attitude Scale. As may be remembered, Arab students rated the statements either in their general form, i.e. not referring to any specific group, or in a form made specifically to refer to Jews. Prothro found that in 36 out of 40 cases the statements were rated as expressing less favourable attitudes when they referred to Jews than when they referred to no specific group. Since one would expect the AL or Arab student subjects to be near the unfavourable end of the attitude continuum for statements referring to Jews, but near the neutral point for statements referring to no specific group, the difference in rating observed in Prothro's experiment is exactly opposite to AL theory predictions. AL theory would predict that the statements should be rated as expressing a more favourable attitude when referring to Jews than when referring to no specific group. But, as we pointed out earlier, the generalized items do not represent a very satisfactory control group. It is not at all certain whether subjects rate items referring to no specific group in the same way as they would rate items referring to a group towards whom they hold a neutral attitude.

The other study which found the effects of judges' attitudes on ratings to be unrelated to the scale position of the item is the study by Ward (1966). His results are fully consistent with AL predictions. In his study, all statements, regardless of their relative positions on the scale, tended to be rated more unfavourably the more favourable the judges. However, since he eliminated a considerable proportion of his subjects according to rather questionable criteria, his results provide only doubtful support for AL theory. It seems therefore to be a reasonable conclusion that, on the whole, studies of the effects of judges' attitudes on ratings of attitude statements do not support AL theory predictions.

AL theory is rather more successful when used to predict context effects due to the composition of the item series. The prevailing AL of a person performing the attitude rating task should not only be determined by residual factors of past experience, but also by focal and background stimuli. A judge's AL, and therefore his ratings, should vary as a function of variations in the item series. Variations in the item series, or in the order of presentation, should result in the same sort of context effects as those demonstrated in psychophysical judgement experiments conducted within the framework of AL theory.

The first person to examine the effects of variations in the item series on judgements of attitude statements was Fehrer (1952), who presented subjects with statements from a Thurstone scale of attitudes towards war. On the basis of Thurstone's original scale values, she was able to vary systematically the content of the item series given to each group. The control scale C consisted of 55 items, five items from each of the Thurstone scale values from 0 (extremely pacifist) to 10 (extremely militaristic). The militaristic series M contained a preponderance of militaristic statements. The series consisted of 48 items, six of each Thurstone scale value from 3 to 10. Thus, the series was truncated at the pacifist end by omitting the most pacifist statements. The third series P was weighted towards the pacifist end. It contained 48 items with scale values from 0 to 7. Twenty-five items, five each with values from 3 to 7, were common to series C, M and P.

Each scale was given to one of three groups of 100 students, every one of them undifferentiated with respect to their own attitude on the issue. The mean judgement of the common items should, according to prediction, have been highest (most militaristic) in scale P, next highest in scale C, and lowest in scale M. The means obtained were in the order predicted, although the differences between them were comparatively small. In fact, the means for scales P and C did not differ significantly from each other. Moreover, where shifts did occur they were limited to certain items. As Fehrer writes:

> Items rated very militaristic, very pacifistic, and neutral on Scale C maintained the same values on Scales M and P. The items whose scale values changed were those near the truncated ends of the experimental scales, namely the moderately pacifistic items on Scale M and the moderately militaristic items on Scale P. As the neutral items were the same on all three scales, the shifts found cannot be attributed to shifts in adaptation

level. Instead, they seem to be related to the fact that the extreme judgment categories were differently defined by the three groups of judges.

1952, p. 188

Fehrer's study thus provides only mild support for AL theory and, as we will point out later, her results are much more consistent with Upshaw's variable-perspective model than with AL theory.

A study which combined an item-order manipulation with a manipulation of judges' attitudes is that of Segall (1959). In his study the issue referred to by the statements was that of the fraternity system. His main manipulations were as follows: first, the subjects (college students) were divided into three groups according to whether they were "pro-fraternity", "moderate", or "anti-fraternity" (as determined from their responses to three questions embedded in a questionnaire administered one month previously). Then, one third of the subjects in each group received 24 "pro-fraternity" statements, followed by 24 "anti-fraternity" statements ("pro-con" condition); for another third the order was reversed ("con-pro" condition), and for the last third, both types were intermingled ("control"). Sixteen items expressing neutral attitudes towards college fraternities were interspersed among these 48 times.

Segall's main analysis concerned the effects of the manipulation of item order and judges' attitudes on subjects' mean judgements of the item series as a whole. According to AL theory, the mean should be lowest (that is nearest to the anti-fraternity end of the scale) for the pro-fraternity judges, intermediate for the neutral judges, and highest for the anti-fraternity judges. Furthermore, judges in the "pro-con" condition should displace their judgements in the "anti" direction and judges in the "con-pro" condition should displace their judgements in the "pro" direction. This should be due to the fact that for the greatest part of the rating task, the AL of the judges in the "pro-con" condition should be on the "pro" side of the neutral point, whereas the AL of the judges in the "con-pro" condition should be on the "con" side. Both the effects of judges' attitudes and of the item order were in the expected direction and statistically significant. Thus, the analysis of the means of the rating of the item series supported AL theory predictions.

The results of a second analysis are only partly consistent with AL theory. In this analysis, Segall inspected the mean ratings of the neutral items in the context of the first half and the second half of each experimental condition. Results for the first half of the testing session, that is when subjects in the "pro-con" condition rated the "pro" items and subjects in the "con-pro" condition rated the "con" items, were consistent with AL theory predictions. Relative to the neutral items in the control condition, the neutral items in the "pro" part of the "pro-con" condition were displaced towards the "con" end of the scale, whereas the neutral items in the "con" part of the "con-pro" condition were displaced towards the "pro" end of the scale. However, the context effects during the second half of the session were not in the predicted direction. The mean judgement of the neutral items of the "pro-con" group was the same in both halves; the mean judgement of the "con-pro" group shifted in the "pro" direction in the "pro" context which is quite opposite to AL theory predictions. Furthermore, judges' attitudes had no significant effect on ratings of neutral items.

With the exception of the ratings of the neutral statements during the second half of the testing session, the effects of the item order manipulation are consistent with AL theory. However, Segall's support for AL theory may have been an artifact of the way he analysed his data. The differential polarization of ratings due to judges' attitudes observed in previous studies can only be detected if the ratings of favourable, neutral, and unfavourable statements are analysed separately and not when only the overall mean effects are analysed. If the effects of judges' attitudes on ratings in Segall's study had been due to differences in judges' AL, the neutral items should have been displaced in the same direction as all the other statements. The fact that judges' attitudes apparently had no effect on mean ratings of the neutral statements is, therefore, inconsistent with AL theory; it supports our suspicion that the differences in the overall mean rating of all the statements may have been caused by differential polarization effects.

The variable series model: an application of the "rubber-band" model to social judgement

The "variable series" or "variable perspective" model of Upshaw (1962) is essentially an application of Volkmann's (1951) "rubber-band" model to social judgement. It is based on Volkmann's position that the stimulus range which the subject takes into account when performing the judgement task (his "psychological range" or "perspective"), the stimulus value, and the number of categories he is instructed to use are the *only* determinants of his judgement. In the attitude rating task, the subject's psychological range, or, as Upshaw calls it, his "perspective", is determined by the most extreme attitude positions on a given issue

he considers in making his judgements. These extreme positions constitute the end-points of the subject's psychological range. The model
assumes that, in performing the attitude rating task, the subject sub-
divides his psychological range into as many subsegments of equal size
as the number of categories he is instructed to use. He then assigns statements to these segments (categories) by assessing the relative distance of
each statement from the two end-points of his psychological range.

With the experimental paradigm used for most of the attitude rating
studies, two of the three parameters of Volkmann's model (stimulus
range and number of response categories) are fixed. The various groups
of judges rate the *same* set of stimuli using the *same* set of categories.
According to the model, the differences observed in the rating of judges
of different attitudes indicate, therefore, a difference in the psychological
range or perspective of these judges. Upshaw suggests that so long as the
range of items presented is sufficiently wide to include statements that
correspond to the judge's own position, his psychological range will be
determined by the extreme statements included in the item series.
Consequently his ratings are not predicted to differ from those of any
other judge whose own position is likewise represented within the item
range. Judges whose own positions lie *within* the range of items presented
to them for judgement are referred to by Upshaw as "in-range" judges.
However, if a comparatively narrow range of items is presented such
that the judge's own position lies *outside* the range of items presented, his
ratings of items will be influenced by his attitude. Under these conditions,
the judge will adopt as end-points for his judgement scale, at one end,
his own attitude on the issue, and, at the other end, the further extreme
of the item series. Upshaw refers to such judges, whose own attitudes lie
beyond the range of the item series, as "out-of-range" judges.

Thus, out-of-range judges are assumed to add their own position to
the item series. Therefore, in effect, out-of-range judges and in-range
judges respond to different series; hence the name "variable series"
model. The alternative name of the model—"variable perspective"
model—refers to the assumed differences in the perspectives of in-range
and out-of-range judges. Since only one end of the out-of-range judge's
psychological range is determined by the stimulus series, whilst the other
end is determined by his own extreme position, the psychological range
of out-of-range judges exceeds the stimulus range; thus, it also exceeds
the psychological range of in-range judges, which is assumed to coincide
with the stimulus range. Hence whilst the centre of the psychological

range of the in-range judge should coincide with the centre of the stimulus range, the centre of the out-of-range judge's psychological range is predicted to be displaced towards the opposite end. Thus, for out-of-range judges, the centre of their psychological range varies as a direct function of the extremity of their own position whilst the average of their ratings varies as an inverse function.

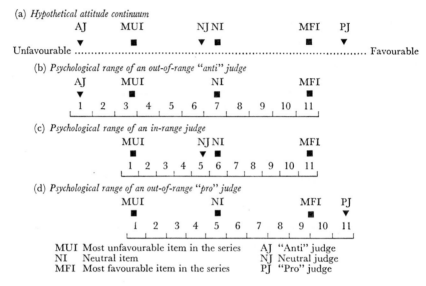

Fig. 5.2. Differences in psychological ranges of "in-range" and "out-of-range" judges.

To clarify this, let us discuss an hypothetical attitude rating study in which three judges, one with an extremely unfavourable attitude (AJ), one with a neutral attitude (NJ), and one with an extremely favourable attitude (PJ) rate a series of attitude statements. This is illustrated in Fig. 5.2. Lines (b) to (d) illustrate the AJ, NJ, and PJ judges' psychological ranges when rating the item series. Each of the psychological ranges is divided into eleven segments, reflecting the subdivision of the rating scale into eleven categories. Since all three judges are instructed to use the same number of categories, the two out-of-range judges AJ and PJ employ broader categories than the in-range judge NJ, as a result of their broader psychological range. If we check, for each of the three judges, the category position of the neutral item NI, we see that the item would receive the most favourable rating by the "anti" judge AJ, and the most unfavourable rating by the "pro" judge PJ, with the judge NJ giving an intermediate rating. The same would be true for any other item in the series.

At least when dealing with relatively extreme judges it is often difficult to determine in advance exactly which judges are out-of-range and which are in-range, granted present methods of attitude measurement. The variable perspective predictions for the classical social judgement paradigm are therefore similar to AL theory predictions. Both models predict that judges with favourable attitudes towards some issue will tend to rate (relevant) attitude statements less favourably than will judges with unfavourable attitudes. However, unlike AL theory, the variable series model does not make the assumption that differences in the ratings given by different groups of judges are necessarily associated with differences in the ways they "perceive" or "interpret" the statements. Instead, Upshaw's model attempts to explain such effects in terms of how the judges define or anchor the extremes of their judgement scale. The effects observed in social judgement are thus assumed to be dependent on the subject's use of the judgement scale, and not the necessary result of any "motivational" processes that influence his "perception" of the items. Furthermore, the assumption that the psychological range of out-of-range judges exceeds the stimulus range at that end of the series which is near the judge's own attitude position implies more than just that the centre of the psychological range of out-of-range judges will differ from that of in-range judges. The assumption that the psychological range of out-of-range judges exceeds that of in-range judges also predicts differences in the size of the segments or categories into which judges divide their psychological range. Since all judges are required to use the same number of categories, category size is predicted to vary directly with the width of the subject's psychological range or perspective. Since out-of-range judges are assumed to have a wider perspective than in-range judges, the size of their categories is also predicted to be greater than that of in-range judges. Therefore, since, in the case of the out-of-range judge, any given category would cover a wider region of the attitude continuum than in the case of the in-range judge, the out-of-range judge would be predicted to concentrate his ratings of any given set of statements into a smaller number of adjacent categories and thus give less polarized judgements than the in-range judge, who requires the total span of the judgement scale to encompass the range of items with which he is presented.

A further difference between the variable series model and AL theory exists in their predictions of the effects of manipulations of the item series on judges' ratings. Unlike AL theory, the variable series model predicts an interaction between a judge's attitude position and the stimulus range on ratings of attitude statements. According to the variable series model, only those changes of the stimulus series which expand or contract a subject's psychological range will affect his judgements of the statements. For example, contraction of the stimulus range, that is, an elimination of some of the most extreme statements, should affect ratings only if this manipulation also contracts the subject's psychological range. Since the psychological range of an out-of-range judge is determined only by the extreme statements opposite his own position, only elimination of these statements should contract his psychological range. Elimination of the extreme statements near his own position should not affect his psychological range, which extends beyond the nearer end of the stimulus range and is anchored to his own position. Again, in view of the difficulty of determining precisely who is an out-of-range judge, this prediction cannot be tested in the absolute form stated above. Even if we do not know how many members of a group of judges with extreme attitudes are in-range and how many are out-of-range judges, we would still expect elimination of all the unfavourable statements from an item series to have a greater effect on the ratings given by a group of judges with extremely favourable attitudes than on those given by judges with extremely unfavourable attitudes. Similarly, elimination of all favourable statements should affect ratings given by unfavourable judges more than ratings given by favourable judges.

Before looking at the research directly concerned with this interaction between item range and judge's attitudes, let us first consider the variable series interpretation of the results of studies employing the classical social judgement paradigm. The typical finding of studies which used statements of attitudes towards Negroes as stimulus material was that pro-Negro judges gave the most polarized ratings, and anti-Negro judges gave the least polarized ratings, with neutral judges being intermediate. According to the variable series model, these findings indicate that the pro-Negro judges employ the narrowest perspective whilst anti-Negro judges employ the widest perspective. That is, in performing the ratings anti-Negro judges are assumed to take into account more extreme statements, both unfavourable and favourable, than pro-Negro judges.

This assumption is somewhat contrary to what one would expect. In most studies, pro-Negro judges held more extreme positions than did anti-Negro judges. Therefore, if the perspectives of extreme pro- and anti-Negro judges were anchored at their preferred end of the scale to their own position and at the rejected end to the most extreme items, one would expect the "pro" judges to hold a broader perspective than the "anti" judges. This should be especially so, since the unfavourable statements included in the item series used in most of these studies (Hinckley, 1932) were more extreme than the favourable statements.

As evidence to support his viewpoint that the perspective of pro-Negro judges is narrower than that of anti-Negro judges, Upshaw cites a study by Ostrom (1966). As part of an experiment which we will discuss later, Ostrom asked his subjects (Negroes and unselected white students) to write two attitude statements which should represent the two extremes of the pro-Negro anti-Negro attitude continuum. They wrote these "perspective statements" after they had rated a series of statements of attitudes towards Negroes. The perspective statements were then categorized in terms of their extremity by a separate group of three judges, and the resulting scores were taken as a measure of the width of each subject's perspective. Assessed by this method, the perspectives of Negro judges were significantly narrower than those of the white subjects. However, there are reasons for doubting whether these results reflect true differences in perspective. When a Negro judge is asked to write a statement about the social position of the Negro, he is in fact writing a statement about himself. It seems quite possible that this fact has something to do with the finding that Negroes wrote less extreme statements. One might be much less reluctant to write that someone else was an idiot or a genius than to use similar terms to describe oneself. As soon as one applies these labels to oneself, they conflict either with modesty or with self-respect.

Furthermore, if the differences found in the ratings of pro-Negro and anti-Negro judges were fully due to differences in their perspective, scales constructed from the ratings of the various groups of judges should have the properties of equal interval scales. This prediction follows from the variable perspective assumption that subjects divide their psychological range into as many equal intervals as they are asked to use categories. If scales computed from ratings of a common set of statements by judges of different attitudes were all equal interval scales, scatterplots relating the work of two groups of judges for a common set of items should be linear. If the two regression lines of such a plot were nonlinear, this finding would constitute evidence that the two groups of judges differ in their judgemental units in ways that are related to particular regions of the scale. Only recently, Upshaw (1969) emphasized again that the variable perspective model requires that scales constructed from the ratings of two groups of judges should be "significantly related linearly and not significantly related by any more complex function" (p. 331). In a test of the relationship existing between scales constructed from the ratings of groups of judges differing in attitudes, some of the data of Upshaw's (1962) and Zavalloni and Cook's (1965) studies were re-analysed (Stroebe, 1968, 1971). In the basic condition of Upshaw's study (the "total series" condition), groups of judges with attitudes towards Negroes ranging from favourable to moderately unfavourable rated a set of statements which supposedly covered the total range from favourable to unfavourable attitudes. A multiple polynomial regression analysis of the scales constructed from the ratings of the two extreme groups indicated that, although the scales were significantly linearly related ($p < 0.01$, $F = 1987.00$, $df = 1/112$), a quadratic function accounted for more of the total variance than did a straight line (quadratic component: $p < 0.01$, $F = 7.61$, $df = 1/111$). However, the difference between the linear and the curvilinear model in terms of the accounted variance was so minimal that it would be dangerous to base too much upon the results of this analysis. More conclusive was a re-analysis of some of the data of the Zavalloni and Cook (1965) study. In this study five groups of judges differing in their attitudes towards Negroes rated the same set of statements of attitudes towards Negroes that had been used in the Upshaw study (two items were omitted). A multiple polynomial regression analysis of the scales constructed from the ratings of the two extreme groups again indicated that, although the scales were significantly linearly related ($p < 0.01$, $F = 559.10$, $df = 1/110$), a quadratic function accounted for about 3 per cent more of the total variance than did a straight line (quadratic component: $p < 0.01$, $F = 25.08$, $df = 1/109$). Further analyses relating to each other the ratings of the less extreme groups always indicated that a quadratic function could account for significantly more of the total variance than a linear model. Visual inspection of the published data of the Selltiz, Edrich and Cook (1965) study seems to indicate the existence of similar curvilinear relationships between the ratings of the extreme groups employed in their study. It should be emphasized, however, that the results of these analyses have to be interpreted with caution. Both sets of scales computed from the ratings of the extreme groups in the Upshaw (1962) and the Zavalloni and Cook (1965) study were significantly linearly related. Descriptively, in both cases, linear F was markedly larger than curvilinear F. Furthermore, the linear correlation between the sets of ratings of the extreme groups was $r = 0.97$ in the Upshaw study and $r = 0.91$ in the Zavalloni and Cook study. Nevertheless, the fact that scales constructed from ratings of groups of judges who differ in their attitudes on the issue investigated are significantly curvilinearly related seems to contradict the equal interval assumptions of the variable series model. It seems therefore, that the differences found in the ratings of pro-Negro and anti-Negro judges cannot be fully accounted for in terms of the differences in judges' perspectives.

Of the studies which used attitude statements towards other issues, only Manis's (1960, 1961) studies yielded results which were clearly different from those of the Negro studies. Manis, who used statements of attitudes towards college fraternities, found that pro- and anti-fraternity subjects gave more polarized ratings than his neutral subjects. According to the variable series model, this would indicate that pro- and anti-fraternity subjects had a narrower perspective in rating the attitude statements than did the subjects with neutral attitudes. Although there is no direct evidence in Manis's papers supporting this view, there is some indirect evidence indicating that the size of the categories employed by "pro" and "anti" subjects was smaller than the category size of neutral subjects. Unfortunately Manis did not test whether the sets of scale values computed from the ratings of the different groups of judges were significantly curvilinearly related; we therefore do not know whether his subjects subdivided their psychological range into segments of equal size.

However, the failure of the variable series model to fully account for the performance of judges in the attitude rating task does not imply that all assumptions of the model are invalid. The curvilinearity observed in scales constructed from the ratings of pro-Negro and anti-Negro judges merely invalidates the variable series assumption about division of the psychological range or perspective into segments of equal size. It does not disprove the variable series assumption that a judge's perspective is an important factor in determining his performance in the attitude rating task.

More direct evidence bearing on the question of whether subjects judge items against their perspective end-anchors comes from studies

E

manipulating the item range. Two such studies (Fehrer, 1952; Segall, 1959) have already been discussed in our section on AL theory. Of these, Fehrer's results seem to be the more consistent with variable series predictions. Fehrer asked judges who were undifferentiated with regard to their attitudes to rate one of three sets of attitude statements. Series C contained statements representing militarist as well as pacifist attitudes. From series P all militarist statements were eliminated, whilst from series M all the pacifist statements were eliminated. If Fehrer's subjects had been in-range judges in all experimental conditions their psychological range should have coincided with the item range of each of the three series. Thus, relative to the mean ratings of the same items in series C, mean ratings of series M should have been more pacifist, while mean ratings of series P should have been more militarist. However, although the mean ratings were in the expected order, the fact that elimination of the militarist statements affected ratings more than elimination of the pacifist statements would suggest (according to the variable perspective model) that the majority of Fehrer's subjects held fairly militarist attitudes. They would thus have been out-of-range judges in the P condition and in-range judges in the M condition. Unfortunately, Fehrer does not report the attitude positions of her subjects. Nevertheless, her finding that the abortion of the item series had the greatest effect on items near the aborted end is consistent with the variable series model. Asymmetric contraction of subjects' perspectives should have the greatest effect on ratings of statements near the aborted end and least effect on ratings of statements near the end of the series which remained unchanged.

Segall's (1959) results are less consistent with variable series predictions. According to the variable series model, the item order manipulations ("con-pro", "pro-con") should have affected the perspectives of "pro" and "con" subjects in different ways. For example, during the first half of the "con-pro" condition, subjects were only presented with unfavourable and neutral items, while being presented with neutral and favourable statements during the second half of the session. Thus, the stimulus range was narrower during the first half of the experimental session than during the second half of the session.[1] Since the attitude of

[1] Since there was no pause or other interruption between the two halves of the testing session we can safely assume that subjects perceived the statements presented during both halves of the testing session as members of the same stimulus series. Therefore, whereas during the first half of the testing session the item series ranged from unfavourable to neutral only, the item series during the second half of the testing series can be said to have ranged from unfavourable to

the "con" judges was near the unfavourable end of the attitude continuum, they should have been in-range judges during both halves of the testing session. Their perspectives, being supposedly anchored to the extreme statements of the item series, should have been expanded with the expansion of the item range. The attitudes of the "pro" judges, on the other hand, were near the favourable end of the attitude continuum. Therefore, they should have been out-of-range judges during the first half of the testing session. Their perspectives should have exceeded the stimulus range at the favourable end to include their own favourable attitudes. Thus, the addition of the favourable statements during the second half of the testing session should not have had any significant effect on their perspectives, nor, therefore, on their ratings. Similarly, the item order manipulation in the "pro-con" condition should have affected the perspectives of "con" subjects less than those of "pro" subjects. Introduction of unfavourable statements during the second half of the "pro-con" testing session should have expanded the perspectives of "pro" subjects but not those of "con" subjects. The perspectives of the "con" subjects should have been broader than those of the "pro" subjects during the first half of the testing session, and equally broad during the second half. Segall's analyses do not support these predictions. In all relevant analyses, the item order by judges' attitude interaction had an F of less than 1.

The interaction between item range and judges' attitudes predicted by the variable series model is demonstrated more clearly in a study by Upshaw (1962). Like Fehrer (1952) he constructed three separate item series. The first of these (the t condition) consisted of the total set of 114 items expressing attitudes towards the Negro used by Hinckley (1932). The second set consisted of the same scale aborted at the pro-Negro end by removal of the 28 most favourable items (the "a + condition"). The third set (the "a − condition") was aborted at the anti-Negro end by removal of the 28 most unfavourable items from the total series.

Each of the series was sorted by one of three large groups of judges (introductory psychology students). After the sorting had been completed, judges were administered a questionnaire on the basis of which they were divided up according to their own attitudes on the issue. These judges whose scores fell within the most prejudiced, the middle, and the

favourable, although no unfavourable statements were presented during the second half. The reader may remember that a similar assumption lay behind Parducci and Hohle's (1957) study (cf. p. 27).

least prejudiced quintiles were used in the analysis. These groups were referred to as the A, N, and P judges respectively.

Since the t series was assumed to cover the entire range of the attitudes held by the judges, Upshaw predicted that the A, N, and P judges in the t condition should have identical perspectives and that their judgements of the statements should not therefore differ systematically. In the a + condition, however, the A and N judges would both be "in-range" judges, since their attitudes would still be represented within the item series, and their judgements should consequently not differ from each other. The P judges, on the other hand, would be "out-of-range", and would thus have a wider perspective than the A and N judges, corres-

TABLE 5.3*

Mean item values

Item subset	Experimental conditions	Attitude of judges		
		A	N	P
Extremely "pro"	t	9.87	10.20	10.30
	a+	—	—	—
	a—	9.79	9.72	9.98
Moderately "pro"	t	8.22	8.56	9.03
	a+	—	—	—
	a—	8.27	8.30	8.61
Midscale	t	6.15	6.23	5.87
	a+	6.64	6.63	5.83
	a—	6.61	5.89	5.40
Moderately "anti"	t	3.98	3.26	3.19
	a+	4.33	3.73	2.93
	a—	3.75	2.93	2.53
Extremely "anti"	t	2.09	1.62	1.53
	a+	2.46	1.79	1.40
	a—	—	—	—

Note. A dash indicates that an experimental manipulation rendered impossible the collection of data otherwise appropriate for a cell in the Table. Dashes appear for both extremely "pro" and moderately "pro" items in the a+ condition and for only the extremely "anti" items in the a— condition because of the generally lower values obtained in the present study as compared with those obtained by Hinckley (1932). Only four of the "anti" items removed in the a— condition, on the basis of the Hinckley data have received moderately "anti" values in the present study.

* Adapted with permission from H. S. Upshaw, 1962.

ponding to the a + range expanded to include their own position. Their judgements of the statements should, consequently, be less favourable than those given by the A and N judges. Conversely, in the a — condition, the P and N judges should be "in-range" and the A judges "out-of-range". The P and N judges should, therefore, give the same judgements as each other, whilst the A judges should judge the statements as more favourable.

Table 5.3 presents the mean judgements of items given by A, N, and P judges under the three experimental conditions (t, a +, a —). The results obtained were in general accordance with Upshaw's predictions. Judges were far less influenced by abortion of the item series at the end of the scale nearest to their own position. The differences between mean item values for t and a + conditions are far larger for A judges than for P judges, whereas the differences between the t and the a — conditions are far larger for A judges than for P judges. This interaction between item range and judges' attitudes strongly supports the variable series model and is quite inconsistent with AL predictions.

According to the variable series model, this differential effect of the item range manipulation on the ratings given by the P, A, and N judges is mediated by differential expansion or contraction of the judges' perspectives. Therefore, the item range manipulation should not only influence the centre of the judges' psychological range but also the size of their categories. As we pointed out earlier, if all judges have to use the same number of categories, category size is related directly to perspective width; the wider a judge's perspective, the greater should be the size of his categories. Thus, if the perspective of P judges in the a + condition was wider than that of the A judges, the width of the P judges' categories in this condition should have been greater than that of the A judges. Similarly, if the perspective of P judges in the a — condition was smaller than that of the A judges, the width of the P judges' categories in this condition should have been smaller than that of the A judges. Furthermore, the category width of P judges in the a + condition should be greater than that of the P judges in the a — condition, whereas the reverse should be true for A judges.

These predictions can be tested in a fairly rough way by inspecting the ratings of A and P judges of those two groups of items ("midscale" and "moderately anti") which were common to both the a + and the a — conditions. The difference in the mean ratings of the two groups of items can serve as a rough index of judges' category width. The greater the size of the categories employed by a given group of judges, the smaller should be the differences in their mean ratings of the two groups of items, as can be shown quite easily. Suppose the distance between two points was measured either in inches (greater category size) or in centimetres (smaller category size). Obviously, the numerical value given for the distance between these two points would be smaller when an inch scale was used rather than a centimetre scale.

TABLE 5.4

Differences between mean ratings of the "midscale" and the "moderately anti" statements for A and P judges (Upshaw, 1962)

Condition	Judges	Mean differences
a+	A	2·31
	P	2·90
a−	A	2·86
	P	2·87

Table 5.4 presents the differences of A and P judges' mean ratings of "midscale" and "moderately anti" items in the a + and a − conditions. According to the variable series model, the size of the categories used by the P judges in the a + condition and the A judges in the a − condition should have been wider (and hence the difference between the means smaller) than that of the A judges in the a + condition and the P judges in the a − condition. The pattern of differences obtained is not consistent with variable series predictions. This is naturally a very rough test of these predictions but the result of this analysis is consistent with the result of a more sophisticated analysis conducted by Upshaw (1965) in a later paper. Thus, the analysis of the effects of the item range manipulation on the size of the categories employed by A, N, and P judges does not support the variable series predictions.

Upshaw's (1962) study was replicated in a somewhat modified form by Ostrom (1966). His subjects were Negro students from a small southern Negro college and unselected white students from a large southern university. Item range was manipulated in a way comparable to Upshaw's study, although with a smaller item pool containing a larger proportion of extremely favourable (Negro superiority) items. The a + range covered positions from white supremacy to equality, the t range from white supremacy to black supremacy, and the a − range from

moderate white supremacy to black supremacy. Although this manipulation resulted in a marginally significant interaction between item
range and judges' race, the interaction did not follow the pattern of
Upshaw's results. The item range by judges' race interaction in Ostrom's
study was apparently due to a greater effect of the item range manipulation on the ratings given by the Negro subjects as compared to the
white subjects. But these results are not necessarily inconsistent with
variable series predictions. If we assume that the perspective of the Negro
subjects was narrower than that of the white subjects, the variable series
model would actually predict the Negro subjects to be more affected by
the item range manipulation than the white subjects. As we pointed out
earlier, Ostrom attempted to measure his subjects' perspectives directly
and apparently found the Negro subjects to have narrower perspectives
than the white subjects. The perspectives of Ostrom's subjects could be
inferred directly from the pro- and anti-Negro statements they were
asked to write down after they had concluded the rating of the item
series. However, as we discussed earlier, there are reasons to doubt the
validity of these statements as indicators of perspective. Furthermore, if
these statements really reflected the judges' perspectives and if the interaction effect of judges' race and item range on ratings was mediated by
perspective, Ostrom should have found the same item range by judges'
race interaction with these "perspective statements". In other words,
the item range manipulation should have influenced the Negro subjects
more than the white subjects not only with respect to how they rated the
items presented to them but also with respect to the extremity of the
"perspective statements" which they themselves constructed. Nevertheless, although Ostrom found that the item range manipulation significantly affected the extremity of the perspective statements in the a +, t,
and a — conditions, there was no differential effect on the subjects of
different races.

So far we have reviewed four studies (Fehrer, 1952; Segall, 1959;
Upshaw, 1962; Ostrom, 1966) which manipulated the range of the item
series. In all four studies the item range manipulation resulted in the
effect predicted by both AL theory and the variable series model, that
items included in a set of predominantly favourable statements were
rated as less favourable than items included in a set of predominantly
unfavourable statements. However, unlike AL theory, the variable
series model predicts that the item range manipulation should also
interact with judges' attitudes. Judges should be less affected by elimi-

nation of statements near their own attitude position than by elimination of statements at the opposite end of the attitude continuum. Since Fehrer did not distinguish between judges on the basis of their attitudes, her study is not relevant to this question. Segall, who manipulated both item range and judges' attitudes, found no evidence of the attitude by item range interaction which Upshaw's model would predict. Upshaw and Ostrom found the item range manipulation to interact with judges' attitudes, but in the case of Ostrom's study it is doubtful whether the interaction effect observed is consistent with variable series predictions. The best we can conclude, then, is that the variable series predictions regarding the interaction between item range and judges' attitudes are only partially supported by the relevant research findings. But, at the same time, the item range by judges' attitude interactions observed in Ostrom's and Upshaw's studies cannot be explained in terms of AL theory, or any other model.

Upshaw (1965) is the first to admit that "a judge's perspective may be determined by a wide variety of influences other than his own attitude and the items of the series" (p. 62). The problem is that, as long as we do not know more about this "variety of influences", it is very difficult to predict judgements of any given series of items. Furthermore, the finding that in some of the studies (Upshaw, 1962; Selltiz et al., 1965; Zavalloni and Cook, 1965) scales constructed from the ratings of pro- and anti-Negro subjects appear to be slightly curvilinearly related seems to indicate that one cannot, as Upshaw (1965) assumes, "completely specify the judgement of a particular item on the basis of knowledge of two perspective parameters (i.e. the stimulus values of the upper and lower end items), the stimulus value of the item, and the number of categories available in the judgemental language" (p. 62).

The assimilation-contrast model

The assimilation-contrast model has been developed by Sherif and Hovland and their co-workers (Hovland and Sherif, 1952; Hovland et al., 1957; Sherif et al., 1958; Sherif and Hovland, 1961; Sherif et al., 1965). This was first suggested by Hovland et al. (1957) as part of a theory of attitude change. As put forward by Hovland et al., the main hypothesis relevant to the question we are considering is as follows:

In evaluations by S of what position is advocated by a communication, the greater the distance between S's own stand and the position advocated by the communication, the greater the displacement *away* from S's position ("contrast effect"). When only a small discrepancy in position exists there will be a tendency for displacement *towards* S's stand ("assimilation effect").   1957, p. 245

Applied to the attitude rating task, the assimilation-contrast model predicts that statements at different positions along the attitude continuum will be displaced in different directions, depending upon their proximity to the attitude of the people judging them. In rating a series of attitude statements judges will "assimilate", that is displace towards their own position, statements expressing attitudes similar to their own. They will "contrast", that is displace away from their own position, statements which express attitudes very different from their own attitudes. Thus, compared with a neutral judge, a "pro" judge will assimilate (judge as more favourable) statements expressing favourable attitudes towards the attitude issue, and contrast (judge as less favourable) neutral and unfavourable statements. An "anti" judge, on the other hand, will assimilate the unfavourable statements and contrast the neutral and favourable statements.

However, Sherif and Hovland do not consider the distance of an item from the judge's own position to be the only factor that determines how it will be judged. In predicting more precisely which items will be assimilated and which will be contrasted, other concepts of major importance to the theory are the "latitudes" of acceptance, rejection and noncommitment. These are defined, respectively, as the ranges of statements to which the judge in question indicates agreement, disagreement and noncommitment. In operational terms, when the judge is required to rate his agreement with each statement in terms of a five-point scale consisting of the categories "strongly accept", "accept", "neither accept nor reject", "reject" and "strongly reject", those statements rated in either of the first two categories are said to fall within his latitude of acceptance, those rated in the middle category into his latitude of non-commitment, and those rated in the last two categories into his latitude of rejection.

Thus, formulated more precisely, the assimilation-contrast model predicts that statements falling into a subject's latitude of acceptance will be assimilated towards the subject's own position, whereas statements falling into his latitude of rejection will be contrasted away from his position. Statements falling into a subject's latitude of noncommitment are likely to be neither contrasted nor assimilated. Sherif and Hovland (1961, p. 129) emphasize that "the latitudes of acceptance and rejection are conceived in motivational terms" and that therefore the "degree of the individual's personal involvement in an issue should be

E*

closely related to important characteristics of his latitudes of acceptance and rejection".

Specifically, the more involved and personally committed the individual is on the issue, the greater is the latitude of rejection in relation to the latitude of acceptance, the number of positions on which he remains noncommittal approaching zero. Conversely, less involved individuals are noncommittal toward more positions in the universe of discourse, and their latitudes of acceptance and rejection are approximately equal or encompass equally small segments of the total range of positions on the issue.

Sherif et al., 1965, p. 14.

It should be pointed out, however, that the assumption that the "more involved and personally committed the individual is on the issue, the greater is the latitude of rejection *in relation to* the latitude of acceptance", does not imply that the subjects' latitudes of acceptance vary to the same degree as their latitudes of rejection. In their studies during the 1960 presidential election, Sherif *et al.* (1965) observed that the size of subjects' latitudes of acceptance varied very little with variation of their involvement. The increase in judges' latitudes of rejection which accompanied increases in levels of involvement seemed to be mainly due to the decrease in the sizes of their latitudes of noncommitment. Thus, compared to uninvolved individuals, highly involved individuals seem to have only slightly smaller latitudes of acceptance but much smaller latitudes of noncommitment and much larger latitudes of rejection.

Since individuals holding extreme attitude positions on a given issue have typically been found to be more highly involved than individuals holding moderate attitudes (e.g. Cantril, 1946; Suchman, 1950), the relative sizes of judges' latitudes of acceptance, rejection and noncommitment are likely to vary with the extremity of their attitudes. Judges with extreme attitudes are likely to have broader latitudes of rejection and narrower latitudes of noncommitment than judges with moderate attitude positions. But it must be emphasized that although extremity of position and involvement are typically correlated and are difficult to separate operationally, they are conceptually different. Extremity of position *per se* is not assumed to be related to the relative size of judges' latitudes of acceptance, rejection and noncommitment. It is only because extreme judges are typically more involved towards the issue investigated than judges with moderate positions that extreme judges usually have wider latitudes of rejection and smaller latitudes of noncommitment than have more moderate judges.

The assimilation-contrast model thus incorporates two principles, a cognitive principle about the anchoring effects of judges' own positions on their ratings, and a motivational principle determining the relative sizes of a judge's latitudes of acceptance, rejection and noncommitment. The cognitive principle states that a judge's own position on an attitude issue constitutes an anchor for his ratings of relevant attitude statements. As an effect of this anchor, items near the anchor will be assimilated while more distant stimuli will be contrasted away. Which items he will perceive as near to his position and which as further away will depend on his personal involvement in the attitude issue. Thus, unlike the two models discussed so far, the assimilation-contrast model predicts ratings to vary not only as a function of judges' attitude position but also as a function of their involvement in the attitude issue. The assimilation-contrast model predicts that, if two judges hold the same attitude position but differ in involvement, the more highly involved judge will assimilate fewer and contrast more statements than the less involved judge.

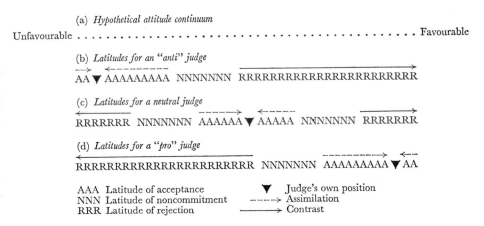

Fig. 5.3. Hypothetical latitudes for judges with different own positions.

Figure 5.3 illustrates the model with a hypothetical example of the relative size and location on the attitude continuum of the latitudes of acceptance, rejection and noncommitment of three judges holding, respectively, extremely favourable, neutral and extremely unfavourable attitudes towards the attitude object. It should be apparent from the Figure that the extreme judges will be rather similar in their ratings, while both will be different from the neutral judge. The extreme judges will rate the extreme statements, the favourable as well as the unfavourable ones, as more extreme than will the neutral judge. The major difference between the ratings of the extreme judges should occur in their judgement of the midscale items which, due to the asymmetry in the relative size of the latitudes of acceptance and rejection of highly involved judges, will be displaced towards the unfavourable end by the "pro" judge and towards the favourable end by the "anti" judge.

According to Sherif and Hovland, the assimilation and contrast of attitude ratings attributed to the anchoring effects of judges' attitude positions represent the operation of essentially the same processes as those invoked to account for the results of the Sherif *et al.* (1958) experiment on lifted weights, discussed in Chapter 3. Even if the interpretation of the latter results was non-problematic, the comparison is an extremely misleading one and detracts from, rather than contributes to, the potential usefulness of Sherif and Hovland's model. The point is simply that the assimilation-contrast model, as applied to social judgement, predicts that items in different positions along the continuum will be displaced in *different directions*, whilst, in the lifted weights experiment, *the stimulus series as a whole* is shifted either towards or away from the anchor. Whatever the merits of saying that the individual uses his own position "as an anchor" while judging attitude statements, it must be borne in mind that the resulting "anchoring effects" are dependent on the relation of each statement taken *individually* to the judge's own position, whereas such effects in psychophysics are dependent on the distance of the anchor from the series *as a whole*. The effects obtained, then, are completely different in the two cases. This difference is far more important, at the theoretical level, than any difference in the "complexity" of the two types of stimuli. The problem is not one that arises from trying to make a single model applicable to different types of stimuli, but one that arises from trying to make a single set of predictions compatible with essentially unrelated sets of results.

In no sense, therefore, do the results found by Sherif *et al.* (1958) for psychophysical judgement constitute an *explanation* of the assimilation and contrast effects found in social judgement. However, this need not necessarily affect the descriptive adequacy of the model. Judges with extreme attitudes may still tend to give more extreme ratings of items at both ends of the scales, though not for the reasons that Sherif and Hovland suggest.

Do judges assimilate acceptable items and contrast items they reject?

In most of the attitude rating studies which are relevant to this question, the effects of judges' own positions have been examined without any attempt being made to assess any independent effects due to involvement. We will discuss these studies first. In a second section we will discuss the few studies in which involvement has been included as a separate variable.

Of all the studies we have discussed which investigated the relationship between judges' attitude positions and their ratings, there are only two studies, namely those of Manis (1960, 1961), which unambiguously support the assimilation-contrast model. In both these studies, anti-fraternity, neutral and pro-fraternity college students rated a series of communications reflecting favourable, neutral or unfavourable attitudes towards the fraternity system. Manis found that the subjects assimilated those communications which advocated a relatively neutral position, such that the pro-fraternity subjects rated them as relatively favourable towards the fraternity system and the anti-fraternity subjects judged them as relatively unfavourable. Since the fraternity system is probably not a highly involving issue for the majority of the subjects, it is reasonable to assume that the neutral communications fell into the latitudes of acceptance for all three groups of subjects. The pattern of rating found for the neutral communications is, therefore, consistent with the assimilation-contrast model. The finding that the pro- and anti-fraternity subjects judged the extreme communications as more extreme than did the neutral subjects is also consistent with assimilation contrast predictions. The neutral subjects are likely to accept the favourable as well as the unfavourable communications. They should, therefore, show a tendency to judge these statements as nearer to their own neutral position. The extreme subjects, on the other hand, should accept and therefore assimilate the extreme communications at their own end of the scale, and should reject, and therefore contrast, the communications at the opposite extreme. Thus, assimilation of the extreme communications by the neutral subjects should lead to a displacement of statements towards the middle of the scale, whilst assimilation or contrast by the pro- and anti-fraternity subjects should lead to a displacement of statements towards the extremes of the scale.

Unfortunately, Manis's (1960, 1961) findings are rather atypical for the results of attitude rating studies. The typical finding, as we pointed out earlier, was that compared to the relatively neutral subjects, subjects with highly favourable attitudes gave more polarized ratings, whereas subjects with unfavourable attitudes tended to give less polarized ratings. Hence, only the findings for the favourable judges seem to conform to assimilation-contrast predictions. The ratings of the unfavourable judges do not seem to conform to the pattern predicted by the assimilation-contrast model.

In a comment on Upshaw's (1962) paper, Manis (1964) points out that the apparent inconsistency of Upshaw's findings with assimilation-contrast predictions could have been due to a failure to include subjects with extremely unfavourable attitude positions in Upshaw's subject sample. Manis argues that Upshaw's findings for his total range condition (t) were reasonably consistent with the assimilation-contrast model, although the displacement effects found by Upshaw seemed to be independent of the discrepancy between the judges' positions and the attitude statements; that is, both pro-Negro and anti-Negro subjects showed assimilation in judging pro-Negro items and contrast in judging anti-Negro items. Manis suggests that this inconsistency may be due to the fact that the judges were mainly distributed towards the "pro" end of the attitude continuum. Even the most anti-Negro judges might be more accurately described as holding neutral attitudes towards Negroes. Thus, the pro-Negro statements, which were relatively close to judges' views, were assimilated, while anti-Negro statements, which were more discrepant, showed contrast.

This explanation is difficult to test, since Upshaw did not measure his judges' attitudes in terms of the same scales[1] in which the items were judged. Fortunately Upshaw presented supplementary data from three groups of subjects who were selected on the same attitude criteria as judges in the main experiment; these supplementary subjects had to indicate their acceptance or rejection of 20 items that had been rated in the main study. On the basis of the scale values of these 20 items in the main experiment, Manis calculated the average position on the eleven-point scale accepted by the members of each group. For the "anti" judges the midpoint of the range of acceptable items was 6.16; for the neutral and "pro" judges the values were 7.44 and 8.70 respectively.

Figure 5.4 presents graphically the control scale values for the five

---

[1] Judges' attitudes were measured with the Murphy–Likert Scale of Attitude towards the Negro. Given only information about an individual's score on a Likert Scale, it is impossible to more than guess his position on an eleven-point Thurstone scale.

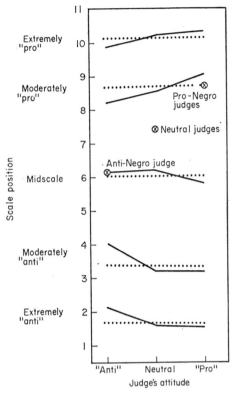

Fig. 5.4. Attitude as a determinant of perceived scale position for five subsets of opinion items. (Reproduced with permission from M. Manis, 1964.)

subsets of statements (dotted lines), the judgements given by the subjects of varying attitude (solid line), and the preferred scale positions of the three groups of judges (circles). The data presented in Fig. 5.4 seem to be fairly consistent with the assimilation-contrast model. As predicted, the neutral group show a tendency to assimilate statements that are relatively close to the judges' own positions whilst contrast appears on those that are farther removed. Some irregularities occur for the pro-Negro subjects. They contrast the moderately "pro" and extremely "pro" items even though these items seem to be relatively close to their own position. Manis (1964) suggests that these "apparent anomalies" may be due to the fact that Fig. 5.4 does not properly reflect the extremity of the attitudes within the pro-Negro group. He writes: "Since all of the pro-Negro judges endorsed the most extreme item in the experiment, the median member of this group would doubtless have endorsed items that were more favourable than those used by Upshaw, suggesting that the group's preferred position may have been somewhat higher on the y-axis than is shown [in Fig. 5.4]." (p. 640.)

Manis's explanation of why the anti-Negro judges consistently assimilated the items towards their own positions, regardless of discrepancy, is also reasonable. He suggested that because of the anti-Negro subjects' position in the middle of the scale, none of the attitude statements were sufficiently discrepant from the subjects' own positions to be contrasted. This explanation is supported by Upshaw's supplementary data which show that a large proportion of "anti" judges found statements near both extremes of the range still acceptable.

However, even if we accept Manis's (1964) reinterpretation of Upshaw's (1962) results, Upshaw's study is only one of several studies which found that judges with favourable attitudes gave more polarized ratings than judges with unfavourable attitudes, and Manis's criticism does not seem to hold for all of these other studies. For example, the most anti-Negro subjects in the Zavalloni and Cook (1965) study were "pledges" of fraternities known to have led a campaign against the admission of Negro students to the university. Although it is possible that these subjects did not hold as extreme attitudes as the most pro-Negro subjects, their attitude position should have been more extreme than those of the two groups (Groups III and IV) with moderate attitude positions. Nevertheless, the anti-Negro subjects seem to have given slightly less polarized ratings than these moderate subjects.

Manis's criticism is even less applicable to the Selltiz et al. (1965) study. As we pointed out earlier, Selltiz et al., in a second analysis of their data, divided the subjects into groups on the basis of an attitude inventory. Subjects from each geographical area were divided into a highly prejudiced, moderately prejudiced, and unprejudiced group depending on their responses to this attitude inventory. For example, the highly prejudiced group of the Border South subjects scored between 7 and 20 on an attitude inventory which ranged from 0 (most prejudiced) to 57 (least prejudiced). Although we do not know precisely how these scores relate to an eleven-point Thurstone scale of equal-appearing intervals, it seems reasonable to assume that a person who scored below 20 on the attitude inventory had a position near the unfavourable end of the attitude continuum. Thus, we would expect such a person to reject, and therefore contrast, at least the extremely favourable statements presented to him in the Selltiz et al. study. Nevertheless, the results followed the familiar pattern with the pro-Negro judges giving more polarized ratings of statements at both extremes than the neutral judges, whereas the anti-Negro judges were less polarized in their ratings of the extreme statements. Regrouping the subjects from other geographical areas according to their attitude inventory scores resulted in the same pattern of ratings.

Eiser's (1971a) study seems to be vulnerable to Manis's criticism, since the subjects with a restrictive attitude towards drug-use held, on average, less extreme positions than the subjects with a more permissive attitude towards the use of drugs. However, in an unpublished re-analysis the restrictive subjects were divided into two groups, one with only moderately restrictive attitudes and one with extremely restrictive attitudes. According to an assimilation-contrast model one would expect the group with only moderately restrictive attitudes to give less polarized ratings than the group with extremely restrictive attitudes. In fact, the observed differences in polarization, though non-significant, were in the reverse direction.

Thus, the failure of at least three studies to find a direct relationship between extremity of attitude and polarization does not seem to have been due to a failure to include subjects with sufficiently unfavourable attitude positions. It seems, therefore, that one has to accept that the assimilation-contrast model fails to account for the pattern of results observed in the studies of Eiser (1971a), Zavalloni and Cook (1965), and Selltiz et al. (1965). One has therefore either to reject the model or incorporate into it additional assumptions which can explain this partial failure.

The effects of judges' level of involvement on ratings of attitude statements

"Ego involvement, in plain terms, is the arousal . . . of the individual's stands in the context of appropriate situations, be they interpersonal relations or a judgement task in actual life or an experiment." (Sherif et al., 1965, p. 65.) In the attitude rating task an individual's ego involvement will be aroused through "the intrinsic importance for him of the issue to which the item or task is related because it concerns his abiding stand on the issue" (Sherif and Hovland, 1961, p. 197).

Like his attitude position, an individual's involvement in an attitude issue can be inferred either from verbal statements or from his actions.

For example, one can ask the individual how strongly he feels about his own position on a given attitude issue, how strongly he feels about the issue, and how much he feels the issue is personally relevant to him. Or one can assume that an individual who feels very strongly about a given attitude issue is more likely to take actions consistent with his attitude position than a person who feels less strongly about the issue.

This behavioural measure of involvement was used by Ward (1965) in an attempt to vary judges' involvement whilst keeping constant the extremity of their attitudes. In this study, 60 subjects, all with "uniform and extremely favourable attitudes towards the Negro", rated a series of statements relating to Negroes. There were 40 such statements, mainly drawn from the Hinckley scale with the addition of a few extremely pro-Negro statements. Of the 60 subjects, 40 had recently picketed local cinemas which practiced segregation. These 40 were divided into two equal groups. Subjects in the first of these—the "pickets-salient" condition—were contacted directly, and the experiment was conducted in such a way as to emphasize the importance of their participation in the picketing. "They were told that the reason for their selection was their membership in the picketing group, and the experimenter identified himself as being also a member . . . " (p. 205.) Before they filled out the questionnaires, the experimenter led a brief discussion on the importance of the group's picketing, the composition of the group's membership, and possible ways to get more people to participate in the picketing in the event that it should be resumed. All this was done to make the subject's membership to the picketing group more salient to the subject and thus heighten his involvement in the attitude judgement task.

Subjects in the second group—the "pickets-nonsalient" condition—were contacted indirectly and told that "they had been selected randomly to participate in a pretest of a national survey of college student opinion" (p. 205). Their membership of the picketing group was not mentioned.

In addition, 20 "non-pickets" were tested; some of these were contacted at the same time as subjects in the "pickets-nonsalient" condition, and the rest were contacted directly after their names had been suggested by subjects in the "pickets" conditions. This was done to ensure that subjects in this condition also held extremely pro-Negro attitudes. All subjects in this condition were given the same explanation for their being selected as had been given to subjects in the "pickets-nonsalient" condition.

Since involvement should leave the size of subjects' latitudes of acceptance relatively unaffected and since all three groups showed the same
attitude position, they should all accept a similar proportion of the most
favourable statements included in the attitude series. However, the
groups should differ in the sizes of their latitudes of rejection and noncommitment. Of the three groups the "pickets-salient" should have the
largest latitude of rejection and the smallest latitude of noncommitment,
while the "non-pickets" should have the smallest latitude of rejection
and the largest latitude of noncommitment. Therefore, the "pickets-
salient" should displace the greatest proportion of statements towards
the unfavourable end of the scale, while the "non-pickets" should displace the smallest proportion.

The results showed that, although the three groups did not differ
significantly in attitude, there were consistent differences in their ratings
of the statements. The series of statements as a whole were judged as
least favourable by the "pickets-salient" group, as slightly more favourable by the "pickets-nonsalient" group, and as most favourable by the
"non-pickets" group. Thus, the effect of the involvement variation on
mean ratings appears to offer reasonable support for assimilation-
contrast predictions. But on closer inspection this evidence turns out to
be rather less conclusive. Ward divided the 40 items into four subsets of
ten items each. The first subset consisted of the ten most unfavourable
items; subsets 2 and 3 consisted of items of intermediate favourability and
subset 4 of the most favourable items. The assimilation-contrast model
would predict that the involvement manipulation should have a differential effect on ratings of the four subsets. Those statements falling into
the latitude of acceptance of all three groups—supposedly most of the
items of subset 4—should not be affected by the involvement manipulation. Items falling into the latitude of rejection of all three groups—
supposedly the items of subset 1 and probably most of subset 2—should
only be slightly affected by the involvement manipulation. The items
most affected should be those which fell into the latitude of non-commitment of the least involved group but into the latitude of rejection of
the most involved group. Without any information about the exact
location of the latitudes of the different groups, it is difficult to say
which items should show this strongest effect, although the items of
subset 3 seem to be the most likely candidates. However, a two-way
analysis of variance (Involvement $\times$ Item Subset) failed to show any
difference between the subsets in the effects of the involvement manipu-

lation. The Involvement × Item Subset interaction only reached a probability level of approximately 0·25. Increased involvement led to increased contrast of all items, even of the items at the favourable end of the scale. This is somewhat inconsistent with assimilation-contrast predictions.

In a second study, already mentioned in our discussion of the effects of judges' attitudes, Ward (1966) extended the design of his first study by varying both involvement and attitude independently. Subjects in this study were presented with a three-part questionnaire. Part I contained 25 statements of attitudes towards the Negro to be rated. Part II consisted of a self-report inventory, measuring subjects' own attitude towards the Negro. Part III consisted of questions designed to measure the degree of subjects' involvement in the attitude issue.

On the basis of their responses to the self-report inventory, subjects were divided into a pro-Negro and an anti-Negro group. Separate analyses of variance were performed for ratings of pro-Negro and anti-Negro subjects. Since Ward discarded the responses of approximately half of his anti-Negro subjects on the basis of rather doubtful criteria (Eiser, 1971b), the results for the anti-Negro subjects will not be discussed. Ward also excluded a sizeable proportion of his pro-Negro subjects (57 out of 261). However, the excluded subjects do not seem to have differed significantly in degree of involvement from those retained for analysis.

Ward divided the pro-Negro subjects into subgroups ranging in attitudes from moderately favourable to extremely favourable. On the basis of their degree of involvement, as indicated by their responses to Part III of the questionnaire, each of these attitude subgroups was further divided into highly involved, moderately involved, and uninvolved subjects. The item series was divided into several subsets varying from favourable to unfavourable. A three-way analysis of variance (Attitude × Involvement × Item Subset), performed on the ratings resulted in a significant Involvement main effect (in addition to the Attitude main effect discussed earlier (cf. p. 98ff.) and the trivial Item Subset main effect). Highly involved judges rated the statements as less favourable towards the Negro than did uninvolved judges. None of the interactions approached significance. Involvement did not interact with either judges' own position (Attitude) or the scale position of the items (Item Subset).

Since the pro-Negro subjects ranged in attitude from extremely favourable to moderately favourable, it is not quite clear whether an

Involvement main effect should have been expected. The assimilation-contrast model would predict an Involvement main effect unambiguously only if all the judges had held positions near the positive end of the scale. For such judges greater involvement should lead to a greater proportion of statements being displaced towards the negative end of the scale. Thus, highly involved subjects with extreme pro-Negro attitudes should tend to rate neutral and anti-Negro statements as more anti-Negro than their uninvolved counterparts. The inclusion of pro-Negro judges with positions near the midpoint of the scale somewhat complicates the predictions. These moderate judges might have rejected statements at both ends of the scale. If that had been the case, rather than an Involvement main effect, the assimilation-contrast model would have predicted an interaction between involvement, judges' attitudes and the scale positions of the items rated (Item Subset). Nevertheless, it is quite possible that the moderate judges still accepted all the favourable items but rejected fewer of the unfavourable statements. If this had been the case, the involvement main effect would have been fully consistent with assimilation-contrast predictions. However, even then involvement should have interacted with the scale position of the items and with judges' attitudes. The finding that involvement did not interact with either of these other variables seems to be quite inconsistent with assimilation-contrast predictions. The other difficulties with this study, though, suggest that a certain amount of caution should perhaps be exercised when interpreting these negative findings.

The results of both these studies by Ward seem to be somewhat inconsistent with assimilation-contrast predictions, and further research on the effects of involvement is needed before conclusions can be drawn with any degree of confidence.

Conclusions

We have seen in the preceding review that as the research on attitude judgement moved from investigating whether a relationship existed between judges' attitudes and their ratings to studying the precise nature of this relationship and finally to testing theoretical formulations which could account for the observed effects, the research methods employed became more and more sophisticated. Judges were no longer eliminated for disproportionate use of extreme categories, care was taken to include judges who held extreme positions at either end of the attitude continuum, and more appropriate ways of analysing the data were used. Under these conditions, an effect of judges' attitudes on ratings has reliably been demonstrated (Hovland and Sherif, 1952; Prothro, 1955, 1957; Manis, 1960, 1961; Upshaw, 1962; Selltiz *et al.*, 1965; Zavalloni and Cook, 1965; Ward, 1966; Eiser, 1971a) and it is now generally accepted that judges' attitudes affect their ratings of attitude statements.

Results of these more recent studies suggest that the effect of judges' attitudes on their rating of any given statement depends on the position of that statement along the attitude continuum. Compared with judges with fairly neutral attitudes towards the Negro, pro-Negro judges rated unfavourable attitude statements as more unfavourable and tended to rate favourable statements as more favourable; judges with anti-Negro attitudes, on the other hand, tended to be less extreme than pro-Negro or neutral judges, in rating both favourable and unfavourable statements. Thus, the major effect of judges' attitudes observed in these studies seems to have been one of differences in polarization. (Upshaw, 1962; Selltiz *et al.*, 1965; Zavalloni and Cook, 1965). Pro-Negro judges gave the most polarized ratings, neutral judges were less polarized and anti-Negro judges gave the least polarized ratings. Similarly, with ratings of statements of attitudes towards drug-use, Eiser (1971a) found polarization of ratings to be highest for judges with attitude positions towards the permissive extreme of the attitude continuum and to be lowest for judges with positions towards the opposite extreme. However, Manis (1960, 1961) in two studies using the issue of attitudes towards the college fraternity system, found polarization of ratings to be highest for judges with extreme attitude positions at either end of the continuum, and to be lowest for judges with neutral attitudes.

Of the three judgemental theories (AL theory, the variable-series model, and the assimilation-contrast model) only two (the variable-series model and the assimilation-contrast model) can predict a relationship between judges' attitudes and polarization of judgement. According to Upshaw's variable-series model, polarization of judgement should vary as an inverse function of the width of judges' perspective. Judges with a wide perspective on a given attitude issue should give less polarized ratings than judges with a narrow perspective. Thus, according to the variable-series model, the finding that pro-Negro judges typically gave more polarized ratings than anti-Negro judges, would indicate that pro-Negro judges employed a narrower perspective than anti-Negro judges; in other words, that the anti-Negro judges took more extreme attitude positions, both favourable and unfavourable, into account when performing their judgements than did the pro-Negro judges. This assumption is not easily reconciled with the fact that the pro-Negro judges typically held more extreme attitude positions than the anti-Negro judges. Furthermore, the somewhat curvilinear relationship observed between the ratings given by pro- and anti-Negro judges in some of these studies is, strictly speaking, inconsistent with the variable perspective assumption that judges divide their perspective into equal intervals.

The assimilation-contrast model predicts both differences in polarization of ratings as a function of judges' attitudes and a curvilinear relationship between the ratings of judges holding different attitude positions. However, the assimilation-contrast model predicts the polarization of ratings to vary with the extremity of judges' attitudes, rather than their favourability. According to the assimilation-contrast model, judges with extreme attitude positions, unfavourable as well as favourable, should give more polarized ratings than judges with positions near the neutral point of the continuum. Therefore, only the results of Manis's (1960, 1961) studies are consistent with assimilation-contrast predictions, whilst the results of most of the studies using the Negro issue (e.g. Hovland and Sherif, 1952; Upshaw, 1962; Selltiz et al., 1965; Zavalloni and Cook, 1965) as well as of Eiser's (1971a) study on the drug issue are inconsistent with the assimilation-contrast model. Furthermore, Sherif and Hovland do not attempt to account for the effects of item range, which seem much more adequately dealt with by Upshaw.

Thus, none of the theories discussed in this chapter can fully account for all of the reported findings, particularly as regards the relationship between polarization of judgement and judges' attitudes. This might perhaps be taken as casting doubt on the validity of any attempt to explain social judgement in terms of principles drawn from psychophysical judgement. On the other hand, it is also possible that these theories are correct in assuming *some* relationship between social and psychophysical judgement, but that when it comes to defining the precise nature of this relationship the accounts which they offer are either inaccurate or incomplete. In the next chapter we shall present evidence in support of this latter interpretation.

6

An Accentuation Theory
Approach to Social Judgement

It will be recalled that in our earlier discussion of psychophysical judgement we distinguished two main classes of context effects. The first were those that arise from manipulation of various parameters of the distribution of stimuli presented for judgement, where these stimuli differ from one another only in terms of the particular attribute being judged. Most of the experiments on lifted weights, for instance, fall into this category; the stimuli typically differ from one another only in terms of weight, and it is their weight alone that is judged. Where such conditions are not fully met (Brown, 1953; Tajfel, 1959b), the results differ from those obtained when the standard procedure is employed. The three main theories of such effects, Helson's (1964) AL theory, Volkmann's (1951) "rubber-band" model, and Parducci's (1963) range-frequency model are all concerned primarily with the phenomenon of contrast. That is, they attempt to explain the unilateral shifts in judgement away from novel stimuli that occur following extension of the stimulus range, introduction of an anchor stimulus, etc. When, exceptionally, the introduction of an anchor stimulus produces a unilateral shift of judgement in the opposite direction (assimilation) such effects are regarded by all except Sherif *et al.* (1958) as a secondary phenomenon. Such unilateral shifts in judgement, with which the major share of research in psychophysical judgement has been concerned, are radically different from the second class of context effects, which arise from differences between the stimuli along dimensions other than the one in terms of which the subjects are instructed to make their judgements. As we saw in Chapter 4, where incidental stimulus variation along a peripheral dimension is correlated with variation along the focal dimension such that stimuli

144

which differ in terms of the focal attribute being judged differ also in terms of the unjudged peripheral attribute, the judged differences between stimuli on the focal dimension tend to be larger than when the same stimuli are judged in the absence of such superimposed cues. Although viewpoints differ regarding whether such effects operate symmetrically at both ends of the judgement scale (Tajfel, 1959a; Holzkamp, 1965), in relative terms such peripheral variation generally produces a *bilateral* shift resulting in increased polarization of judgement.

When one moves on to consider the results of social judgement experiments, the picture which emerges is in many respects very similar. The effects resulting from manipulation of the item range in studies such as those of Upshaw (1962) and Ostrom (1966) seem directly comparable to those found in psychophysical judgement as a result of variation in the stimulus range, and the inverse relationship between judges' attitudes and overall mean judgement of the item series as a whole is certainly reminiscent of the unilateral contrast effects found in psychophysical experiments (although it may arise simply from asymmetrical polarization). On the other hand, there is a relationship between judges' attitudes and polarization of judgement, suggesting that differences in attitude may lead to bilateral judgemental effects; these latter effects do not appear to be explained entirely satisfactorily by the models reviewed in Chapter 5.

The models proposed to account for these findings are all based upon principles originally formulated to account for the first class of psychophysical context effects, namely the unilateral shifts which occur for stimuli varying along a single dimension only. No consideration is given to the principles put forward to explain the bilateral shifts arising from incidental stimulus variation along peripheral dimensions. This is particularly evident in Segall's (1959) and Upshaw's (1962) approaches. It is also true of Sherif and Hovland's (1961) assimilation-contrast model, for, although they manage to produce a prediction of a bilateral shift in judgement, they derive it by a suspect line of reasoning from the principle of anchoring which, in psychophysics, is used both by other researchers and by themselves (Sherif *et al.*, 1958) to produce predictions of unilateral shifts.

Sherif and Hovland's own discussion makes it clear that the distance of any given attitude statement from the judge's own position (his "anchor") is of only secondary importance in determining whether that statement is "assimilated" or "contrasted". What is important is whether the statement falls within the judge's latitude of acceptance, rejection, or non-commitment. As they write, when considering the rating behaviour of extreme judges:

> *The reference scale of acceptance-rejection*, with its narrow latitude of acceptance and wide latitude of rejection, *is reflected in the categorization of the items* according to their favorableness and unfavorableness on the issue; intermediate items fall within the latitude of rejection and are lumped together in the extreme category opposite to the individual's own stand [our italics].
>
> 1961, p. 162

What this means essentially is that judges are predicted to *accentuate the differences* between the items they accept and those which they reject, in much the same way as subjects in a psychophysical judgement experiment concerned with the effects of incidental stimulus variation accentuate the differences between the stimuli which fall into distinct classes in terms of some additional attribute. The focal attribute is the favourability of the statements towards the issue; the peripheral attribute their acceptability to the judge. Although such an interpretation would seem prima facie to provide a far more coherent basis for Sherif and Hovland's predictions than their own idiosyncratic application of the concept of anchoring, at no stage do they make this parallel explicit. The remainder of this chapter will therefore be concerned with what may be called an accentuation theory approach to social judgement, the central hypothesis of which is that an individual's own opinions and system of values provides him with additional cues on the basis of which he may categorize attitude statements in terms of their favourability towards a given issue. This hypothesis rests upon two assumptions, which will be examined separately: firstly, that correlated peripheral variation produces accentuation effects in the judgement of attitude statements; and secondly, that an individual's own agreement and disagreement with the items he has to judge may be considered as a peripheral attribute superimposed on the focal dimension of favourability–unfavourability to the issue in question.

Incidental stimulus variation and the judgement of attitude statements

Before it can be argued that an individual's levels of agreement and disagreement function as a superimposed classification in judgements of attitude statements, it must be seen whether or not accentuation effects occur in the same way as they do with physical stimuli when correlated peripheral variation is superimposed experimentally on an item series. The study which bears most directly on this question is that by Eiser (1971a), which was mentioned in the last chapter. The principal aim of this study was to test the following hypothesis:

> When a classification in terms of an attribute other than that of favorability towards the issue in question is superimposed on a series of attitude statements in such a way that statements from one part of the scale tend to fall consistently into one class, and those from the other part into the other class, this will tend to lead to an accentuation of the judged differences between the distinct classes, as compared with the judgements given to the same series of statements, on which such a classification has not been superimposed.
>
> p. 4

For this purpose, 128 students were presented with 64 statements expressing varying degrees of "permissiveness" or "restrictiveness" towards the non-medical use of drugs. For half the subjects (the control group) the only departure from the standard Thurstone procedure was that they were told (incorrectly) that the statements were all "drawn from newspapers", and that they would be asked some more general questions about their reactions to the statements at the end of the experiment. The statements were then rated in terms of an eleven-point scale from "extremely permissive" to "extremely restrictive". For the other half of the subjects (the Experimental group), however, the statements were presented in the form of quotations from two newspapers, referred to by the fictitious names of "The Gazette" and "The Messenger", each statement being printed in quotation marks, with one of the two newspaper names printed immediately below it. Subjects in this group were told: "These statements have all been drawn from two newspapers. However, to control for any personal biases you may have, the real names of the newspapers will not be used . . . While judging the statements, please pay especial attention to the newspapers from which they are drawn, since you will be asked some more general questions about your reactions to the newspapers at the end of the experiment." Of the 64 statements, the 32 most "permissive" (all of which had received scale values of less than 6·0 in a pilot study) were presented as coming from "The Gazette", and the 32 most "restrictive" from "The Messenger". The supposed source of the statements thus constituted a special case of a superimposed cue, analogous to the alphabetic labels used by Tajfel and Wilkes (1963) in their study on judgements of length of lines.

In other parts of the questionnaire, subjects were asked to rate their own attitude towards drug use on the same eleven-point scale, and also their own levels of agreement with each of the 64 statements, having been assured of anonymity. To control for possible order effects, half the subjects reported their levels of agreement before they gave their ratings of the statements on the permissive–restrictive scale, and the other half performed the tasks in reverse order. The statements in the list were presented in one of two random orders.

In order to test for accentuation of interclass differences, each subject's ratings were averaged separately over the 32 more permissive items attributed to "The Gazette" and the 32 more restrictive items attributed to "The Messenger". As predicted, the differences between these means were significantly larger in the experimental than the control group; in other words, as compared with the control subjects, the experimental subjects tended to judge the permissive items on average as more permissive and the restrictive items as more restrictive.[1] The assumption that superimposed classifications may produce accentuation of interclass differences and hence increased polarization would thus seem to hold as well for judgements of attitude statements as for judgements of physical stimuli.

In order to see whether the attribution of the statements to the two newspapers produced a reduction of intraclass differences, i.e. a tendency to judge the items *within* each half of the scale as more similar to each other, a measure of the dispersion of each subject's ratings, the interquartile range, was calculated separately for the 32 permissive and the 32 restrictive items. If we extend Tajfel and Wilkes's (1963) assumptions to this situation, the prediction would be for these interquartile ranges for both sets of items to be smaller in the experimental group than in the control group. However, although the differences observed were in the predicted direction, they failed to approach significance. As with the effects of comparable manipulations in psychophysical experiments, therefore, the evidence for a reduction of intraclass differences is at best equivocal. The principal result of superimposing a classification on a series of statements appears to be an accentuation of interclass differences.

---

[1] It is also worth noting that this measure of the *average* interclass differences is in some respects a more cautious measure of polarization than that used by Tajfel and Wilkes (1963), who based their analysis on ratings of stimuli at the class boundaries; in some situations it may happen that accentuation effects occur for stimuli at the class boundaries without an increase in the differences between the average ratings given to each stimulus class as a whole (cf. Campbell, 1956).

Agreement-disagreement as a superimposed cue

To show that superimposed cues produce accentuation effects in the judgement of attitude statements does not, of course, establish that all differences in polarization, particularly those associated with differences in judges' attitudes, are to be explained in terms of principles of this kind. All we know is that an individual's own levels of agreement with the statements he has to judge *could* function as a superimposed cue. In order to be surer, we must determine whether the observed effects of judges' attitudes on their ratings are consistent with such an interpretation.

The two issues which at first sight would seem relatively critical are the question of linearity, and the asymmetry between the rating behaviour of pro-Negro and anti-Negro judges. One point which Upshaw claims as support for his variable perspective model as compared with Sherif and Hovland's approach is the finding that scales constructed from the ratings given by different groups of judges tend to be highly linearly related to each other (Upshaw, 1964). As we saw in the last chapter, the data relating to this question are not always as clearcut as they might appear. It is true that the linear correlation coefficient computed between different sets of scale values is typically very highly significant, but it is also true that, in some cases at least, a curvilinear component may also be significant. Even bearing this in mind, the *absolute* departures from linearity typically observed are not generally very marked. Now, if a superimposed classification leads to accentuation of interclass differences and also to reduction (or at any rate no accentuation) of intraclass differences, the relationship between ratings of a set of stimuli on which a classification has been superimposed and ratings of the same stimuli in the absence of such a classification should be curvilinear. However, it does not necessarily follow that such curvilinearity will be reflected to any very noticeable extent in the value of the linear correlation coefficient. This point comes out very clearly when one compares the ratings given by the experimental and control subjects in the Eiser (1971a) study. When the median scale values for each statement are calculated separately for the experimental and control groups, and the two sets of scale values are compared, the value of the correlation coefficient is 0·981; in other words, almost perfectly linear. Yet, as the previous analyses have demonstrated, the experimental group showed markedly greater interclass differences and very slightly smaller intraclass differences in their ratings than the control group. One is therefore left with a situation in which the correlation analysis implies a linear relationship, whilst the analyses of mean differences and interquartile ranges point to significant differences between the ratings given by the experimental and control groups which are suggestive of a curvilinear relationship.

The situation is complicated even further when a similar comparison is made between the ratings given by the different attitude groups in the Eiser (1971a) study. The 128 subjects were divided into two groups on the basis of their rating of their own position on the permissive–restrictive scale, group P consisting of the 60 most permissive subjects in terms of this measure, and group R consisting of the 68 most restrictive. The analysis of the interquartile ranges of each subject's rating of the statements in each half of the scale indicated a significant Item Group × Attitude interaction, whereby group P showed small interquartile ranges (less intraclass differentiation) in the more permissive than in the more restrictive half of the scale, whilst group R showed less differentiation among the more restrictive than the more permissive items. This effect is, if anything, contrary to that which would be predicted by the assimilation-contrast model. It is also inconsistent with the variable perspective model, which requires that the extent to which judges differentiate between different items should be constant over all regions of the scale. This analysis quite clearly implies a curvilinear relationship, but again the value of the correlation coefficient is 0·978.

Perhaps the main reason for this apparent inconsistency is the fact that the correlation analysis involves summarizing the scores for each item taken separately, over all the individuals in each subject group, whilst the analysis of mean differences and individual measures of discrimination involves summarizing the scores for each individual taken separately, over all the items in each item group. Effects that are apparent when the data are inspected on a subject-by-subject basis may therefore be concealed when *group* responses to individual items are compared.

There is also another reason why the linearity evidence may be less crucially relevant for an accentuation theory approach than might at first appear. So far we have only considered the case of *discontinuous* peripheral variation, where the items being judged can fall into only two distinct classes in terms of the peripheral attribute. In the experimental condition of the Eiser (1971a) study, the items were all attributed definitely to one of the two newspapers; there was no distinction, for instance, between "strongly Gazette-like" and "moderately Gazette-like" statements. However, when one thinks of the acceptability or unacceptability of the items to the judge as a peripheral attribute super-imposed on the focal dimension of favourability–unfavourability to the issue in question, it would seem somewhat more reasonable to talk of a superimposed *continuum* rather than a superimposed classification. One would expect that, if required, judges could distinguish between "defi-nitely acceptable", "moderately acceptable", and "just about accept-able" statements. If one is dealing with *continuous* peripheral variation, the question of a reduction of intraclass differences does not really arise. What one finds is typically an accentuation of judged differences be-tween successive members of a stimulus series resulting in an increased polarization of judgement over the whole scale. With estimates of coin sizes, for instance, the more extreme stimuli (as least at the high value end) tend to show the greatest shifts. As a result, when one compares the estimated size of coins with their actual size, the relationship appears almost perfectly linear (cf. McCurdy, 1956). Similarly, where value is associated experimentally with either end of a stimulus series, Tajfel writes, this "results in an increase in the judged differences between the stimuli at or near the opposite ends of the series. This increase seems to be a direct function of the nearness of the stimuli to the ends of the series." (1959b, p. 301.) Such findings would appear to suggest that superimposed peripheral variation, particularly when it is continuous, may produce shifts in judgement which do not necessarily show any very marked departures from linearity, although they may do so under certain circumstances.

The asymmetry between the rating behaviour of judges at opposite ends of the scale raises a more serious problem for an accentuation theory approach. For the anti-Negro judge, one would expect an inverse relationship between the favourability of the statements towards Negroes and their acceptability to the judge. His own agreement–disagreement with the statements would therefore seem to constitute a case of corre-lated peripheral variation which should lead him to make more polar-ized judgements than a more neutral judge. The differences observed, however, are in the reverse direction. Furthermore this finding does not appear to be restricted to the Negro question. In the Eiser (1971a) study, the more restrictive subjects (group R) gave less polarized ratings than the more permissive subjects (group P), and although it is arguable that group R included more moderate judges than group P, further sub-division of group R into moderate and extremely restrictive judges showed that the more extreme members of that group in fact gave slightly less polarized ratings than the more moderate members.

On the other hand, there are a number of important differences between judgements of attitude statements and the kind of situation facing a subject in a typical psychophysical experiment. For a start, the acceptability–unacceptability of the statements to the judge is not quite the same kind of super-imposed cue as, for instance, the alphabetic labels in the Tajfel and Wilkes (1963) experiment. It does not merely imply a distinction between statements in different parts of the scale: it implies that these statements may be distinguished *evaluatively* in terms of their compatibility with the judge's own attitudes and system of values. In addition, the focal dimension along which the items are to be rated is not quite the same as dimensions like size and heaviness. What makes social judgement "social" is precisely the fact that such judgements are made within the context of social norms and values—norms and values which are implicit in the judgement scale itself. For this reason, the focal dimension in most social judgement experiments is rarely one that calls for mere descriptive ratings of an objective attribute of the stimulus items. Instead, the judge is required to assess the positions of the items along an essentially *value-laden* continuum.

If one considers the social context in which the studies on the Negro question were conducted, it seems reasonable to suppose that overtly racialist attitudes would tend to be condemned, at any rate professedly, by most members of the student populations from whom the subjects were drawn. Within such a context, to describe someone as anti-Negro would be more or less equivalent to calling him prejudiced or racialist: it would imply, in other words, that one evaluated that person negatively. Similarly, the British students used in the drug study were drawn from a population among whom restriction of individual liberty for its own sake would tend to be strongly condemned. The term "restrictive" would thus be one which could be assumed to carry relatively negative connotations for most of the judges used as compared with the term "permissive" which would imply a somewhat more positive evaluation. Viewed in this way, the situation confronting the pro-Negro or permissive judge would appear to be radically different from that confronting the anti-Negro or restrictive judge. The former would be able to rate the statements with which they agreed as lying nearer to the end of the scale marked by a term with evaluatively positive connotations, and those with which he disagreed as nearer to the evaluatively negative end of the scale. The latter, on the other hand, would be in the position where the statements with which he agreed would lie closer to the evaluatively negative end of the scale and those with which he disagreed would lie closer to the positive end. To illustrate this point somewhat more clearly, suppose we asked a sample of American students to rate a set of statements concerning the Vietnam war along some such dimension as "peace-loving–war-mongering". One would suspect that subjects who were opponents of US policy in Vietnam would be quite happy to describe the kinds of opinions which they themselves would accept as "peace-loving" and quite prepared to describe the positions they themselves would reject as "war-mongering". In their case, the approval and disapproval implied by the judgement scale terms would be consistent with their own acceptance and rejection of the items in the various regions of the scale. Supporters of US intervention, on the other hand, would be in the position of having to describe opinions which they themselves accepted as "war-mongering" and those which they rejected as "peace-loving". If, on the other hand, the same statements had to be rated along some such scale as "patriotic–unpatriotic", it would be the anti-war judges who could rate statements which they accepted as closer to the end of the scale with the more positive value connotations. It would seem plausible that in such a situation the pro-war judge would be more prepared than the anti-war judge to discriminate between the statements on a scale like "patriotic–unpatriotic", whereas the anti-war judge would be more prepared than the pro-war judge to discriminate between the statements on a scale like "peace-loving–war-mongering". We might expect, therefore, that the pro-war judge would give more polarized ratings than the anti-war judge on the "patriotic–unpatriotic" scale, whereas the anti-war judge would give more polarized ratings than the pro-war judge on the "peace-loving–war-mongering" scale.

If then we are to consider the individual's own agreement and disagreement with the statements as a superimposed cue, we must also take account of the relationship between his own evaluations and the implicit value connotations of the judgement scale terms. Indeed, it could be argued that such value connotations are themselves a superimposed cue since they serve to distinguish different parts of the attitude continuum from one another in terms of the additional attribute of value. If this is so, we then have a situation in which the statements are judged in the presence of not one but two superimposed cues, both of which imply a

F

distinction in terms of value. In the case of the pro-Negro judge, statements near the favourable end of the scale may be classified as "better" than those at the unfavourable end both because the judge himself accepts them, and because they lie closer to the end of the scale with the more positive value connotations: the relationship, "the more pro-Negro the better," holds true both when" better" means more personally acceptable to the judge and when it means nearer the more positively labelled extreme of the scale. The two sets of cues, in other words, are *congruent* with each other. In the case of the anti-Negro judge, however, they are *incongruent*. The relationship, "the more pro-Negro the better", holds true only when "better" is taken to mean closer to the more positively labelled extreme. When "better" is defined in terms of the judge's own levels of agreement and disagreement, the relationship is reversed.

If, therefore, we make the assumption that the combined effect of these two sets of cues should be additive, i.e. that it should be a function of the *net* difference in value superimposed on the attitude continuum, then they should reinforce each other in the case of the pro-Negro or permissive judge, but inhibit or cancel each other out in the case of the anti-Negro or restrictive judge. The result should be the observed effect that pro-Negro and permissive judges give more polarized ratings than anti-Negro and restrictive judges on the scales employed. This assumption may be formulated in terms of the following more general hypothesis:

> If the judge's own evaluations of the statements are congruent with the connotations attached to the regions of the scale from which they are drawn, he will tend to accentuate the differences between the statements he accepts and those he rejects: if his evaluations are incongruent with such connotations, he will tend to reduce these differences.
>
> Eiser, 1971a, p. 3

If this approach is correct, then we would expect the relationship between judges' attitudes and polarization of judgement to vary depending on how the judgement scale is labelled. As in our hypothetical example about the Vietnam war, we would expect a different pattern of results depending on whether we labelled the continuum "patriotic–unpatriotic" or "war-mongering–peace-loving". This implies that what appears, in the results of the studies so far considered, to be an effect of differences in judges' attitudes may in reality be produced by an interaction between judges' attitudes and the value connotations of the judgement scale terms. But such an interaction cannot be demonstrated so long as only one of the factors under consideration is manipulated. In the next section, therefore, we will discuss the results of two studies in which both judges' attitudes and the value connotations of the judgement scale terms were varied independently.

The role of "value connotations"

The hypothesis that polarization of judgement should be affected by the value connotations of the judgement scale terms was tested in a further study by Eiser (1972), again using the issue of students' attitudes towards the use of drugs. For this purpose, a total of 71 male and female students were presented with 30 items based on the item series used in the Eiser (1971a) study, each item being rated on each of the following five scales: "extremely immoral–extremely moral"; "extremely liberal –extremely authoritarian"; "extremely broadminded–extremely narrow-minded"; "extremely permissive–extremely restrictive"; and "extremely decadent–extremely upright". For each scale, the first term referred to category 1 and the second to category 11. The questionnaire was laid out so that each page contained one of the 30 items with each of the five scales printed beneath it. At the bottom of each page, subjects were also required to indicate their own agreement or disagreement with the item in terms of the five categories: strongly agree, agree, undecided, disagree, strongly disagree. The first section of the questionnaire concluded with subjects being required to rate their own position on each of the five scales. This was followed by a second section, designed to provide a measure of the value connotations of each of the scale terms. This consisted of ten questions of the form: "If you were to describe an opinion as . . . , how likely is it that you would approve of it?" The blank in each question was filled in by one of the ten scale terms.

On the basis of the results of the previous study, it was predicted that the more polarized ratings on the permissive–restrictive scale would be given by the more permissive judges, and also that there would be an overall tendency for the judges as a whole to say that they would be more likely to approve of opinions described as "permissive" than of opinions described as "restrictive"; in other words, for the term "permissive" to carry the more positive value connotations. On two of the other scales, "liberal–authoritarian" and "broadminded–narrow-minded", it was anticipated that the presumably more pro-drug terms (liberal, broadminded) would carry more positive value connotations than their opposites, and therefore that the relationship between judges' attitudes and polarization should be in the same direction as that predicted for the "permissive–restrictive" scale. On the other two scales, it was anticipated that the presumably more pro-drug terms (immoral, decadent) would carry more negative value connotations than their opposites, and therefore that the relationship between polarization and judges' attitudes should be in the opposite direction, with the more "pro-drug" judges giving the least polarized ratings. Judges were divided into three attitude groups on the basis of their own positions on the "permissive–restrictive" scale, their own positions being defined as the average of the scale values of those items with which they indicated agreement or strong agreement. Group I (the most permissive) consisted of 24 judges with own positions of less than $5 \cdot 3$; group II consisted of 23 judges with own positions between $5 \cdot 3$ and $6 \cdot 1$; and group III consisted of 24 judges with own positions of more than $6 \cdot 1$. This measure of judges' own positions on the "permissive–restrictive" scale correlated highly significantly ($p < 0 \cdot 001$) with equivalent measures on each of the other four scales, and also with judges' self-ratings of their own positions on the "permissive–restrictive" scale (the measure used in the previous study).

The standard deviation (SD) of each judge's ratings of the 30 items was calculated separately for each of the five scales to provide a measure of polarization on each scale. On the "permissive–restrictive" scale these scores were higher for group I than group III, as predicted, although groups I and II were almost identical. Comparison of judges' scores on the other four scales, however, revealed two main tendencies, over and above any associated with differences in attitude. On the one hand, the average SD's for the total sample of judges were higher on certain scales than others. The highest was the "broadminded–narrow-minded" scale (mean SD: $2 \cdot 80$), followed by liberal–authoritarian ($2 \cdot 78$), "permissive–restrictive" ($2 \cdot 62$), "decadent–upright" ($2 \cdot 43$) and "immoral–moral" ($2 \cdot 31$). On the other hand, there appeared to be considerable individual differences in these SD scores, such that some judges seemed to show relatively high degrees of polarization on all five scales, whilst others apparently showed relatively low degrees of polarization. To separate out these differences, therefore, judges' SD's were first converted to rank form, with the lowest SD on each scale receiving a rank of 1 and the highest a rank of 71. A measure of judges' *overall* extremity of judgement was then derived by taking the sum of each judge's ranked SD scores on the four scales other than "permissive–restrictive". The 71 judges were then divided into 35 "high polarizers" and 36 "low polarizers" on the basis of these summed scores, which showed no apparent relationship to judges' own positions.

The scores on the four scales other than "permissive–restrictive" were then analysed by first calculating for each subject the sum of his ranked SD scores on the "liberal–authoritarian" and "broadminded–narrowminded" scales, minus the sum of his ranked SD scores on the "immoral–moral" and "decadent–upright" scales. This difference score represents the extent to which each judge showed greater polarization on the former than on the latter two scales, relative to the amounts of polarization shown on each of the scales by the subjects as a whole. If our hypothesis concerning a possible interaction between value connotations and judges' attitudes is correct, this difference should be directly related to the permissiveness of the judge's attitude, being highest for group I and lowest for group III. The results support this prediction. Treating the division of judges into the three attitude groups, and into high and low polarizers as a 3×2 factorial design, the mean difference scores for each group were as follows: I-High: 18·04; I-Low: 20·13; II-High: 9·29; II-Low: 2·68; III-High: $-18·23$; III-Low: $-23·19$. An analysis of variance performed on these scores showed that the Attitude main effect was highly significant $(F = 14·54, df = 2/65, p < 0·001)$, the other main effect and interaction yielding F ratios of less than 1. A similar analysis performed on judges' ranked SD scores on the "permissive–restrictive" scale indicated a highly significant main effect for High versus Low polarizers $(F = 97·07, df = 1/65, p < 0·001)$, showing that judges who gave relatively highly polarized ratings on the other four scales also tended to show relatively high degrees of polarization on the "permissive–restrictive" scale, irrespective of their attitude. A significant Attitude main effect $(F = 4·50, df = 2/65, p < 0·02)$ reflected the tendency for group III to give less polarized ratings than the other two attitude groups, the interaction again being non-significant $(F < 1)$. Inspection of judges' responses to the second section of the questionnaire confirmed the assumptions concerning the value connotations of the particular terms for the judges as a whole. In addition, it was observed that the more permissive the judge's own attitude, the greater was his preference for the more "pro-drug" and the lesser was his preference for the more "anti-drug" term in each pair.

This study thus supported the main hypothesis concerning the inter-action between judges' attitudes and the value connotations of the judge-ment scale terms. At the same time, these results provide a cautionary note against any simple assumption that *all* differences in polarization may be explicable in terms of an accentuation theory approach. On an individual basis, there are the marked differences between high and low polarizers on all five scales and in all three attitude groups. It might be reasoned that these differences could reflect differences in "ego-involve-ment" between the different groups, on the assumption that the high polarizers were the more involved. Subsidiary analyses revealed little evidence to support such an interpretation. Alternatively, they may represent what Upshaw (1965, 1969) would consider to be differences in "perspective" which either might be specific to the particular attitude issue under consideration, or might reflect more general individual differences in cognitive style, e.g. Pettigrew's (1958) notion of Category Width. The emphasis throughout this book has been intentionally and explicitly on general principles of judgement rather than on individual differences and response biases. The importance of such factors, how-ever, should not be underestimated when one is concerned with predict-ing judgemental behaviour at an individual level. Our prime concern in the latter half of this book has been with the effect of judges' attitudes, and it is therefore worth noting in this context that these marked overall differences in extremity of judgement, whatever their explanation, neither interacted with, nor were predictable from, differences in judges' own positions.

Apart from these individual differences in extremity of judgement, it is also clear from this study that different labellings of the attitude continuum may lead to different amounts of polarization in judgements of a given set of items, over and above any effects resulting from differ-ences in judges' own positions. Unless two pairs of terms are com-pletely synonymous, it is unlikely that they will be seen as completely equal in applicability to the particular statements being judged. When this is the case, what is crucial for a test of the interpretation proposed in this chapter is not necessarily the absolute amount of polarization shown by a given judge on each scale, but how the polarization of his ratings on any given scale compares with that shown by other judges. What this approach requires, and what the results of this second study on attitudes towards the use of drugs appear to indicate, is that differences between judges in terms of the *relative* amounts of polarization shown by them on the various scales are a function both of judges' attitudes and of the value connotations of the judgement scale terms.

A second study along these lines was conducted by Eiser and Mower White (in preparation). Seventy-five schoolchildren, aged 14 to 15, were presented with ten statements concerned with the general question of adult authority over children, how much freedom teenagers should have, and whether teenagers should always obey their parents and teachers. These statements were rather longer than those used in the studies so far considered, and were phrased more informally than typical Thurstone scale items. Five statements were designed to be relatively pro adult authority, and five to be relatively anti adult authority. The five "pro" statements were as follows:

1. If everybody was a rebel, then nobody would know where they were; life wouldn't work at all if everyone did things their own way. You should try and fit in with others and take advice from older people—that's the only way to get the best from them. Perhaps it sounds a bit dull, and it would be nice if life was a bit more exciting, but I've got more respect for my parents than that.

2. If everyone spent all their time trying to do something new and original the result would be complete and utter chaos. Of course you need some people who've got new ideas from time to time, but you also need other people to steady things down a bit; sometimes change can be exciting, but often it can be very dangerous and frightening. Young people often don't see the dangers, but older people do, so it's not surprising that they prefer things to stay the way they are.

3. I think the most important thing is to be happy and I'm sure that all these people who don't conform with others can't be happy, because they're always saying something's wrong. I know you have to move with the times but I still feel people should respect their elders and keep calm when they think something's wrong—otherwise you just add to the trouble.

4. I think life can be just as exciting if you do what you're told. Teachers and parents generally know best and they often have good ideas. Also if you're polite and do what they say you usually come off best in the end. I think you should support them because they've probably done quite a lot for you.

5. You can learn a lot from people older than yourself. After all, they've had much more experience and have a better idea of right and wrong that young people have. Many young people just rebel for the

sake of rebelling—I think this is stupid. It upsets your parents and in the end everyone suffers. I reckon you owe it to your parents to do what they say.

The five "anti" statements were as follows:

1. Teachers are quite often wrong so it probably does them good to be contradicted once in a while—of course you can go too far—I don't believe in being different just for the sake of it, but I do get tired of having to obey rules and not having time to do what I want.

2. Teenagers nowadays don't really need to be looked after by their parents any more, and it's time parents, and adults generally, realized this. Young children obviously need to be looked after, but after you get to 13 or 14 you could easily look after yourself if you could afford it. I'm sure most families would be much happier if parents didn't keep telling their children what they should do and what they shouldn't do, but instead let them do what they wanted.

3. School's a bit dull really—always being told what to do and having to work with other people. It makes life easy, but it would be nicer to be free and go off and do things on my own. Sometimes I think I should help teachers and other people, but that's not very interesting.

4. If everyone always did what they were told, there would never be any progress. Adults are only interested in keeping things the way they are now—they aren't interested in what will happen in the future. We should never feel guilty if we do something we enjoy doing, even if our parents disapprove of it, as their ideas are rooted in the past and have no relevance to the way things are today.

5. Nobody has the right to tell anybody else what to do with their lives. It's up to each individual to decide what he wants to do, and what he wants to be, and to discover life in his own way. You have to break free from authority if you want to discover your true self, even if this means offending people in the process. If you think your parents or teachers are wrong, you shouldn't be afraid of saying so.

Subjects were told that these were comments made by young people and were asked "to read these statements and then imagine what sort of person made them". They were then asked to describe the sort of person they imagined made each statement in terms of ten semantic differential-type scales. On five of these scales (scale group I) the presumably more "pro authority" term was evaluatively positive, and the presumably more "anti authority" term was evaluatively negative. These were:

"impatient–patient", "uncooperative–cooperative", "hot-headed–level-headed", "ill-mannered–well-mannered", and "disobedient–obedient".
On the other five scales (scale group II) the direction of evaluation was presumed to be reversed. These were: "progressive–old-fashioned", "independent–dependent", "unconventional–conventional", "adventurous–unadventurous", and "imaginative–unimaginative". Instead of the usual eleven-point scale, each scale consisted of a continuous line, 100 mm long with the "anti authority" term printed above the left-hand end and the "pro authority" term above the right-hand end. Subjects were instructed to make their responses by marking a cross at the appropriate point along the line, and each response was scored from 0 to 100 depending on its distance (in millimetres) from the left-hand extreme. The mean ratings for each statement on each scale confirmed the author's assumptions regarding which statements were "pro" and which were "anti authority". Also the correlations between all the ten scales were extremely high, suggesting that subjects treated all scales as referring to essentially the same underlying continuum.

Before rating the ten statements, subjects were also required to rate the following four concepts in terms of the same ten scales: "Any one person whom I know well" (a warm-up item), "Me as I really am", "Me as I would like to be", and "The kind of person I most admire". The last two of these were included to provide a measure of the "value connotations" of the scale terms, it being assumed that, for example, if someone said that he would like to be adventurous rather than unadventurous, and admired adventurous people more than unadventurous people, then the term "adventurous" could be considered to carry more positive value connotations for him than the term "unadventurous". In general, subjects' responses to this part of the questionnaire confirmed the expectations on which the selection of terms was based. The only exception was "unconventional–conventional". Anderson (1968) reports a higher mean "likeableness" rating for "unconventional" than "conventional", and on this basis it was expected that "unconventional" should have more positive connotations than "conventional". In fact the reverse was true; however, since "conventional," had less positive connotations than any of the "pro authority" terms in the five scales of group I where the "pro authority" term was assumed to be the more positive, the results for this scale will be grouped together with those for the other four scales of group II where the "anti authority" term was assumed to be the more positive for the purpose of the analyses

F*

reported here. (This would, in fact, reduce the chances of finding any differences in judgement between the different types of scales.)

There were thus basically two groups of statements and two groups of scales. In addition, subjects were divided up into three groups of 25 on the basis of their own agreement or disagreement with the statements. This was measured by requiring subjects to indicate their own agreement or disagreement with each statement along a 100 mm scale from "Agree very much" (0) to "Disagree very much" (100). The sum of each subject's agree–disagree ratings for the five "anti authority" statements was then subtracted from the sum of his agree–disagree ratings for the five "pro authority" statements. This difference score (essentially comparable to a Likert measure) would tend to be negative for subjects endorsing the "pro authority" statements, and positive for subjects endorsing the "anti authority" statements. Fortunately, these scores produced a more or less symmetrical distribution with an overall mean close to zero. For once, then, the problems posed by an uneven distribution of judges' attitudes do not apply. Subjects were therefore split into a "pro" group, consisting of the 25 with the most negative own position scores, a "neutral" group of 25, and an "anti" group consisting of the 25 with the most positive own position scores. An incidental finding was that girls tended to be more "pro authority" than boys. The number of boys and girls in each group were as follows: "pro" 11 boys, 14 girls; "neutral" 14 boys, 11 girls; "anti" 20 boys, 5 girls. (Chi-square = 7·00, $df=2$, $p<0.05$.) The questionnaire was administered during a school classroom period. Subjects were assured of anonymity, and told that their answers would not be seen by anyone except the experimenters.

The main hypothesis was that the "pro" group should show relatively more polarization on the five scales where the "pro authority" term was the more positive than on the other five scales. This difference should be reversed in the case of the "anti" group, with the "neutral" group showing no clear "preference" for either type of scale. The measure of polarization used in this study was as follows: for each subject, the sum of his five lowest ratings on any one scale was subtracted from the sum of his five highest ratings on that scale. The greater the difference, the higher is the degree of polarization. As in the Eiser (1972) study, however, subjects' polarization scores were typically higher on some scales than others. These scores were therefore converted to rank form, with a rank of 1 being given to the lowest polarization score and 75 to the highest polarization score on any single scale. Each subject's ranked polarization scores were then summed separately over the two groups of scales. The means of these summed ranks for each scale group in each of the three attitude groups were as follows: "pro", group I 41·26, group II 36·61; "neutral", group I 31·19, group II 37·02; "anti", group I 36·56, group II 40·37. A 3×2 (Attitude $\times$ Scale group) analysis of variance indicated a significant Attitude $\times$ Scale group interaction ($F = 8·32, df = 2/72$, $p < 0·001$), the attitude main effect being non-significant. The main hypothesis, that individuals should give more polarized judgements on scales where their own evaluations of the statements are congruent with the value connotations of the judgement scale terms, was thus substantially confirmed, although not all the scales in either group completely conformed to the overall pattern.

"Value connotations" and overall mean judgement

Our discussion so far might be taken to imply that the *denotative* meanings of such terms as, say, "imaginative" and "impatient" are broadly equivalent. In other words, that though these terms may imply different *evaluations*, any opinion that could be *described* as "very imaginative" could equally well be described as "very impatient". Such a viewpoint would imply that we had a situation of the kind represented in Fig. 6·1, with (in the present case) the various statements arranged along a single underlying psychological continuum which may be approximately defined as ranging from extremely "anti authority" to extremely "pro authority", and with terms such as "imaginative" and "impatient" being used as alternative.

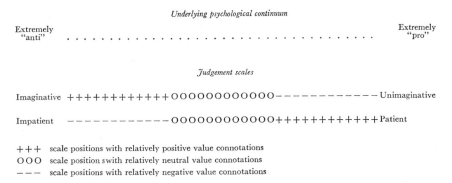

Fig. 6.1. Hypothetical locations of different scale terms on the underlying psychological continuum: first viewpoint.

labellings of the "anti" extreme and terms such as "unimaginative" and "patient" applied to the "pro" extreme. In other words, the sets of terms "imaginative–unimaginative" and "impatient–patient" would have different value connotations but equivalent *ranges of application*.

The notion of a single underlying psychological continuum implies that the kind of judgements made are essentially unidimensional, i.e. that the ratings given to the statements on the different scales are all highly intercorrelated. For simplicity of exposition, we will proceed upon this assumption for the time being, although it is not a necessary assumption for the purpose of accentuation theory. (This criterion of strict unidimensionality is in fact not fully met in the second study on attitudes towards drug-use (Eiser, 1972).) It should be remembered that the kind of statements used in Thurstone scales are deliberately selected so as to satisfy this assumption. Just because two scales are found to be highly correlated when applied to a specific set of statements, therefore, there is no reason to suppose that they will necessarily be as highly correlated in all contexts.

However, even if the assumption of a single underlying continuum holds, and the different scales are highly correlated, we do not have to assume that terms such as "imaginative" and "impatient" occupy the same location along that continuum. Evidence from the area of trait inferences (Peabody, 1967) implies that trait words which refer to relatively extreme characteristics of a person tend to carry more negative value connotations than trait words describing relatively moderate characteristics. Thus if we were describing how prepared various people were to spend their money, we might use such words as "miserly", "thrifty", "generous", and "extravagant". In general, we would expect someone described as "miserly" to spend less than someone described as "thrifty", and someone described as "extravagant" more than someone described as "generous". We would tend to apply negative evaluations both to people who spend too much money and those who spend too little. This is consistent with Aristotle's concept of "good" as implying moderation, and of "evil" as implying either deficiency or excess. Applying this idea to the present case, the relationship between differently labelled judgement scales and the underlying psychological continuum would now become approximately as represented in Fig. 6.2.

In terms of this second viewpoint, ratings of statements on the "imaginative–unimaginative" scale would remain correlated with their ratings on the "impatient–patient" scale, but the two scales would differ in their range of application. As represented in Fig. 6.2, the first scale would apply to the most "pro" two-thirds of the underlying continuum,

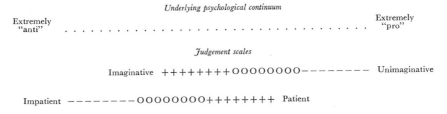

Fig. 6.2. Hypothetical locations of different scale terms on the underlying psychological continuum: second viewpoint.

and the second to the most "anti" two-thirds (these proportions are, of course, entirely hypothetical). If this is so, then we would expect differences in the overall means of an individual's ratings of a given set of statements on the two scales. Statements, the "true" positions of which were near the centre of the underlying psychological continuum, would be judged as closer to the left-hand end of the "imaginative–unimaginative" scale and closer to the right-hand end of the "impatient–patient" scale. The overall mean of a given subject's judgements of a set of statements should thus tend to be higher on scales such as "impatient–patient" than on scales such as "imaginative–unimaginative"; in other words, the mean of a judge's ratings should be drawn towards the positively labelled end of the scale. This prediction is confirmed very strongly in the Eiser and Mower White results. All these attitude groups showed much higher mean judgements on scales of type I than on scales of type II. There is also some evidence of a similar effect in the second drug study (Eiser, 1972), although the differences here are very slight. It is not inconceivable that this phenomenon might be somehow related to the effects of assimilation towards the more valued end of the continuum mentioned at the end of Chapter 4.

This prediction of a "positivity bias" does not take account of the possibility that judges may "redefine" the scale terms so as to match the end-points of their scales to the end-points of the range of items with which they are presented. Whilst the evidence reviewed in Chapter 5 suggests that such a "range principle" may not always be quite as powerful in social judgement as in psychophysical judgement, it would seem likely that the more subjects are presented with statements which cover *both* extremes of the underlying continuum, the more they should define their scales of judgement in a manner comparable to that represented in Fig. 6.1 rather than in Fig. 6.2. This would act against the possibility of observing any such "positivity bias". Nor does this prediction take account of the possible influence of judges' own attitudes on their overall mean judgements, whether this influence is conceived of in terms of different judges perceiving a given set of statements as occupying different locations on the underlying psychological continuum, or in terms of differences in attitude leading to differences in perspective. None the less, the idea that moderate positions along the underlying continuum may tend to be more positively evaluated than extreme positions might be taken to suggest a tentative re-interpretation of the inverse relationship typically found between judges' attitudes and overall mean judgements. AL theory predicts this relationship by assuming (a) that individuals use their own position as an "anchor" or comparison point against which to judge the statements presented to them, and (b) that their AL, or point of perceived neutrality, is drawn towards their own position, so that they see their own position as more moderate or neutral than it "really" is. There is nothing basically implausible about either assumptions, at least when phrased in these general terms. It is quite reasonable to suppose that individuals compare others' attitudes with their own, and see their own opinions as less extreme than others see them, at any rate in certain circumstances, and, although this approach cannot predict *all* observed effects of judges' attitudes (particularly differences in polarization), it as least predicts *some* of them. The question is not whether this is so, but why. What appears somewhat counterintuitive about the AL theory approach to social judgement is the assumption (which remains relatively unchallenged by Sherif and Hovland and also, to some extent, in the earlier version of Upshaw's model) that an individual's own position functions more or less as though it were just another stimulus to which he was exposed, and to which he would automatically "adapt". The slightly different viewpoint, that judges with "pro" attitudes tend to have more "pro" AL's because they have been exposed to more "pro" statements in the past, again is merely an assumption. In either case, it is left very unclear what exactly constitutes "exposure" and "adaptation" in this context.

If, on the other hand, it is generally true that moderate positions are seen as "better" than extreme positions, the assumption that individuals see themselves as more moderate than they "really" are implies that they should also see themselves as *better* than they "really are", or at least wish to present themselves as such in the task of judgement. If then we assume that individuals are generally motivated to maintain a positive self-evaluation, and/or to present themselves in positive terms to others, the notion of any adaptation process becomes redundant: individuals behave as though they see themselves as more moderate, not because they have become "adapted" to a particular set of beliefs, but because moderate positions are more positively evaluated. This approach would have the added advantage of *not* having to predict overall contrast as opposed to overall assimilation effects in all circumstances. It is conceivable that there might be situations in which the extremes of the underlying psychological continuum might be more positively evaluated than the centre. In such cases, individuals should tend to see and/or present themselves as more extreme than they "really" are, and a *direct* relationship between overall mean judgement and own position should result. Unfortunately, the results of the Eiser and Mower White study provide no clarification on this point. A direct relationship between attitude and overall mean judgement (assimilation) is found on all scales of group I and on the "unconventional–conventional" scale, i.e. on all six scales where the "pro authority" term is the more positive, whereas the more common inverse relationship (contrast) is found on the remaining four scales of group II. At present, we would not wish to hazard a guess as to how this rather curious finding might be reconciled with the results of previous studies.

Conclusions

The approach to social judgement outlined in this chapter is primarily designed to account for the relationship between judges' attitudes and polarization of judgement. Essentially, it is assumed that such effects arise from subjects accentuating the judged differences between the statements most and least acceptable to themselves, the acceptability of the statements to the judges being treated as a special case of correlated peripheral variation. Other things being equal, this should result in judges with more extreme opinions at either end of the scale giving more polarized ratings than judges with more moderate opinions. This is basically the same prediction as that made by the assimilation-contrast model, although the suggested explanation is different. However, the finding that extremity of own position is directly related to polarization only among judges with attitudes towards one end of the favourability–unfavourability continuum for at least two kinds of issues (attitudes towards Negroes, and towards drug-use), calls for a consideration of certain principles which are not incorporated in Tajfel's (1959a) application of accentuation theory to the judgement of physical stimuli.

An exclusive prediction of the approach suggested in this chapter is that the relationship between own position and polarization should vary as a function of how the favourable–unfavourable continuum is labelled. Specifically, it is predicted that, when the continuum is labelled in such a way that one end of the scale is marked by a term with relatively positive value connotations and the other end marked by a term with relatively negative value connotations, individuals whose own positions lie closest to the positive end of the scale should give the most polarized ratings, whilst those whose own positions lie closest to the negative end of the scale should give the least polarized ratings. This involves the assumption that individuals will tend to perform the judgement task in such a way as to maintain and/or present a positive self-image. In support of this prediction, we have outlined the results of two studies in which the direction of the relationship between own position and polarization was shown to depend on the evaluative labelling of the judgement scale. These findings demonstrate that such differences in polarization cannot be completely attributed to any hypothesized individual differences in categorizing style.

Regarding the results of previous studies in which the value connotations of the judgement scale terms were not directly manipulated, we have argued that the differences in polarization found between the ratings given by pro-Negro and anti-Negro judges may be explained along similar lines, if it is assumed that, in the social context in which the studies on attitudes towards Negroes were conducted, the term "favourable" (towards Negroes) would generally have more positive value connotations than its opposite. Similarly, in the Eiser (1971a) study on students' attitudes towards drug-use, the observed differences in polarization between the more "permissive" and more "restrictive" judges are compatible with the assumption that the term "permissive" carried the more positive connotations—an assumption which seems supported by the results of the Eiser (1972) study obtained from a comparable sample of subjects. This line of argument does *not* require that the implicit value connotations which particular scale terms hold for a given individual should be completely unaffected by his own attitude. On the contrary, when an attempt is made to measure such connotations, evidence of such a relationship can easily be observed. However, the point is that differences between individuals in their perceptions of the implicit value connotations appear, on present evidence, to be considerably smaller than differences between them in terms of their own attitudes. Reversals of the connotative value of a given scale, as would occur if an "anti-drug" judge rated the term "authoritarian" more positively than the term "liberal", seem comparatively rare, at least for the types of scales used so far. The more typical finding is for the "anti-drug" judge to evaluate the term "liberal" rather less positively, and the term "authoritarian" rather less negatively, than the "pro-drug" judge, but still to evaluate "liberal" more positively than "authoritarian". Moreover, there may well be issues or dimensions where such connotations are either absent altogether, or else of negligible importance as compared with differences in judges' attitudes. A possible example is Manis's (1960) study on attitudes towards fraternities, where judges with attitudes at either extreme of the continuum gave more polarized ratings than more moderate judges. If it is assumed that terms like "pro-fraternities" and "anti-fraternities" do not carry any very strong value connotations irrespective of judges' attitudes, then the question of the congruity between an individual's own evaluations of the statements and the implicit value connotations of the terms by which the judgement scale is labelled would not arise. The greater degree of polarization shown by both pro- and anti-fraternity judges as compared with more moderate judges would thus be compatible with a more simple application of accentuation theory principles. Where a systematic relationship exists between an individual's own evaluations of a set of statements and their relative positions along the attitude continuum (and the connotative values of the judgement scale terms are negligible), his levels of agreement and disagreement with the statements constitute a special case of correlated peripheral variation and should thus lead to enhanced polarization of judgement.

It is not proposed that accentuation theory principles are the only ones that operate in a social judgement context. As Upshaw has shown, the distribution of statements presented for judgement may affect both subjects' overall mean judgement and the degree of polarization of their ratings. In addition, there is the inverse relationship often (though not universally) observed between own position and overall mean judgement. Accentuation theory is primarily concerned only with bilateral shifts in judgement. However, the notion that individuals attempt to present or perceive themselves in positive terms implies that they should tend to present or perceive their own positions as lying closer to the centre of the underlying psychological continuum than they "really" are, if it is assumed that extreme positions tend to be negatively evaluated. If this were so, then an inverse relationship between own position and overall mean judgement would be predicted without having to postulate the operation of any adaptation processes.

7

Social Judgement and Phenomenal Causality

In this monograph we have attempted to explore in some detail the ideas and research relating to a limited number of specific topics, whilst other questions, among them no doubt many to which some readers might have expected us to give more attention, have been ignored completely, or passed over with only a cursory mention. In deciding which issues to discuss and which to ignore, we ourselves have performed an act of categorization. Like most other acts of categorization, its purpose has been to allow us to treat our field of interest as a relatively unified structure distinguishable from other areas. Yet the value of social psychological research does not depend simply on the coherence of the answers it may provide to certain specific and isolated questions, but also on the relevance of these specific questions and answers to more general areas of concern. From this point of view, the question of the judgement of attitude statements, which has been the focus of much of our attention, is *not* simply a problem of scaling methodology. It is one aspect of the more general question of how individuals perceive and construe their social world.

So far we have considered judgemental behaviour in situations where experimental subjects have been presented with series of distinct stimuli for assessment and comparison. We have seen how so-called "absolute" judgements are not absolute at all, but vary considerably depending on the context in which a given stimulus occurs, and on the categories, if any, to which it belongs. The kinds of social judgements we make in our everyday lives, however, are often much more than simple ratings of "single stimuli". They represent an attempt to give meaning to *configurations* of phenomena which we see as somehow interdependent and related to each other. When rating lengths of lines, we may decide, for instance, which of two lines is the longer, and by how much, but there it more or less ends. On the other hand, if we decide which of two people is, say, the more influential, we are not simply assigning them to different locations on some descriptive dimension, but saying something about the actual or potential relationships between them. Moreover, such judgements serve both an explanatory and a predictive function. A statement like "Tom is more influential than Jim" might, depending on the context, serve as an explanation of the fact that, for example, Jim was more eager to make Tom's acquaintance than vice versa. It might also enable us to make predictions about how Tom and Jim would be likely to behave towards each other, or towards a third person. In addition, it might predispose us to infer that Tom was not only more influential than Jim, but also more likely than not to be more success-ful, confident, skilful, wealthy and so on. Such explanations and infer-ences, of course, need not be correct, but we none the less often see them as implied.

It must be stressed at the outset that when we talk of "configurations" we are not talking about things as they "really are", but as they appear to the individual who perceives them. The kinds of "structures" with which we are concerned are cognitive, not physical. The same two events may be seen by one person as dependent on one another, and by another person as totally unrelated. Thus, in order to predict an in-dividual's response to one element in a structure from a knowledge of his response to another element in the same structure we must be able to assume that he sees the different elements as related to one another in the way we suppose. In examining how individuals appraise con-figurations of social stimuli, therefore, a major problem is that of determining how individuals infer the presence of any relationships between separate elements of a structure in the first place. In many ways, this is the same kind of question as the problem of stimulus rele-vance which we discussed in Chapter 3. In this chapter, we shall consider it in terms of the balance theory concept of "unit relations".

Once an individual sees the different elements of a configuration or structure as interrelated, the question then arises as to what kinds of relationships, and hence what kind of structure, he perceives. Cognitive consistency theory asserts a preference for structures where the relations between the different elements are "balanced", that is, internally consistent with each other, whilst the phenomenon of "positivity bias" reflects a preference for structures containing positive and self-enhancing relations, even at the price of some inconsistency. This applies both when the different elements in a structure are different people or concepts, and also when they are different characteristics of the same individual—when the "configuration" in question is, in fact, a single person. We tend to assume a degree of consistency among the various aspects of an individual's personality; in other words, we formulate "implicit personality theories".

Just as individuals seek to simplify their perceptual world by the use of categories, so the perception of configurations provides categories appropriate for such simplification. The same is true when our concern is with our experience of social phenomena. Consistent cognitive structures provide us with schemata in terms of which we can anticipate and predict the relation of one element in the structure to another. As with perceptual categories, they serve to highlight the more "redundant" aspects of our experience by rendering salient those similarities and differences between objects of judgement which are (or are assumed to be) predictive of other similarities and differences along different dimensions. When we talk of different elements in a cognitive structure being related to one another, therefore, we mean that they are related to each other in terms of certain salient dimensions: it is not required that they should be related in terms of *all* possible dimensions.

The question then arises as to which dimensions an individual will see as salient in any given situation. We shall mention evidence which suggests that individuals tend to make greater use of those dimensions in terms of which they can achieve both descriptive and evaluative consistency in their judgements and inferences, and also results which imply that individuals presented with information that is contradictory in terms of one dimension will engage in a search for new dimensions in terms of which the contradiction can be resolved. This leads on to a consideration of personal construct theory, which states that the individual perceives the world in terms of his own unique set of cognitive dimensions or "constructs". The value of personal construct theory is limited by its inability to generate precise predictions about the ways in which the construct systems of any two individuals will differ from one another, or about the kinds of dimensions that are likely to be salient for any given individual in a given situation. We shall argue, however, that one determinant of the salience of particular dimensions for an individual may be his own attitude towards the objects or concepts he

is judging, and that the degree of polarization of an individual's judgements along a given dimension may be taken as an index of the salience
of that dimension for him personally.

The ways in which we appraise configurations of social stimuli are
more than just discriminations. They represent an attempt by us to
render our experience intelligible, predictable and explicable. Balanced
structures are preferred to imbalanced ones not only because they are
balanced, but because they provide us with more consistent information
on the basis of which to make inferences and attributions. An individual
is presumed to develop certain personal constructs rather than others
because they enable him to "anticipate events". A theory of social
judgement must therefore be at least partly a theory concerning what
various authors have referred to as "phenomenal causality", "naive
psychology", "psycho-logic" or "lay conceptions of personality". In
this final chapter, therefore, we shall consider three approaches to the
problem of phenomenal causality. A full discussion of any one of these
three areas, *cognitive consistency*, *attribution*, and *personal constructs*, could
easily fill a monograph by itself. Our purpose here is simply to provide a
summary of the basic concepts involved, and a highly selective account
of some of the research to which they have given rise, so as, on the
one hand, to suggest some of the possible ways in which social judgement
may be relevant to other areas of social psychology, and, on the other
hand, to see how far the study of phenomenal causality may contribute
to an understanding of judgemental behaviour in the kinds of situations
we have discussed in previous chapters.

Cognitive consistency

The basic idea of cognitive consistency is perhaps the best known of all
theoretical concepts in social psychology. In simple terms, it is assumed
that individuals attempt to organize their feelings, attitudes and beliefs
into structures which are internally consistent, and that when they
experience cognitions which are incompatible with existing cognitions,
they will be motivated to reduce, resolve, or avoid the apparent contradiction. This notion is basic to the "balance theories" of Heider (1946,
1958) and Newcomb (1953), Rosenberg and Abelson's (1960) theory of
"affective-cognitive consistency", Osgood and Tannenbaum's (1955)
"congruity theory", Festinger's (1957) theory of "cognitive dissonance",
and all the various reformulations of these theories too numerous to

mention. It is also influential in current "cognitive" approaches to motivation (e.g. Zimbardo, 1969).

For present purposes, we shall discuss cognitive consistency mainly within the general framework of Heider's theory of cognitive balance—not because this is necessarily the most sophisticated of the various formulations of consistency theory, but because it is the one from which most of the others (and more recently, attribution theory) have developed. Balance theory is essentially an attempt to describe a part of what Lewin calls the "life space", or what Heider (1958) calls the "subjective environment" of an individual "perceiver" p. This subjective environment consists of certain *entities* and certain *relations* between these entities, *as perceived by p*. The classic example incorporates three entities, p, o and x, where p is the perceiver, o is another person perceived by p, and x is an impersonal entity such as an object or opinion (in some instances this third entity may be another person, in which case he is referred to as q.) Any pair of entities may be connected by either of two kinds of relations, referred to as *unit* and *sentiment relations*. A positive unit relation (U) indicates that the two entities in question are linked to each other by some kind of associative bond, whilst a negative unit relation $(-U)$ indicates that the two entities are somehow segregated, dissimilar or disassociated. Sentiment relations may likewise be either positive (L) indicating liking, agreement, admiration, etc., or negative $(-L)$, indicating dislike, disagreement, contempt, etc.

A *triad* consists of three entities linked by three relations, each of which can be a unit relation and a sentiment relation as well. Triads are said to be balanced when all three relations are positive, or when two are negative and the third is positive. Triads with one negative and two positive relations are defined as imbalanced, whilst those with three negative relations are treated as "ambiguous" by Heider, and as "imbalanced" by Cartwright and Harary (1956) and Rosenberg and Abelson (1960). Heider predicts that individuals will prefer balanced situations to imbalanced ones, and will therefore be motivated to take action to change the sign of a relation to restore balance where a state of imbalance exists. In addition, when individuals have knowledge of two relationships in a triad, and are required to infer the third, it is predicted that they will tend to infer the kind of relationship which produces a balanced as opposed to an imbalanced triad. This reflects the assumption that the preference for balance is essentially a preference for situations in which attributions can be made reasonably easily, and for which explanations are comparatively simple to find. As Heider writes:

> Attitudes towards persons and causal unit formations influence each other. An attitude towards an event can alter the attitude towards the person who caused the event, and, if the attitudes towards a person and an event are similar, the event is easily ascribed to the person. A balanced configuration exists if the attitudes towards the parts of a causal unit are similar.
>
> 1946, p. 107

There are a number of areas where subsequent research has called for revision or elaboration of Heider's original formulation of balance theory. One such extension which we shall not consider directly is the attempt to deal with different *degrees* of liking or disliking, as exemplified in Osgood and Tannenbaum's (1955) congruity model. A congruent (or balanced) state exists if two "objects of judgement" which are positively associated are evaluated equivalently by an individual, i.e. if (as seen by that individual) they occupy the same location along an evaluative dimension, which may be represented as a bipolar scale ranging from $+3$ to -3, in a manner analogous to the "good–bad" scale of the semantic differential. Thus, a congruent state would exist if one's best friend ($+3$) shared one's admiration for one's favourite composer ($+3$). Congruity theory deals only with sentiment, and not with unit relations, and although it takes account of the degree of sentiment relations, this applies only to the *po* and *px* relations and not to the *ox* relation. None the less, this particular formulation is especially interesting from the point of view of social judgement in that it explicitly treats such evaluations as constituting a *judgemental frame of reference*. We shall be returning to this point later in the chapter. However, the two aspects of balance theory which are perhaps most relevant to social judgement are the problems of positivity bias and unit relations.

Positivity bias

The first major demonstration of "positivity bias" was in Jordan's (1953) test of Heider's model. If one considers the case where one has a triad consisting of three entities (p, o and x), each of which can be linked to another by any of four kinds of relations (U, $-U$, L, $-L$), 4^3 or 64 different kinds of triads can be constructed. Jordan presented subjects with very simple verbal descriptions of each of these 64 triads. The symbol p was replaced by "I", with the symbols o and x being maintained for the other two entities. L and $-L$ relations were formulated respectively as "like" and "dislike", and U and $-U$ relations as "has some sort of bond or relationship with" and "has no sort of bond or relationship with". Thus the triad $(pLo) + (p-Lx) + (oUx)$ was presented in verbal form as "I like o, I dislike x, o has some sort of bond or relationship with x". Subjects were instructed to take the role of "I" (i.e. p) and rate each of the 64 triads in terms of pleasantness. In accordance with balance theory predictions, balanced triads were generally rated as more "pleasant" than imbalanced ones. However, triads containing negative relations tended to be rated as "unpleasant", even in the case of balanced triads consisting of one positive and two negative relations. This preference for positivity, or "positivity bias" as it has come to be called, was more marked for sentiment than for unit relations, and was particularly important in the case of the po relation, i.e. the relation between the two personal entities. A similar pattern was observed by Rosenberg and Abelson (1960), who found that subjects who were instructed to take the role of the owner of a department store (in which the rug department manager was planning to mount a modern art display which might have either beneficial or detrimental effects on sales) showed a preference for information which implied that sales would improve, even when this produced imbalanced cognitions.

Another area in which such positivity effects have been observed is one which may be loosely referred to as "interpersonal evaluation". As in the classic balance theory situation, one is concerned with two individuals, p and o, each of whom evaluate a third entity, x. Typically, the problem is one of predicting the po relation from knowledge of the other two. In this case, however, the third entity is actually p's own view of himself, and not some impersonal object or issue, or a third person. The question being asked is: How far is our evaluation of, or liking for, another person influenced by our perception of whether the other person likes us, and how far is this dependent on our own self-concept?

According to Secord and Backman's (1965) application of balance theory to this question, individuals who evaluate themselves positively should prefer others who also evaluate them positively, and dislike others who evaluate them negatively. For such individuals, in other words, liking should be reciprocated. However, where individuals hold *negative* views of themselves, they should prefer others who dislike them rather than others who like them. A person is thus predicted to like others who confirm his own evaluation of himself, whether this evaluation is positive or negative. An alternative viewpoint, recently termed "signification theory" by Skolnick (1971), postulates that one will prefer other people who evaluate one positively, whether or not such evaluations are congruent with one's own opinion of oneself. In other words, one will prefer others whose evaluations of oneself serve to support or enhance one's self-esteem. Essentially, therefore, this latter approach predicts a *tendency towards positivity* in interpersonal evaluations. For individuals high in self-esteem, this tendency is consistent with a tendency towards balance. In the case of low self-esteem individuals it leads, at any rate initially, to a state of imbalance.

Although a number of studies have shown that liking will be reciprocated in the case of high self-esteem individuals, there is scant support for balance theory predictions in the case of individuals who hold negative opinions of themselves. Deutsch and Solomon (1959) conducted an experiment in which their subjects (female telephone operators) were led to believe that they had either succeeded or failed on a series of tasks. Each subject then received a note, supposedly from another member of her "team", in which her performance and desirability as a team-mate was evaluated either very positively or very negatively. Subjects who were led to believe that they had succeeded indicated greater liking for their supposed "team-mate" when this evaluation was positive than when it was negative, whereas subjects who believed that they had failed showed little difference in their reactions to positive and negative evaluations. Deutsch and Solomon ascribed these findings to the operation of two tendencies, one towards positivity and the other towards balance, and inferred that the reason that no differences were found between subjects in the "failure" conditions was that these two tendencies cancelled each other out.

More recently, however, Skolnick (1971) failed to replicate Deutsch and Solomon's findings. The most important departure from the original procedure was an increase in the ambiguity of the tasks which subjects were required to perform, which were designed to leave them very confused about how they had actually performed. Subjects were then given three conditions of feedback by the experimenter. Each subject in the "success" condition was given a score card apparently showing that his performance was the best in his group. In the "failure" group, the score card presented his own score as the lowest in the group, and in the "no feedback" condition, each subject received a score card supposedly showing the distribution of scores in his group but with no indication which score was his own. Each subject then received a note, supposedly from another member of his group, evaluating his own performance and value as a team-mate either positively or negatively. Another difference between this and Deutsch and Solomon's study was the use of male and female college students as subjects. Skolnick found a preference for positive evaluators in all three feedback conditions. In other words, subjects indicated greater liking for someone who evaluated their own performance positively, irrespective of whether they themselves felt that they had succeeded or failed, or had no idea of their own performance. (This preference for the positive as compared with the negative evaluator was actually *largest* in the "failure" condition.) Skolnick argues that subjects in the Deutsch and Solomon study may have been less "ego-involved" than his own, and also may have felt so certain about their own performance that they viewed evaluations which contradicted their own opinions about their performance with suspicion or incredulity. Skolnick (1971) suggests that effects compatible with balance theory predictions "are more likely to occur where ego involvement is minimal and suspicion and incredibility are high; alternatively, a signification model is likely to be supported where there is high ego involvement and suspicion is minimal" (p. 66).

Further evidence of both a positivity and a congruity tendency comes from an unpublished study by Berscheid and Walster (1968) in which the perceived accuracy of an evaluator's impression of the subject was varied independently of its favourability. Each subject was required to indicate his liking for each of four evaluators who had supposedly formed impressions of the subject from a "set of biographical materials". The subject was told that all four evaluators had said that they liked him "extremely much", and had each listed eight traits which they thought he possessed. One of them (who tended to be the one liked most) listed eight traits which the subject regarded as both desirable and characteristic of himself; the next most preferred listed eight characteristic traits one of which was undesirable; the next most preferred listed eight uncharacteristic desirable traits; the least preferred listed eight uncharacteristic traits, one of which was undesirable. The effects of the perceived accuracy and the perceived favourability of the evaluations on subjects' liking for each evaluator were both significant (the former being more so), and they did not interact significantly. However, the fact that favourability was manipulated by varying only one of the eight traits, and that all evaluators indicated extreme liking for the subject, means that no general conclusions can be drawn from this study concerning the relative importance of the tendency towards balance and the tendency towards positivity, since the manipulations were of unequal strength.

Fairly similar results were obtained in a study by Eiser and Smith (1972). Subjects rated each of 50 personality trait words in the following terms: (a) how likely it would be that they would like someone whom they described as possessing the trait in question; (b) how accurately the trait adjective in question described them personally; and (c) how likely it would be that they would like someone whom they overheard describing them as possessing the trait in question. For each subject separately, the trait words were classified as positive and negative on the basis of that subject's first set of ratings and as accurate and inaccurate on the basis of his second set of ratings. Subjects indicated most liking for a hypothetical evaluator who described them in terms which they considered both positive and accurate, and least liking for one giving negative and inaccurate descriptions. Contrary to the Berscheid and Walster findings, however, inaccurate positive descriptions were preferred to accurate negative ones, i.e. the effect of positivity was stronger than that of accuracy (congruity). As in the Berscheid and Walster study, the two effects did not interact. This study differs from the others we have mentioned in that the evaluator was purely imaginary and hypothetical, as opposed to being supposedly a real person with whom the subject was likely to interact. Although this procedure has obvious limitations, it nevertheless constitutes a situation in which *both* ego involvement *and* suspicion are minimal, yet where both the tendency towards balance, and, more markedly, the tendency towards positivity can be seen to operate.

The tendency to maintain a positive self-evaluation, and/or to prefer situations in which cognitions are experienced which are consistent with a positive self-evaluation, would thus appear to be an important aspect of interpersonal attitudes. This may be related to the argument we put forward in Chapter 6, that the need to present or perceive oneself in positive terms may be an important factor in influencing an individual's judgements of attitude statements. But it is not entirely obvious how such a tendency towards positivity should be interpreted. According to Heider, the tendency towards balance may reflect both a *preference* for balanced states (imbalance leads to "tension") and an *hypothesis* or expectation about reality (we expect our experiences to be consistent with each other). Similarly, it would be consistent with the evidence presented so far to consider the tendency towards positivity either as a preference for positivity (negative relations are unpleasant) or as an hypothesis about reality (negative relations are exceptional), or both. A study by Jacobs *et al.* (1971) suggests that a preference for positivity may operate even where negative relations are more expected. They argue that individuals who are low in self-esteem may be more likely than high self-esteem individuals to assume that others will dislike them, and hence will be more likely to misinterpret affectionate overtures from others. This would appear to constitute an expectation of negative interpersonal relations in the case of low self-esteem individuals. At the same time, however, low self-esteem individuals appear to show a greater need for approval and are more receptive than high self-esteem individuals to affection, once they realize that it is being offered. This would appear to constitute a preference for positive interpersonal relations. On the other hand, evidence from work on the use of evaluative language suggests that language is primarily geared towards the expression of positive rather than negative relations. Boucher and Osgood's (1969) "Polyanna hypothesis" suggests that this may reflect an *expectation* that positive relations and characteristics will predominate over negative ones. (See Peeters (1971) for a fuller discussion of these and other related issues.)

Unit relations

One of the major problems of Heider's theory is the ambiguity that surrounds the concept of unit relations. Although Heider distinguishes between unit and sentiment relations, he does not really treat them as though they were different in any important respects. Both can supposedly be positive or negative, and the presence of either a positive or a negative unit relation can supposedly lead to a state of balance or imbalance. However, although verbal equivalents can easily be found for positive and negative sentiment relations, as opposite points along the continuum for liking to disliking, this is much more difficult in the case of unit relations, especially *negative* unit relations. The negative unit relation $(p-Uo)$ effectively means "There is no reason to talk of both p and o in the same context", but if this is so, then it is not easy to see why anyone should ever choose to *assert* a negative unit relation, except in situations where a positive unit relation might otherwise be expected. The reason for this is that, whereas a negative sentiment relation is the *opposite* of a positive sentiment relation, in the sense that "dislike" is the opposite of "like", or "disapprove" the opposite of "approve", a negative unit relation is the *complement* of a positive unit relation: it merely negates the presence of a positive unit relation. It does not refer to a different kind of relation, but states simply that no relation exists.

This line of argument implies that, since balance is dependent on the presence of (signed) relations between entities, the question of balance or imbalance does not arise when entities are linked by a negative unit relation. Put another way, if a negative unit relation is not really a relation at all, but the absence of a relation, then it cannot be said to constitute an effective part of any structure, or render any structure either balanced or imbalanced. For this reason in Cartwright and Harary's (1956) reformulation of Heider's model in terms of graph theory, relations such as liking, disliking, etc. are represented graphically as lines which link pairs of points representing entities. The negative unit relation, however, is represented as the absence of a line. In terms of their model, this means that it cannot constitute part of any balanced or imbalanced structure or "cycle". To test this interpretation, Cartwright and Harary re-examined the results of Jordan's (1953) study. Of Jordan's 32 "balanced" triads, 14 contained no $-U$ relations and can therefore still be regarded as balanced. These 14 achieve a mean "unpleasantness score" of 39. The other 18 contain at least one $-U$ relation and are therefore defined as "vacuously balanced" by Cartwright and Harary. These achieve a mean unpleasantness score of 51. Of Jordan's 32 "imbalanced" triads, 19 are similarly "vacuously balanced" in that they contain at least one $-U$ relation. The mean unpleasantness score for these is again 51. This leaves 13 triads which remain imbalanced, and achieve a mean unpleasantness score of 66. In other words, the ratings given to the various triads in terms of "pleasantness–unpleasantness" do not serve to distinguish between triads defined as balanced or imbalanced in terms of Heider's model, where these triads contain one or more $-U$ relations.

Another reformulation of balance theory, that of Jaspars (1965), carries a similar implication. Adopting the framework of Coombs's (1964) theory of data, Jaspars argues that balance theory only applies when a single cognitive dimension (in Coombs's terms, a "J-scale") underlies an individual p's preferences for o and x (the po and px sentiment relations).

In other words, balance theory applies only when p's degree of liking for o and x is based upon a common underlying attribute or dimension. Where this is so, the degree to which the entities o and x possess the attribute in question would be represented by their location on the same underlying J-scale. If they were similar they would be located close to each other, and if dissimilar they would be located at some distance from each other. The individual p's preferences for either entity is then determined by its distance on the J-scale from an *ideal point P*. This *ideal point* could vary from individual to individual, in much the same way as an individual's "own position" along an attitude continuum. If small distances between points on the J-scale represent positive relations and large distances represent negative relations, then it is possible to represent five different types of triads in terms of such a unidimensional preference space. These include the triad with three positive relations, the three triads containing one positive and two negative relations, and also an instance of a triad with three negative relations, where P occupies an intermediate position on the J-scale, and o and x occupy positions at opposite extremes. (This might occur if o and x were two politicians, o being a communist and x a fascist. If p conceived of such opinions as extreme points on a unidimensional scale, with the ideal point being at the centre, then he could disapprove of both o and x, and expect o and x also to disapprove of each other.)

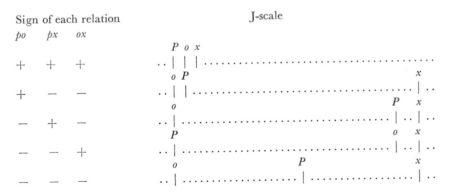

Fig. 7.1. Representation of triads in a unidimensional preference space.

The first four of these triads that can be represented in terms of a unidimensional preference space are all balanced. The fifth also describes an instance when a triad with three negative relations might be regarded as balanced. Imbalanced triads (i.e. triads with two positive and one negative relation, or with three negative relations and an *ideal point P* close to either extreme) *cannot be represented in a unidimensional preference space.* In other words, it is impossible to locate the three points P, o and x so that they lie on a single straight line, and also represent an imbalanced triad. From this point of view, a preference for balance would be compatible with the general principle of economy in cognitive functioning in that it would represent a preference for structures which could be represented in terms of simple rather than complex cognitive maps. Similarly, differences between individuals in their preference for simple as opposed to complex cognitive structures should be reflected in differences in their preferences for balanced as opposed to imbalanced states. Moreover, to the extent that individual differences in cognitive "simplicity–complexity" may be generalizable over different kinds of situations, individual differences in preference for balance as opposed to imbalance should be similarly generalizable. To the extent that individual differences in cognitive "simplicity–complexity" may apply only to certain situations, individual differences in preference for balance should also be situation-specific.

In what situations, then, will a single cognitive dimension underly an individual's preferences for particular objects of judgement? A simple answer would be when the objects of judgement share a common attribute, and the individual bases his preferences on the differences between these objects in terms of this attribute. An example would be if someone preferred fast cars to slow cars and ignored all other attributes of cars except their speed. His *ideal point* would lie at the "fast" end of the "slow–fast" J-scale, and the more similar two cars were in terms of their speed (their positions on this J-scale), the more similarly he would evaluate them. If the same person chose a fast, expensive car because of its speed and also a slow, cheap car because of its low price, then his preference for the two cars could not be represented in terms of the same J-scale. Put another way, considering either speed or price alone, his choice of the two cars would appear imbalanced. This definition, however, is too simple. On the one hand, not all objects which share a common attribute can be represented within a single unidimensional preference space, even if this attribute provides the basis for a given individual's preferences of the objects in question. Consider the attribute "sweetness". It is quite possible for someone to prefer sweet chocolate to bitter chocolate, dry sherry to sweet sherry, sweet white wine to dry white wine, and not to take sugar in his coffee. Although chocolate, sherry, wine and coffee all share the attribute of sweetness, the individual may employ different *ideal points* for different classes of objects. On the other hand, balance theory also seems to apply to situations where the common "attribute", if it can be so called, is not any objectively definable characteristic shared by the elements in question. If one considers the three elements in Rosenberg and Abelson's (1960) study, "Fenwick", "Modern Art" and "Sales", it is not that they share any single common "attribute" but rather that they are seen as somehow *interdependent*. A modern art display might affect sales, and Fenwick might therefore affect sales through putting on such a display; moreover, since Fenwick is responsible for sales in his part of the store, his proposal to put on a display must be judged in terms of its likely effect on sales and not in terms of some extraneous criterion. In other words, the situation is such that it makes sense to talk of the three elements in the same context, as related to each other, in such a way that they *form a unit*. For two elements to be represented on the same cognitive dimension, therefore, it is neither sufficient nor necessary that they can be compared in terms of some objective attribute; what is important is that the individual perceives a *unit relation* between them.

A study which brings out the importance of unit relations is that by Stroebe *et al.* (1970), who presented subjects with information about a "Dr M" who was represented as either supporting or opposing a certain scientific theory, and as either having recently married or recently divorced his wife. Additional information stated that, *as a scientist*, Dr M was either "outstanding" or "inadequate" and that, *as a person*, he was either "warm, friendly and likeable" or "cool, distant and unlikeable". Subjects were then asked to evaluate both the theory and Dr M's wife on a number of semantic differentials. The results indicated that subjects differentiated quite clearly between "Dr M as a scientist" and "Dr M as a person": when evaluating the theory they took into account Dr M's expertise as a scientist, irrespective of his likeability as a person, and when evaluating his wife they ignored his expertise and attended only to his likeability. In terms of our present discussion, one could interpret these results as implying that subjects inferred unit relations between the concepts "theory" and "Dr M as a scientist" and also between "wife" and "Dr M as a person", but not between "theory" and "Dr M as a person", or "wife" and "Dr M as a scientist". Here again, this is not merely a matter of shared attributes but of perceived relevance.

G

Cognitive consistency theory is thus essentially a statement about how we organize our appraisals of elements that are regarded as interdependent or relevant to each other within a given context. Appraisals of elements regarded as relevant to each other influence each other; appraisals of unrelated elements do not. As Osgood and Tannenbaum (1955) express it: "Changes in evaluation are always in the direction of increased congruity with the existing frame of reference" (p. 43), or "Judgmental frames of reference tend toward maximal simplicity" (p. 42). Cognitive consistency theory thus applies only to elements that can be evaluated within a common *frame of reference*, or located along a common cognitive dimension or J-scale. This problem is similar in many ways to that which we considered in Chapter 3 in our discussion of the question of stimulus relevance in psychophysical judgement. We saw then that subjects' scales of judgement typically do *not* reflect the pooled effect of all past and present stimulation along a given sensory dimension, as Helson assumed, but are affected only by those stimuli which subjects regard as relevant to the kinds of judgement they are making. Not only do we adopt different standards for the judgement of different classes of objects on a common physical dimension (as when judging the weight of pipes and ash-trays), which Helson himself admits, but our judgements of stimuli in one class are typically unaffected by exposure to stimuli belonging to another, irrelevant, class. In the studies reviewed in Chapter 3, both "relevant" and "irrelevant" stimuli shared a common attribute, such as weight or size, which was the same as the attribute in terms of which the stimuli were being judged. This, however, was not sufficient to lead subjects to treat the different types of stimuli as belonging to a single frame of reference. In the same way, where we are dealing with elements between which no unit relation exists, and which cannot therefore be included within a single frame of reference, the question of balance does not arise.

Attribution

An area which makes a particularly direct attempt to examine "lay conceptions of personality" is that concerned with how individuals attribute personality characteristics to another person. Work in this area falls into two more or less distinct parts. The first, that of *trait inferences*, is concerned with the question of what kinds of traits one will infer that another person possesses, if given information that he possesses certain others, and with the related question of how the combination of traits one is told that another person possesses affects one's overall impression of his personality. The second, that of *attribution theory*, is concerned more specifically with the question of how and when one will attribute personality characteristics to another person (or even to oneself) on the basis of observed behaviour or its consequences.

Trait inferences

Since the early work by Asch (1946) a large number of experimenters have attempted to study attribution processes by examining individuals' reactions to personality trait words. The phrase "personality trait" should not be interpreted all that technically. More or less any adjective from ordinary language that could be used to describe a person's characteristics qualifies as a possible "personality trait" for the purposes of these experiments. In general, the responses subjects are required to make take the form either of inferences, where they may be asked questions such as "If someone is considerate, how likely is it that he is also truthful?"; or of ratings, where they have to rate trait words, either in isolation or in combination with other trait words, in terms of semantic differential scales that are generally (though not necessarily) evaluative in nature (see, for instance, Anderson's (1968) list of "likeableness" ratings for 555 such words). For the purpose of our present discussion, this distinction between inferences and ratings is not all that crucial. To rate a trait such as "truthful" as very "likeable", is not too different from inferring that someone who is "truthful" will also tend to be "likeable". We shall therefore consider both kinds of studies under the same general heading of "trait inferences", even though, strictly speaking, many involve "trait ratings".

   The clearest overall result of these studies is that subjects seem to base their inferences and impressions upon an assumption of a kind of intra-personal consistency. In other words, they appear to assume that someone who is possessed of one "good" trait will be possessed of other "good" traits also (the classic "halo effect"). This is compatible with Heider's (1946) hypothesis that "a balanced state exists if any entity has the same dynamic character in all possible respects" (p. 107). The question arises, however, as to whether the assumption of intra-personal consistency reflected in such judgements and inferences is purely a matter of *evaluative* consistency, or whether it represents an attempt to maintain descriptive

G*

consistency as well. In other words, do individuals make inferences to traits which are similar to those with which they are originally presented simply in terms of their affective or evaluative *connotations*, or do they also select traits which have similar *denotations?* The common emphasis on evaluation in trait inferences has been questioned by Peabody (1967), who argues that in such studies evaluative and descriptive similarity are typically confounded. One cannot be sure, therefore, whether inferences to similar traits are made generally on the basis of evaluative or descriptive consistency or both, unless one deliberately constructs a set of traits in which evaluation and description are unconfounded. Peabody therefore proposes the following scheme for unconfounding evaluation and description. Suppose one has in mind a particular attribute X. It is necessary to find two different terms to denote X, one positive in evaluation, and one negative. One then needs to find antonyms for these two terms; in other words, one selects two terms to denote "un-X", one negative in evaluation and one positive. Thus, if we defined the attribute X as a disposition to take risks, we might select the traits "bold" (+) and "rash" (−) to denote X, and "timid" (−) and "cautious" (+) to denote un-X. This is the same logic as lay behind the labelling of the different judgement scales in the Eiser and Mower White study on children's attitudes towards adult authority described in Chapter 6. If X means a disposition to question adult authority, terms like "imaginative" (+) and "impatient" (−) would denote X, and terms like "unimaginative" (−) and "patient" (+) would denote un-X. By selecting traits in this way, it is possible to compare the roles of evaluative and descriptive similarity by requiring subjects to make inferences from a trait such as "cautious" either to an evaluatively similar but descriptively dissimilar trait such as "bold", or to an evaluatively dissimilar but descriptively similar trait such as "timid". In judgemental terms, this involves requiring subjects to rate the concept "cautious" on the semantic differential "bold–timid".

In all such cases where evaluative and descriptive similarity are unconfounded in this way, referred to as "critical inferences", Peabody found that descriptive similarity was decisive over evaluative similarity, i.e. "cautious" was taken to imply "timid" rather than "bold". He also reported that when the inferences were factor analysed none of the factors were evaluative. Rosenberg and Olshan (1970), however, have disputed this last conclusion, pointing out the presence of an artifact in Peabody's factor analysis:

The absence of an evaluative dimension in Peabody's factor analysis seems simply to be the result of scoring all the bipolar scales in the same direction with respect to evaluation and then correlating across the scales.

p. 624

When Peabody's data are re-analysed with this artifact removed, a strong evaluative factor reappears. In response to these findings Peabody (1970) has modified his position so as to take account of both descriptive and evaluative factors, concluding:

(a) In analysis of general relations based on the covariation of many traits, descriptive and evaluative relations are of comparable importance; (b) in analyses of separate trait inferences, descriptive relations are more important where they are specifiable; (c) in the combining of several traits, preliminary evidence shows that descriptive relations are even more important than for single traits.

p. 645

Similar evidence of attempts by subjects to maximize both descriptive and evaluative consistency comes from a study by Felipe (1970), who concludes:

Present evidence suggests that two consistency-producing mechanisms, appearing in a definite sequence, may be involved in trait inferences. The first, discovered by Peabody, consists of testing for similarity in the descriptive contents of trait terms . . . Traits similar in such descriptive attributes, regardless of their evaluative contents, are judged to have more likelihood of occurring together in a person than traits that are evaluatively similar, but descriptively different . . . Although descriptive similarity is the first requirement to be satisfied in trait interferences, achieving descriptive similarity may not terminate cognitive operations. On the other hand there seems to be an evident pressure to also achieve evaluatively consistent trait cognitions. Traits which are both descriptively and evaluatively balanced have a greater likelihood of occurring together than traits which are only descriptively, but not evaluatively, balanced . . . In other words, when an individual has a chance to express descriptively consistent cognition in an affectively balanced way, that will be undertaken. When one tests for descriptive consistency and fails to achieve it, he generally proceeds to apply the second mechanism, attempting to achieve affective balance, at least. Thus, in inference . . . involving concepts and scales with reduced descriptive overlaps, the individual apparently forms cognitive structures in a manner predicted by traditional balance theories, balancing signs of concepts.

p. 635

At least at a general level, this conclusion is in close accordance with the interpretation of social judgement data proposed in Chapter 6, and with the results of the Eiser and Mower White study. It may be remembered that when the mean ratings of the attitude statements on each scale are compared, all ten scales showed high positive correlations with each other. Since the ten scales were all arranged with the left-most term denoting the "anti-authority" end of the continuum, and with the right-most term denoting the "pro authority" end, irrespective of their value connotations, the fact that these correlations were all highly positive reflects a strong tendency on the part of the subjects to maintain consistency at a descriptive level between their ratings on the different scales. On the other hand, the differences in polarization between the different scales as a function of their value connotations reflect an additional tendency by the subjects to maintain consistency at an evaluative level between their own personal evaluations of the statements and their ratings of those statements on any given scale. At one level, they attempt to rate the more "pro" statements towards the more "pro" end of the scale, and thus maximize descriptive consistency. At another level, they attempt to rate the statements with which they personally agree as closer to the more positively valued end of the scale, and thus maximize evaluative consistency.

A further result from Peabody's (1967) study, to which we have already alluded in Chapter 6, is the finding that negative traits are typically, but not always, treated as descriptively more extreme than positive traits. Peabody reports that pairs of negative traits, such as "rash" and "timid", which are descriptively opposite to each other, are rated as more dissimilar to each other than corresponding pairs of positive traits, such as "bold" and "cautious". Subsequent work, notably Rosenberg and Olshon's (1970) finding of an evaluative factor which was independent of any descriptive dimension, has called for modification of Peabody's (1967) original contention that "evaluation is typically based on a descriptive judgement of the degree of extremeness" (p. 15). None the less, there would appear to be a relationship between evaluative judgements and judgements of descriptive extremity, even if it is difficult to infer its causal direction. This is particularly interesting in relation to the phenomenon of positivity bias discussed earlier in this chapter. Considering positivity bias as a *preference* for cognitive structures which are consistent with a positive self-evaluation, when combined with the notion that moderate positions along a descriptive dimension tend to be more positively evaluated, leads to the prediction of contrast effects for social judgement data, as suggested towards the end of Chapter 6. In addition, the negative evaluation of more extreme positions, if combined with an assumption that extreme positions are relatively exceptional by comparison with more moderate positions on most descriptive dimensions, would be consistent with viewing positivity bias as reflecting an *expectation* that objects of judgement will tend to be positive rather than negative.

Another aspect of trait inferences which has attracted considerable attention is the question of how *combinations* of traits lead to overall impressions, or inferences to other traits. Here the problem is basically one of predicting the implicational properties of a combination of traits from a knowledge of the implicational properties of the individual traits in the combination. Thus, a typical question might be: What is the probability that someone who is "beautiful" and "truthful" will also be "considerate" if someone who is beautiful has a probability p of also being "considerate" and someone who is "truthful" has a probability q of also being "considerate". This area owes much to the pioneering work of Bruner *et al.* (1958) who proposed a model for predicting inferences from trait combinations based upon a simple additive principle. Subjects were presented with four traits and required to estimate the probability that someone possessed of these traits, either singly or in combination, could also be described by each of a list of 59 trait words. Subjects made their responses in terms of the five categories: "very often are", "tend to be", "may or may not be", "tend not to be", and "seldom are". The first two categories were defined as definite positive inferences and the last two as definite negative inferences. Bruner *et al.*'s results showed firstly:

> Where two (or two out of three) traits, given singly, point in the *same inferential direction*, the inference from the combination of two (or three) will point in the same direction. Where two traits singly generate inferences to a specific trait that are, respectively, *positive and negative*, the combination of the two will show the same signs as the trait that in isolation led to a larger number of definite inferences in a given direction.
>
> 1958, p. 283

In addition, combinations of traits which, if taken singly, all produced inferences of like sign to a specific trait, produced a larger number of definite inferences over a group of subjects than the number of definite inferences produced by any of the component traits in isolation in 41 per cent of the cases of such trait combinations. In 91 per cent of the cases the number of definite inferences produced by the combination was greater than the average number of definite inferences produced by the component traits in isolation. It is worth noting that these results are not restricted to purely evaluative inferences.

Many attempts have been made to develop more quantitative models

---

[1] We do not wish to imply that this is the only information required to make this prediction.

to predict such effects. Simple linear models based upon summation (Fishbein and Hunter, 1964), or weighted average formulations (Anderson, 1965), have met with a considerable amount of descriptive success, although more sophisticated models based on principles of set theory (e.g. Hays, 1958) have at least comparable predictive power (cf. Warr and Smith, 1970). Instead of attempting to compare these various models in detail we shall consider briefly a specific area in which the adequacy of simple linear models may be called to question, namely the problem of inferences from combinations of *inconsistent* traits.

There is already some evidence in the study by Bruner *et al.* that combinations of inconsistent traits may not always produce the effects one might anticipate. Consider, for instance, what one might intuitively expect about the certainty of inferences made from inconsistent information. The most obvious thing to expect would be that such inferences tend to be made with less certainty than inferences based on consistent combinations. But apparently this is not necessarily so. Bruner *et al.* report that in 70 per cent of the cases with combinations of traits which lead singly to inferences of *unlike* sign, the number of definite inferences produced by the combination exceeded the average number of definite inferences produced by the component traits, and in 40 per cent of the cases also exceeded the number produced by any single component. In other words, the same effect occurs as with consistent trait combination, although not to quite the same extent. Combinations of traits, whether consistent or inconsistent, apparently lead to more definite inferences on average than do single traits. However, Bruner *et al.* point out: "While conflictful information may often produce an increase in the number of definite inferences, this gain is *not* as often accompanied by a corresponding increase in agreement as to the sign of the inference." (p. 286.)

More substantial evidence of the inapplicability of simple linear models to inconsistent combinations comes from a series of studies by Cohen (Cohen and Schümer, 1968, 1969; Cohen, 1971). Cohen points out that the kinds of ratings or inferences which subjects are typically required to make in such studies involves their having to respond to inconsistent combinations in terms of the very dimension which contains the contradiction. Suppose, for instance, we had a subject who considered that someone who was "generous" was likely to be "kind" and that someone who was "arrogant" was likely to be "unkind". How would such a subject respond to the combination "generous and arrogant"? The answer suggested by models incorporating an additive or averaging principle is that either he will discount one of the two components or he will respond to some kind of "compromise" impression. In other words, he will tend, on average, to rate the combination as close to the neutral point on the "kind–unkind" dimension, that is, as close to the average of the scale values of the two component traits on that dimension. Cohen argues that this prediction is indeed generally correct, but only because the subject is forced to make his response on the "kind–unkind" continuum, i.e. because he is forced to make a *single* response to the combination on the very dimension in terms of which the combination is contradictory. From this point of view, a neutral rating on the "kind–unkind" continuum *might* convey an impression like "Someone who is generous and arrogant is of average kindness", but it might equally well convey something like "Such a person is *both* kind *and* unkind", or "I cannot rate such a person on this dimension" or, more positively, "Such a person is neither simply kind, nor simply unkind, *but something else.*" As Cohen (1971) puts it:

Only when one forces a judge—we assume—to give an estimate, say, of the intelligence of a student who does excellently on written exams but dreadfully on orals, or to rate the aggressiveness of a murderer who happens to be a pacifist as well: only in such cases will the judge, of necessity, make his judgement on that contradiction-laden dimension. If, however, he were allowed the opportunity to express himself freely, a large portion of the variance of his judgments would fall on dimensions other than the contradiction-laden one: in the case of the first example above the judge might refer to "difficulties of verbal expression" or "examination anxiety", while in the second example he would talk about "neurotic reaction formation" or "guilt feelings". In analogy to the ethologists' "substitute behaviors" or the psychoanalytic model of the neuroses, it may be anticipated that when judgments of contradictory items of information are made only a small portion of the variance of the judgments will fall, as the linear model suggests, on that dimension which reflects the contradiction of the individual items, while the major portion of the variance will fall on dimensions independent of this one. Further, it appears reasonable to assume that under conditions of free expression the subject will interpret the contradiction itself as an item of *further* information and as a signal to switch his judgments to a dimension which is independent of that on which the contradictions exist.   pp. 476–477

   Cohen (1971) reports three parallel experiments which lend strong support to this point of view. In the first of these, subjects were presented with eight copies of a rating form containing 36 semantic differential scales. These included two scales which were highly intercorrelated, i.e. which showed highly similar patterns of correlation with the other scales. These were "cheerful–sober" and "optimistic–pessimistic". On the first four of the eight rating forms presented to the subjects, one of these four adjectives was checked off. Subjects were instructed to imagine as accurately as they could a young man of about 20 years old who could be described by the adjective checked off on each form, and then to rate this young man on the other scales of the semantic differential. Ratings were thus obtained from each subject for each of these four traits considered in isolation. (On the basis of this data, subjects who failed to treat the two scales as intercorrelated, i.e. failed to treat the pairs of terms "cheerful–pessimistic" and "sober–optimistic" as contradictory, as required by the hypotheses, were excluded from the analysis.) The remaining four ratings forms each had two of these four adjectives checked off, so as to produce the two consistent trait combinations, "cheerful"+"optimistic" and "sober"+"pessimistic", and the two inconsistent or contradictory combinations, "cheerful"+"pessimistic" and "sober" + "optimistic". In these cases, subjects were told that these were judgements of the young man made by two different people, both of whom were equally well acquainted with him and who generally agreed in their judgements about other people, and that both the characteristics checked off were of equal importance. Subjects then rated the trait combinations in the same manner as the single traits.

These ratings were then intercorrelated across the scales (Q-technique) and factor analysed separately for each subject; in addition they were submitted to an analysis of variance for each scale separately. It was found that, where consistent traits were combined, the major portion of the variance of subjects' judgements fell on the same dimension as those on which most of the variance of their judgements of the single traits also fell. In other words, consistent combinations led to qualitatively similar impressions to those produced by the individual traits in the combinations. However, for contradictory combinations, the major portion of the variance fell on dimensions other than those which characterized the contradiction, i.e. those which accounted for most of the variance of the single trait judgements. In other words, contradictory combinations produced qualitatively very different impressions to those produced by the component traits in isolation. Subjects apparently were able to deal with the "contradictory" information presented to them by the experimenter by appraising the stimulus person in terms of dimensions where such information ceased to be contradictory. Moreover, there was substantial consistency between the different subjects with respect to those dimensions onto which they "displaced" their judgements of the contradictory pairs, suggesting that these pairs were not treated, as simple additive or averaging models would assume, as "neutral" or "ambiguous" stimuli but as items of information in their own right with definite implicational properties. Cohen therefore concludes that the adequacy of simple linear models for the prediction of judgements of trait combinations decreases markedly and steadily the more the component traits are experienced as contradictory. These conclusions are supported in two other experiments reported in the same paper, with different pairs of adjectives being used to describe the stimulus person.

Subsequent work by Cohen and Schümer (1968, 1969) using short behavioural descriptions instead of trait words to depict the stimulus person substantially confirmed these findings. Again, there was considerable intersubject agreement regarding the dimensions used to describe contradictory combinations of behaviour. Combinations of hostile and friendly behavioural descriptions led to judgements on scales interpreted as denoting "neuroticism", whilst combinations of extrovert and introvert behavioural descriptions led to judgements on scales interpreted as denoting "outer-directedness". There is also evidence that the amount of contradiction (i.e. the absolute differences between the judgements of the component behavioural items on those dimensions which account for most of the variance of the judgements of the components considered in isolation) may also be a predictor of which dimensions will be used for judgements of the contradictory pairs.

These findings provide yet more evidence for the "assumption of intrapersonal consistency" which appears to characterize most trait inferences. Their chief value, however, is in showing what may occur when subjects are presented with information which violates this assumption, when they are given apparently contradictory descriptions of a single stimulus person. According to balance theory, imbalance should lead to cognitive restructuring aimed at resolving the inconsistency. An individual confronted with a state of imbalance may, of course, simply "give up" trying to resolve the inconsistency, but, equally well, he may not. If he does not, then he will seek to *explain* the inconsistency, and the search for explanation may involve a search for a dimension or frame of reference in terms of which such inconsistency is minimized, and where the previously conflicting items of information can be represented within a common cognitive space. Cohen's work is especially interesting in that it suggests that this search for explanation and for new dimensions may proceed in a systematic and predictable fashion.

Attribution theory

This kind of explanatory function of attribution processes is the main concern of research centred around a set of theoretical principles that have come to be known as "attribution theory". In the work on trait inferences, the question to which most attention has been paid is that of how different personality traits (or more precisely, personality trait *descriptions*, which are not necessarily quite the same thing) are conceived of as implying one another. From the standpoint of "attribution theory", however, a statement like "That person is generous" is interesting not so much because it "implies" other statements like "He is honest" or "He is considerate", but because it proposes a reason for why the person acts the way he does. Attribution theory is concerned primarily with how individuals attribute *causes* to events in their experience, in particular, to the behaviour of themselves and others. Here the emphasis is often not so much on *which* personality characteristics are likely to be attributed to a given person, but whether *any* characteristics can be attributed to him on the basis of his behaviour, the primary question being whether the cause of his behaviour lies in some personality characteristics which he may possess, or in the influence of external pressures and constraints over which he has relatively little control.

The two main theoretical statements of attribution theory, both based on the ideas put forward by Heider (1958) in "The Psychology of Interpersonal Relations", are those of Jones and Davis (1965) and Kelley (1967). Since these formulations are compatible with each other in most general respects, we choose to phrase our discussion primarily in terms of Kelley's version of the theory. Kelley lists four types of criteria which, if violated, will reduce the probability that an individual will seek to explain behaviour by attributing specific personal characteristics or intentions to the actor. These he defines as distinctiveness, consistency over time, consistency over modality, and consensus.

The criterion of *distinctiveness* requires an adequate specificity of the situation in which a given attribution is made. Thus, if we made a statement like "That person is generous", and someone then pointed out to us "But you always think people are generous", we might feel required to justify our statement more specifically.

The criterion of *consistency over time* requires that the actions on the basis of which we attribute certain personal characteristics to the actor should be reasonably typical of the behaviour he could also be observed (or expected) to show at different times and in different situations. The less frequently we can observe (or the less confidently we can expect) replications of the behaviour in question, the more likely we are to attribute the cause of such behaviour to temporary aspects of the external situation in which it occurs.

The criterion of *consistency over modality* requires that all aspects of the behaviour in question should be consistent with each other. In other words, at whatever "level" or through whatever "channels" we observe the behaviour our impression should be the same.

The criterion of *consensus* is the familiar variable of most conformity and attitude change studies. If we learn that other people do not generally agree with our description of a person's behaviour as "generous", then we are less likely to feel that our impression is correct.

Thus, applied to the specific question of how we infer an individual's intentions or dispositions from his actions, attribution theory predicts that we should apply a number of "tests" before attributing the cause of his behaviour to his intentions or to some feature of his personality, rather than to some feature of the external environment or to any other extraneous factor. First, we test for whether the intentions or personality of the actor can be regarded as a *relevant* causal factor influencing his behaviour and its observed consequences. If we come to the conclusion that the person would have acted in the way he did, or that his behaviour (whatever form it has taken) would have had the same consequences, even if his intentions had been different, we cannot consider his intentions to be a relevant causal factor in the situation, and therefore cannot infer what his intentions or personality might be simply from an observation of his behaviour in that situation. (Jones and Davis's (1965) discussion of this point is somewhat more extensive than Kelley's.) Similarly, if we observe that the impression we have of the actor's personality is in no way distinctive, i.e. no different from the impressions we normally form of other people whatever their behaviour or the consequences of their behaviour, we again cannot consider his actual intentions or personality to be a relevant cause of our impression. Having satisfied ourselves that the actor's intentions or personality could be considered a relevant causal factor, we may then test for whether the impression we have formed is consistent with the impressions we would form if we observed his behaviour at different times, or in different ways, or with the impressions formed by other people. In other words, we treat a person's intentions or personality, his behaviour, and our own impressions as constituting a causal unit only when the criteria of relevance and consistency are satisfied.

As with cognitive consistency theory, however, such validation procedures do not always operate in a perfectly "logical" manner. One effect, which would appear to be closely related to the phenomenon of "positivity bias", is the tendency of individuals to claim their successes and disown their failures. Thus, when supervisors can exercise some measure of control over the behaviour of subordinates by the use of reward and punishment, they make different attributions depending on how well the subordinates perform. If the subordinates perform well, the supervisors are more likely to attribute this to the success of their own supervision. If the subordinates perform badly, they are more likely to be blamed for their poor performance by the supervisors (Kite, 1964). Similar results have been found by Johnson et al. (1964), who report that improvement in the performance of a pupil influenced teachers' evaluations both of the child's ability and of their own skill at teaching, and also by Streufert and Streufert (1969). As in other instances of "positivity bias", therefore, subjects arrange their cognitions into causal units which are not simply balanced but consistent with a positive self-evaluation.

One important instance of where the criteria for attributing the causes of a person's behaviour to "internal" factors, such as his intentions or personality, are not fully met is where the person is seen as constrained to act the way he does. Nemeth (1970) found that subjects will indicate greater liking for another subject (a confederate) who helps them with a task than for one who does not help them when his decision to help or not help is apparently voluntary. However, when his decision is compulsory (i.e. when the experimenter instructs the subject and confederate either to help or to withhold help from one another), the confederate is slightly (not significantly) preferred when he withholds help. Similar results were found by Eiser et al. (in press). Subjects participated in a type of bargaining game in which they played against a simulated partner whose apparent behaviour produced either favourable or unfavourable outcomes for themselves. The pay-off matrices were arranged so that the partner appeared either to be relatively free to choose whether to assign favourable or unfavourable outcomes to the subject at low cost to himself, or to be forced to act the way he did by the constraints of the pay-off matrix, or to be acting in spite of the pay-off matrix (i.e. deliberately incurring high costs). The partner was seen as more likely to act competitively in a future interaction when assigning unfavourable than when assigning favourable outcomes under conditions of apparent free choice, whereas no difference was observed when the partner appeared to be acting under the constraints of the pay-off matrix. When the partner appeared to be acting in spite of these constraints, the results were intermediate between those of the other two conditions.

A recent study by Jones *et al.* (1971) also shows that perceived freedom of choice may affect the attitudes we attribute to another person on the basis of what he says. Subjects were presented with an essay, supposedly written by the target person, which was either strongly favourable, moderately favourable, moderately unfavourable or strongly unfavourable to the legalization of marijuana. In the "choice" condition, subjects were told that the target person had been allowed to choose whether to write for or against marijuana. In the "no choice" condition, they were told that he had been instructed by the experimenter to take the stand he did. When the essay was strongly favourable or strongly unfavourable the attitude attributed to the target person was more in line with that expressed in the essay in the choice than in the no choice condition, although there was still a tendency in the no choice condition for subjects to see the target person's attitudes as corresponding to those which he expressed. However, when the target person produced a moderate essay under conditions of no choice, he was seen as holding an opposite attitude to that which he expressed. Subjects' prior expectations of the target person's attitudes also influenced their attributions.

Just as individuals differ in the extent to which they organize their cognitive structures in accordance with the precepts of balance theory, so we can expect individuals to differ in terms of how they make attributions in any given situation. A large body of research, essentially concerned with such individual differences in "attributional style", is that centred around Rotter's (1966) notion of "locus of control". Approaching the problem from the standpoint of social learning theory, Rotter argues that the effect of reinforcement on an individual's behaviour does not depend simply on the occurrence (or non-occurrence) of such reinforcement, but on how it is construed by the individual. Of especial importance is the extent to which the individual sees the reinforcement as following from, or contingent upon, his own attributes or behaviour, as opposed to being controlled by external forces (e.g. chance) which operate independently of his own behaviour. Rotter postulates that, as a function of their social learning history, individuals will develop *generalized expectancies* as to whether the "rewards" they receive will tend to be contingent on their own behaviour, or a result of forces outside their control. Rotter conceives of individual differences in such generalized expectancies as lying along a dimension which he refers to as that of "internal versus external control". At one end of this dimension, individuals with "internal" expectancies are predicted to attribute the cause of the reinforcements they receive in a variety of situations to their own behaviour or attributes; at the other end, "external" individuals are predicted to see their own behaviour as having no effect on whether or not they receive "reinforcements".

Although Rotter formulates his theory in terms of such "learning theory" concepts as "reinforcement" and "expectancy", there is comparatively little evidence that directly supports his idea that particular (that is, identifiable) events in an individual's social learning history influence his adoption of an "internal" or "external" orientation (cf. McArthur, 1970). It has also been argued that "externality" may at least partly represent a feeling of social and political "powerlessness" (Thomas, 1970; Seeman, 1971). Whatever its basis, however, locus of control has been shown to be an important predictor of subjects' behaviour in a variety of situations.

Jones et al. (1971), for example, report a follow-up study in which they presented 21 "internals" and 23 "externals" with the strong pro-legalization essay used in their main study under either "choice" or "no choice" conditions. They found a significant interaction between locus of control and the choice variable, indicating that "internals" were more sensitive to the choice variable than "externals".

Differences in attributional style of a somewhat different kind have been reported by Kelley and Stahelski (1970). Basing their argument largely on studies of dyadic interaction in mixed-motive games, they suggest that competitive individuals typically fail to discount the causative role of their own behaviour in shaping the responses of their partner. As a result, they uniformly tend to attribute competitive intentions to their partner, as compared with cooperative individuals who are more "heterogeneous" in their attributions of competitiveness or cooperativeness. It is perhaps open to question whether such differences in attributional style are situation-specific, or, as Kelley and Stahelski (p. 66) suggest, reflect the different "views of their worlds" adopted by cooperative and competitive "personalities". Nevertheless, it is useful to look at attribution processes as they operate in these and other kinds of interactions, rather than only restricting one's attention to the implicational properties of particular sets of personality descriptions. Whereas the study of trait inferences throws light on the kind of psychological assumptions which people make when describing the behaviour and characteristics of others, work on attribution theory lays greater stress on the explanatory nature of these descriptions.

When we attribute certain attitudes, intentions or characteristics to another person, therefore, we are not simply locating that person along some descriptive dimension. We cannot "observe" a person's attitudes or character directly. All we can do is to infer them from the things he says and the way in which he behaves. Why then are we so ready to make such inferences? The answer suggested by work on attribution theory is that we do so in order to be able to predict and explain our experience, and thereby render it more simple and intelligible. In doing so, we pay attention to the same criteria of relevance and consistency which are basic to the definition of cognitive balance. As with the ways in which we receive imbalance, however, the ways in which we make attributions in any given situation conform to rules of "psycho-logic" and not necessarily to rules of logic. There appear to be "stylistic" differences between individuals in the kinds of attributions they make. The phenomenon of "positivity bias" translates itself into a preference for self-enhancing attributions (although this cannot be assumed to be the case for all individuals). Moreover, since the characteristics we attribute to others (and to ourselves) to a large extent direct the way in which we behave towards them, our own behaviour may frequently make our attributions self-fulfilling. In a Prisoner's Dilemma game, a cooperative subject faced by a competitive partner is likely to be forced to act competitively out of self-defence, and so confirm his partner's expectations. In the same way, a teacher who decides that a particular pupil is especially "promising" is likely to give him extra attention and encouragement as a result of which such promise is confirmed. A racialist government which believed in the inferiority of Negroes would be likely to pursue policies that discriminate against them. The further study of attribution processes might hopefully provide a useful link between theories of social judgement and an understanding of such aspects of social behaviour.

Personal constructs

Just as individuals differ in the manner in which they attribute causes to events in their experience, so it is reasonable to expect that they may also differ in the cognitive dimensions in terms of which they appraise such events. In other words, different individuals may see different aspects of the same events as being the most relevant or salient, and may therefore attempt to explain such events in terms of different frames of reference or causal units. This assumption (albeit phrased in somewhat different terms) is basic to a rather different kind of theory from those we have so far considered, namely G. Kelly's (1955) theory of personal constructs.

The starting point of Kelly's theory is a conception of man "as a scientist", attempting to explain, predict and control events in his experience. The individual thus is assumed to adopt an essentially *active* role *vis-à-vis* his experience, formulating and testing hypotheses against experience rather than *passively* responding to incoming stimuli. His behaviour is not determined simply by "real" or "objective" situations but by his own perception or judgement of these situations, which will be a function of his current cognitive structure or "contruct system". "Constructs" are conceived of as bipolar dimensions, peculiar to each individual, through which he interprets events in his experience. Their function is to define the relevant ways in which different objects of judgement resemble or differ from one another. Contructs are regarded as differing from "concepts" in that (a) they are more elaborate, embodying notions of polarity, (b) they enable the individual not only to label, but also to predict his experience, and (c) they are related and organized in a hierarchical structure. Kelly presents his theory in terms of the following fundamental postulate, and eleven corollaries:

Fundamental postulate A person's processes are psychologically channelized by the ways in which he anticipates events.

Construction corollary A person anticipates events by construing their replications.

Individuality corollary Persons differ from each other in their constructions of events.

Organization corollary Each person characteristically evolves, for his convenience in anticipating events, a construction system embracing ordinal relationships between constructs.

Dichotomy corollary A person's construction system is composed of a finite number of dichotomous constructs.

Choice corollary A person chooses for himself that alternative in a dichotomized construct through which he anticipates the greater possibility for extension and definition of his system.

Range corollary A construct is convenient for the anticipation of a finite range of events only.

Experience corollary A person's construction system varies as he successively construes the replications of events.

Modulation corollary The variation in a person's construction system is limited by the permeability of the constructs within whose range of convenience the variants lie.

Fragmentation corollary A person may successively employ a variety of construction subsystems which are inferentially incompatible with each other.

Commonality corollary To the extent that one person employs a construction of experiences which is similar to that employed by another, his psychological processes are similar to those of the other person.

Sociality corollary To the extent that one person construes the construction processes of another, he may play a role in a social process involving the other person.

As the reader may by now have realized, one of the more unusual features of personal construct theory is the terminology in which it is expressed, and it is perhaps partly for this reason that much work on personal construct theory has proceeded in relative isolation from other approaches. This is particularly unfortunate, since, although Kelly's ideas may have been somewhat unorthodox by the standards of psychology in the mid-fifties, by now much of the assumptive base of his theory, at least at a general level, is quite consistent with theorizing in many of the more conventional areas of psychology. Consider, for instance, the following quotation:

> All perception involves categorizing. If you see something you have never seen before you will already have categorized it as "something I have never seen before". At birth (and before) stimuli are categorized in the sense that the nervous system deals differently with light and sound stimuli, and so on. At the other extreme, in complex social behaviour, categorizing is very evident. A person reacts to others depending on how he has categorized them. Probably the most general dichotomous social category is "Us versus Them".

No, this passage was *not* written by Bruner of Tajfel, nor is it an extract from one of the earlier chapters in this book! It comes instead from the editorial foreword to Bannister and Fransella's (1971) paperback on personal construct theory. However, the simple proposal that "people categorize" is not a theory in any real sense of the word unless and until one can formulate empirically testable predictions concerning *how* people will categorize in any given situation and *which* aspects of the situation will be treated as the basis for classification. By the same token, the notion that perceptual experience involves the formulation and testing of hypotheses is consistent at a general level with such concepts as "analysis-by-synthesis" (Neisser, 1967) and "TOTE" (Miller *et al.*, 1960), but it cannot be *simultaneously* translated into both of these and still make unambiguous predictions about how such a process of hypothesis-forming and hypothesis-testing takes place.

The same plausibility at a general level, combined with imprecision with regard to any specific detail, is apparent in the various corollaries of Kelly's fundamental postulate. The "construction corollary" implies that the attributional criterion of consistency over time is assumed to be satisfied in our appraisals of events, whilst the "experience corollary" implies that the individual's construct system will be affected by the extent to which this assumption turns out to be valid. Just to say that "experience", in the form of validation and contradiction, may lead to modification of one's current set of predictions (and hence one's construct system) does not get us very far unless one defines more precisely the specific steps which an individual will take to resolve the state of imbalance occasioned by the invalidation of his construct system.

The "organization corollary" asserts the existence of relationships between different constructs within an individual's cognitive system, whilst the "fragmentation corollary" allows for a degree of inconsistency between different parts of the system. Here the notion of "subsystems which are inferentially incompatible with each other" seems very close to Cartwright and Harary's (1956) concept of "local balance". The "dichotomy corollary", taken literally, is not easily reconciled with the evidence that individuals undoubtedly *can* rate objects as occupying intermediate positions on judgemental continua. However, the implication that individuals may *prefer* to make dichotomous categorizations is not implausible. As Osgood and Tannenbaum put it:

> Since extreme, "all-or-nothing" judgments are simpler than finely discriminated judgments of degree, this implies a continuing pressure toward polarization along the evaluative dimension (i.e. movement of concepts toward either entirely good or entirely bad allocations).
>
> 1955, p. 44

Again, the "dichotomy corollary" is not developed into an empirical prediction concerning *when* judgements in terms of constructs will be most "dichotomous".

The "range corollary" refers to the familiar problem of "relevance", "universes of discourse", "unit relation", etc. The point is simply that it is only meaningful to call for judgements of a finite selection of objects or events in terms of any given construct or cognitive dimension. For any given construct or dimension there will be an infinity of objects or concepts to which it does not apply. Consequently, the less the referential ambiguity of an individual's set of constructs, the less easily will it be modified by experience ("modulation corollary"). However, to recognize the problem of relevance, though commendable in itself, is not the same as being able to answer the multitude of questions to which it gives rise. By what criteria does one decide to treat a given element as relevant to a given construct or dimension? Are judgements of relevance "all-or-nothing" decisions, or do we allow for degrees of relevance? Is the "range of events" to which an individual applies a given construct a function of the range of events or elements which the experimenter presents to him in the testing situation?

The "commonality" and "sociality corollaries", taken together, predict, among other things, that individuals who are cognitively similar (i.e. have similar construct systems) will be able to communicate more effectively with each other. This prediction is reasonably well supported by experimental data, but the overall conclusion from research in this area is that it would be premature to claim that any single parameter of cognitive similarity is the only major determinant of communication effectiveness. Rosenberg and Cohen (1966) present a stochastic model of referential processes in terms of which cognitive similarity is defined as the "homogeneity" of the individual's response repertoires. Other definitions are based upon the nature of the psychological dimensions used by different individuals when appraising either events in general or the particular set of objects about which they are attempting to communicate. Triandis (1960a) used an adaptation of the repertory grid test to determine "attribute similarity", i.e. the extent to which individuals generally use the same dimensions "when examining events in their environment". He distinguished this from "communication similarity", i.e. the similarity in the dimensions used by individuals "in the actual process of communication" (p. 176), which he measured by means of a content analysis of subjects' messages in a communication task. He found that, although the two kinds of similarity were not

H

correlated with each other, both led to greater communication effectiveness. Regarding "communication similarity", he concludes: "It is
desirable from the point of view of communication effectiveness, that
two people use the same dimensions when they attempt to communicate.
However, communication is still possible when they use different dimensions." (p. 181.) A second study (Triandis, 1960b) provides more
evidence for the importance of "communication similarity", this time
as measured by a semantic-differential technique. Here he makes the
further observation: " . . . given the two Ss use the same dimensions, it
is also important to consider whether they agree when assigning events
to positions along these dimensions. The greater their agreement, the
more likely it is that they will communicate effectively." (p. 295.)

This last conclusion is somewhat different from that put forward by
Bonarius (1965) in his review of research relating to Kelly's theory. He
states:

> It is important to realise that commonality of construing is not identical with simi-
> larity in the evaluation of an event along the common construct dimension . . . Thus
> where many would stress consonance in the evaluation of an event in order to achieve
> communication, the theory of personal constructs postulates only commonality of the
> construct dimensions.
>
> p. 39

As support for this argument, Bonarius cites a study by Runkel (1956)
who asked psychology students and their teachers to indicate their
orders of preference for five statements indirectly related to the content
of their course. By an application of Coombs' unfolding technique,
Runkel distinguished those students who were "noncolinear" with their
teacher, i.e. who appeared to be basing their preferences on different
underlying attributes or J-scales, from those who were "colinear" with
their teacher (Coombs (1964) uses the more cautious term "compatible"),
i.e. whose preferences *could* be based on the same underlying attribute
or "J-scale", even though they might have a different "ideal point" on
that attribute from their teacher. Runkel found lower course performance among students who were "noncolinear" as opposed to "colinear"
(or "compatible") with their teachers, a result which he interprets as
indicating that greater cognitive similarity between teacher and student
led to better exchange of information between them, and hence to
improved performance by the student. Coombs (1964) stresses the
following point:

> It is not agreement with the teacher on which statements are the best that makes the

difference in quiz grades; rather it is judging the statements according to the *same underlying attribute*, regardless of whether the student agrees with the teacher about the most desirable point on the attribute.

p. 129

However, there are important differences between the notion of a J-scale and a construct. A J-scale denotes the *underlying* attribute on which an individual's set of preferences in based; it does not denote the preferences themselves. It is not required that individuals should be able to give a verbal description of this attribute in order to base their preferences on it, but if they do not, then it cannot be elicited as a "construct" in a repertory grid. Moreover, Bonarius is unfortunately ambiguous when he talks of similarity in *evaluation* of events along a given construct. By definition, J-scales are descriptive, not evaluative. The question of evaluation only arises when one defines the location of a given individual's "ideal point" on a given "J-scale". The "J-scale" can then be "folded" about this "ideal point" to produce an evaluative "I-scale". Nevertheless, constructs can be, and in practice often are, very highly evaluative. Even "good–bad" is perfectly admissible as a construct. Where this is so, "commonality of construing" will be far less distinguishable from evaluative congruity than Bonarius implies.

Apart from the difficulty in deciding on any single definition of cognitive similarity, there is the question of interpreting its effects. Does cognitive similarity lead to greater communication effectiveness because it enables one individual to "tune in" to another's cognitive structure (cf. Zajonc, 1960)? Or does it depend on the "decentering ability" of the individuals concerned (Feffer and Suchotliff, 1966), or the degree of correspondence in the "coding rules" which they employ (Mehrabian and Reed, 1968)? Kelly's theory is quite consistent, at a *general* level, with evidence in the communication area. The value of a scientific theory, however, does not depend simply on such general plausibility, but also on its ability to generate *specific* predictions in specific situations.

In some ways the most important but at the same time one of the least well defined of Kelly's corollaries is the "individuality corollary" that "persons differ from each other in their constructions of events". At a simple level, this is bound to be correct, unless it can be shown that *everyone* employs an identical construct system to everyone else. This emphasis on the uniqueness of the individual is immediately counterbalanced by some of the other corollaries. The "commonality" and "sociality corollaries" assume that different people may to some extent share or be able to adopt each other's constructions of events, and the "experience corollary" implies that individuals whose experiences are dissimilar will employ more dissimilar construct systems than those with similar experiences (since similar experiences should serve to validate similar hypotheses about reality). All this suggests that some individuals are likely to be "more unique" than others, at least in so far as their construct systems are taken as a measure of their individuality.

There is also the curious paradox of "supplied" personal constructs. The original version of the repertory grid test was designed to elicit from subjects their own verbal descriptions of the cognitive dimensions in terms of which they appraised events in their experience, the supposed merit of this technique as compared with more standard rating procedures being that it got at the subjects' own *personal* constructs. In practice this can sometimes be a rather time-consuming and chancy business, and there is a growing tendency for researchers to supply subjects with constructs instead of attempting to elicit them separately from each individual (e.g. Bannister and Fransella, 1966). Whilst this allows for rather easier comparisons between individuals, it is essentially the same as any other technique which involves administering standardized bipolar rating scales. This can be particularly embarrassing when it turns out that, for some purposes at least, the reliability of measures calculated from such "supplied" constructs is rather higher than from "elicited" constructs (Tripodi and Bieri, 1963). Similarly, Triandis's (1960a) finding that "attribute similarity" and "communication similarity" did not correlate emphasizes the unremarkable, but none the less important, point that individuals may employ different cognitive dimensions when appraising different kinds of objects and events, and that two individuals who are similar when making one kind of judgement may not necessarily be similar when making another.

There is evidence that individuals make more extreme judgements on constructs elicited from them personally, or rated by them as more personally relevant or meaningful, than on constructs supplied by the experimenter (Cromwell and Caldwell, 1962; Bonarius, 1965; Landfield, 1968). Although Warr and Coffman (1970) failed to confirm this effect, they themselves suggest that this may have been because the supplied constructs were still comparatively relevant or meaningful. When they later manipulated the perceived importance of the concepts subjects were required to judge, they found greater extremity of judgement on semantic-differential scales for concepts perceived as more important. Further evidence for this kind of relationship comes from a study by Tajfel and Wilkes (1964) using a rather different procedure. Subjects were required to give free descriptions of other people, and the relative priority and frequency with which they mentioned particular attributes was recorded. Tajfel and Wilkes reasoned that those attributes which featured most prominently in an individual's free descriptions would be of greater "salience" or "subjective importance" to him than those which featured less prominently (an assumption which they were later able to confirm). When subjects were then required to rate photographs on rating scales based on attributes elicited from their own free descriptions, they gave more extreme or polarized ratings on the more salient than on the less salient dimensions.

From the point of view of social judgement, these results are of great importance, since they suggest that the pattern of judgements (specifically the degree of polarization) shown by an individual when rating a given set of objects or concepts along a given construct or dimension may be taken as an index of the "personal relevance" of that dimension to the individual—although they do *not* allow us to infer that the same dimensions will be salient or relevant to a given individual whatever objects he is judging. Moreover, if Kelly is correct in assuming that personal constructs are not mere descriptions of experience but also an attempt by the individual to predict and explain his experience, then a knowledge of the dimensions that are most salient for a given individual should also tell us something about that individual's explanations of those parts of his experience to which such dimensions refer. Unfortunately, personal construct theory cannot take us beyond this point. No definite indication is given as to the reason why, or the manner in which, the construct system of two individuals may resemble or differ from one another. Yet without more specific predictions of this kind, the simple assertion that "individuals differ" is little more than a motto.

Dimensional salience

The notion that different dimensions, issues or events will be more "salient" or "personally relevant" for some individuals than for others is by no means peculiar to personal construct theory. On the contrary, the concept of "salience" in one form or another is implicit in most theories in social psychology, and indeed in many areas of general psychology as well. Like the concept of a stimulus, the term "salience" is more easily employed than defined. If a stimulus is something that elicits a response, then a salient attribute of a stimulus is an attribute that elicits the response most intensely or emphatically. In the context of a judgement task, it is commonly assumed that individuals will discriminate more between different objects of judgement in terms of attributes they consider salient than in terms of those they consider non-salient, and hence that a given dimension can be said to be particularly salient for an individual if he gives particularly extreme or polarized judgements along it. However, it is circular to argue that differences in polarization are due to differences in salience unless we can define independently which dimensions are likely to be more salient for a given individual. Operational definitions are to some extent provided by the personal construct theory distinction between "elicited" and "supplied" constructs and by Tajfel and Wilkes' (1964) criterion of priority and frequency of mention. The point here is that one can decide which dimensions are to be treated as salient for a given individual *before* looking at his judgements. But these approaches do not provide an answer to the question of *why* a particular dimension or stimulus attribute is more salient than another.

Most attempts that have been made to answer this question have consisted merely in a restatement of the question in different terms. Bonarius (1965) takes the differences in polarization observed on different types of constructs as showing convincingly that "the individual prefers to express himself and to describe others by using his own personal constructs than provided dimensions" (p. 26), yet he offers no explicit guidance on why this "preference" should exist. Other researchers have generally done little more than to suggest that salient dimensions are salient because they are "emotionally significant", "subjectively important", "ego-involving", "personally relevant", "associated with value" and so on. Yet this only puts the question one stage back: Why should particular dimensions be "emotionally significant" to an individual? Without an answer to this question we are left with the rather unsatisfactory conclusion that salient dimensions are important to the subject because of their subjective importance.

Nevertheless, from this list of partial synonyms, two clues emerge. The first is implied by the term "ego-involving". As we have seen, there is comparatively little direct evidence regarding the effects of involvement on social judgement, although there is rather more in studies we have not reviewed regarding the effects of involvement on attitude

change (Sherif *et al.*, 1965). In Sherif's system, a high degree of involvement on an issue is presumed to enhance the "anchoring" effects of an
individual's own position, to broaden his "latitude of rejection", and to
increase his resistance to influence. Although Sherif does not always
draw a sharp distinction between involvement and the extremity of own
position, implied in the notion of involvement is the idea that the
individual's self-esteem is somehow bound up with and committed to a
particular position on the issue in question, so that a challenge to an
individual's attitude on that issue represents a challenge to the individual
himself.

The second clue is contained in Tajfel's use of the terms "salience"
and "value". According to Tajfel, the association of value with a particular attribute is a special case of superimposing a classification on a
series of stimuli: it enhances the salience of the attribute with which it is
associated, and, as with other instances of correlated incidental stimulus
variation, leads to increased polarization of judgement along the focal
dimension. Although the effects produced by value are assumed to be
no different in kind from those produced by other superimposed cues,
they are predicted to be of greater magnitude, since value is of "emotional significance". Thus, the greater the "value differential" of a given
dimension (i.e. the more the differences along that dimension are
systematically related to differences in value), the more salient is that
dimension. This implies, in other words, that a salient dimension is *par
excellence* a dimension that is relevant to an individuals' evaluations of
the stimuli he is required to judge.[1]

The concept of salience, therefore, appears to be concerned in some
way both with evaluative discriminations of objects of judgement, and
with commitment to one's self-esteem, i.e. to an evaluation of oneself as
positive. How does this help us predict which dimensions will be salient
for a given individual? To answer this question, let us recap on some of
the earlier arguments of this chapter. The notion that individuals discriminate between objects of judgement in terms of those dimensions
which are salient to themselves is basically a statement about how
people attempt to interpret their experience. As such, it may be directly

---

[1] This should not be taken to imply that all judgements are necessarily evaluative, but only that
where evaluation is relevant to a judgement task it is a prime determinant of the salience of a
particular dimension. In non-evaluative psychophysical judgement tasks the salience of a
particular dimension can be manipulated experimentally by prior training (Davidon, 1962).
Here, however, the task of finding an "objective" basis for differences in salience is somewhat
more clearly defined than in social judgement.

compared with other hypotheses about phenomenal causality, such as that individuals attempt to organize their cognitions into balanced structures, and to see events as related to each other in terms of causal units. Research relating to the questions of how people achieve and maintain cognitive balance and how they attribute causes to events in their experience may thus at least partly suggest how the concept of salience may be defined less tautologically.

One of the most important points to come out of research on balance theory is the importance of self-evaluation. The unqualified formulation of cognitive consistency theory assumes a positive self-concept. Consider, for example, Osgood and Tannenbaum's (1955) congruity model. Among its assumptions are (a) that objects of judgement which are equally evaluated by an individual may be located at the same position on an evaluative scale, and (b) that maximal congruity exists when objects of judgement which are "associatively linked" are located at the same position on an evaluative scale and objects of judgement which are "dissociatively linked" occupy opposite locations. Thus, if we wished to represent the relationship "Tom thinks very highly of his friend Jim" in terms of a congruity model, treating Tom as the "perceiver", we would have little hesitation in assigning Jim to a location close to $+3$ on Tom's evaluative scale. In doing so, however, we have already made an important assumption. Since there is an "associative link" between Tom and Jim, if Tom were required to locate himself on the same evaluative scale congruity would obtain only if he also evaluated himself towards the positive end of the scale. Thus, the "straightforward" prediction that we should like others who like us is derivable from balance theory only when granted the assumption of a relatively positive self-concept. Where this assumption is not met, research on interpersonal evaluation implies that a preference for positivity with respect to self-evaluation may be more powerful than a preference for congruity, particularly, as Skolnick (1971) has suggested, when ego-involvement is high. Other manifestations of "positivity bias" in research on both cognitive consistency and attribution processes points in a similar direction. We may conclude that an important feature of the individual's "naïve psychology" is that he attempts to maintain and present a positive view of himself in relation to other objects and events in his experience.

If we move on to consider work on the unit relation and on trait inferences, we find evidence that enables us to consider particular kinds of cognitive *structures* in terms of particular kinds of cognitive *dimensions*. We see that individuals do not necessarily evaluate different elements or objects of judgement in relation to all other elements simultaneously, but are able to differentiate relevant elements from irrelevant ones (Stroebe *et al.*, 1970). There is then the argument that balanced structures can be represented on a single cognitive dimension or J-scale, whereas imbalanced structures cannot (Jaspars, 1965). This in turn suggests that the perception of imbalance may initiate a cognitive restructuring, involving a *search for new dimensions* in terms of which the structure may be seen as balanced: a suggestion which receives substantive support from the work of Cohen (1971). In other words, the hypothesized tendency to prefer balanced to imbalanced cognitive structures may manifest itself in a tendency to construe particular sets of relationships along certain kinds of dimensions rather than others, that is to *see as more salient* those dimensions in terms of which a given structure may be seen as balanced. However, as the work on positivity bias indicates, it is not just consistency which is important, but consistency with a positive self-evaluation. In other words, it would be predicted that individuals should see as most salient those dimensions in terms of which their evaluations of interdependent objects of judgements are most consistent with each other, and with a positive evaluation of themselves.

At this point, we may return to a consideration of the effects of judges' attitudes on the judgement of attitude statements, where we concluded that the interaction effect shown between judges' attitudes and the value connotations of the judgement scale was compatible with the assumption that subjects' behaviour in a social judgement task is directed towards the maintenance and/or presentation of a positive self-concept. Where an individual's own evaluations of the statements he is required to judge are *congruent* with the value connotations of the judgement scale terms—in other words, where the statements with which he agrees lie closer to the end of the scale marked by a term with relatively positive connotations, and those with which he disagrees lie closer to the evaluatively negative extreme—he will tend to give relatively more polarized ratings than on scales where his own evaluations of the statements are *incongruent*. This is consistent with work on evaluative versus descriptive aspects of trait inferences, where it has been found that individuals attempt to achieve consistency at an evaluative level even after consistency at a descriptive level has been achieved (Felipe, 1970). It is also compatible with the more general principles of categorization which we

H*

have discussed in previous chapters. Thus, whilst on the one hand research on phenomenal causality leads us to certain conclusions regarding the kinds of dimensions which should be relatively "salient" for a given individual, and also suggests that greater salience should be reflected in greater polarization of judgement, on the other hand research on social judgement indicates that it is indeed these kinds of dimensions on which judgements tend to be more polarized.

Approaching the problem of dimensional salience from the standpoint of the psychology of judgement thus leads to an equivalent conclusion as approaching it from the standpoint of phenomenal causality. Salient dimensions are dimensions along which the individual can present the relationships between relevant objects of judgement in a way that is both descriptively accurate and evaluatively congruent. The phrase *relevant* objects of judgement is extremely important. Perception and judgement must of necessity be selective. It is impossible to simultaneously appraise the relationships between every object in one's experience, even where these objects may share many physical attributes in common, and still make the kind of *decision* that is involved in any act of judgement. As we saw in the earlier chapters of this book, the AL theory hypothesis that context effects in psychophysical judgement represent the pooled effect of *all* past and present stimulation is quite indefensible. Even in tasks as "uninvolving" as the judgement of lifted weights, subjects are able to exclude from consideration objects which they regard as having nothing to do with the stimuli they are required to judge. Consequently, it would be extremely surprising if subjects could not make a similar differentiation in social judgement situations when confronted with stimuli more central to their own feelings and beliefs. We should not fall into the error of assuming that just because an individual prefers to use certain dimensions rather than others when judging a particular set of stimuli (e.g. attitude statements on a given issue, facial photographs, or a list of relatives and acquaintances), these dimensions or "personal constructs" will remain equally salient for him whatever the nature of the stimuli he is judging. Dimensions which are found to be salient for a given individual in one situation will not necessarily be salient for him in another. This is not to deny that "attitudes cluster", or that individuals may frequently construe seemingly dissimilar objects or concepts in similar ways. We are not asserting that there is *never* likely to be any correspondence between the way in which someone "construes" one set of events and the way in which he "construes" another set: the very existence of descriptive language assumes the possibility of such generalization, whilst at the same time setting limits to how far such generalization can extend. The point is simply that one cannot draw a map of the world just by looking out of one's window, however "typical" the view which one sees. The same is true of "cognitive maps". A subject's judgements of a particular set of stimuli provide a window through which we can view a specific area of his "cognitive world". It may well be that many of the features we see there may partially repeat themselves in other areas also; indeed we would expect this to be so. But what we are not entitled to assume is that the totality of his experience is included within the horizons of our particular field of vision.

This question of relevance is just as important from the standpoint of phenomenal causality. The tendency towards balance in cognitive organization is not just a kind of aesthetic "preference" for symmetry. It represents an attempt by the individual to construct meaningful *causal units* out of events which he sees as interdependent. As we have argued, where no interdependence is assumed, the question of balance does not arise. The individual does not only try to depict his experience, he tries to explain it. By the same token, therefore, salient dimensions should be salient not simply for purposes of description, but also for purposes of explanation. In Chapter 6 we suggested an hypothetical experiment in which American students would be asked to rate a series of statements about the Vietnam war on scales such as "peace-loving–war-mongering" and "patriotic–unpatriotic", and an anti-war subject would be more prepared to discriminate on the "peace-loving–war-mongering" scale. In other words, we would expect the "patriotic–unpatriotic" dimension to be more salient for the pro-war subject, and the "peace-loving–war-mongering" dimension more salient for the anti-war subject. This is not to deny, of course, that some subjects may choose to escape from the dilemma posed for them by the experimenter by wholly or partly reversing one or other scale to render it more congruent with their own evaluations. The pro-war judge might reverse the "peace-loving–war-mongering" scale by arguing: "In Vietnam we are fighting for peace; to oppose US involvement in this war is to support Communist aggression." Similarly, the anti-war judge might reverse the "patriotic–unpatriotic" scale by arguing: "US policy in Vietnam is wrong: it is therefore unpatriotic to support the war, and patriotic to oppose it." Such processes of redefinition would act against the interaction between judges' attitudes and value connotations predicted from the model proposed in Chapter 6. However, the point is that these are special cases—they are ways of getting out of a dilemma, but the dilemma itself is still real enough. To say that the pro-war judge is more likely to see the "patriotic–unpatriotic" dimension as salient, therefore, is not merely a statement about the probable degree of polarization of his judgements: it is to say that he is more likely to see the war as an issue of patriotism. He is more prepared to use the word "patriotic" not just descriptively, but with gerundive and explanatory force. One *should* support the war, he might argue, because it is patriotic to do so, and if we want to know *why* some people support the war and others do not, well, that is at least partly because some people are patriotic and others are not. The anti-war judge, on the other hand, might argue that if one loves peace one should oppose the war, so that the reason why some people oppose the war and others support it is at least partly because some people love peace more than others.

If this is so, then it suggests not only that individuals with different attitudes may sometimes *see* a particular issue in terms of certain dimensions rather than others, but also (since such dimensions provide a frame of reference for explanation as well as description) that they may seek to *explain* the attitudes of different people towards this issue in different terms. What is more, by looking at the kinds of explanations which an individual gives for the attitudes of other people towards a given issue, we may come a little nearer to knowing why he himself holds the attitude he does. The pro-war judge may be pro-war *because* he sees Vietnam as an issue of patriotism; the anti-war judge may be anti-war *because* he sees peace as all-important. If the dimensions that are salient to an individual are those in terms of which he sees his own position as most securely positive, then they may also be those that touch most closely upon the system of values in terms of which he considers his own attitude to be justified. In so far as an individual's interpretation of his own experience influences, and is influenced by, his attitudes and behaviour, then a study of "naïve psychology" may eventually provide a psychological explanation of attitudes and related behaviour which is not so "naïve" after all.

Concluding remarks

We have travelled a long way from our starting point in psychophysical judgement. In the course of this journey we have come across many important differences between social and psychophysical judgement, but we have also found many important similarities. Whether we are dealing with judgements of the heaviness of lifted weights, or of the likeableness of personality traits, we find experimental subjects actively attempting to structure and interpret the information with which they are presented. Judgements, be they social or psychophysical, are much more than mere passive responses to stimulation and theories which fail to take account of this fact are fundamentally inadequate. The following remarks which Allport made about AL theory apply equally well to many other similar approaches:

> Any method that is centred on the purely quantitative aspects of phenomena, no matter how important, or how truly part of the whole picture these may be, is bound to lose sight of much that is both general and significant . . . The perceived object or situation cannot be all dimensions; there must be some type of *aggregate*, or structure, in order to give significance to the dimension itself . . . Adaptation-level, like all frame of reference manifestations, implies a judgmental structure; and to understand this structure may be one of the conditions of understanding adaptation-level itself.

1955, p. 252

If this is true of simple perceptual judgements, then it is even more applicable to social judgement. Simply viewing social judgement from the point of view of scaling methodology may enable us to make reasonably precise predictions about the effects of *certain* variables under *certain* conditions, but it does not necessarily tell us which other variables it might be important to consider, nor how the effects which we have observed should be interpreted.

Both social and psychophysical judgements reflect an attempt on the part of the individual to simplify the almost impossibly complex phenomena of his perceptual world through processes of comparison and categorization. But in addition social judgements reflect, to a greater extent than do psychophysical judgements, an attempt by the individual to achieve consistency in his descriptions and evaluations, to perceive and present himself in generally positive terms, and to explain his own and other people's behaviour. Social judgements are made within an implicit social context, and if we are to understand them we must first understand their structure.

References

Adorno, T. W., Frenkel-Brunswik, E., Levinson, D. F. and Sanford, R. N. (1950). "The Authoritarian Personality". Harper Row, New York.

Ager, J. W. and Dawes, R. M. (1965). The effect of judges' attitudes on judgment. *Journal of Personality and Social Psychology*, **1**, 533–538.

Allport, F. H. (1955). "Theories of Perception and the Concept of Structure". John Wiley, New York.

Anderson, N. H. (1965). Averaging versus adding as a stimulus-combination rule in impression formation. *Journal of Experimental Psychology*, **70**, 394–400.

Anderson, N. H. (1968). Likableness ratings of 555 personality-trait words. *Journal of Personality and Social Psychology*, **4**, 272–279.

Asch, S. E. (1946). Forming impressions of personality. *Journal of Abnormal and Social Psychology*, **41**, 258–290.

Ashley, W. R., Harper, R. S. and Runyon, D. L. (1951). The perceived size of coins in normal and hypnotically induced economic states. *American Journal of Psychology*, **64**, 564–572.

Bannister, D. and Fransella, F. (1966). A grid test of schizophrenic thought disorder. *British Journal of Social and Clinical Psychology*, **5**, 95–102.

Bannister, D. and Fransella, F. (1971). "Inquiring Man: the Theory of Personal Constructs". Penguin Books, Harmondsworth.

Baumgardt, E. and Smith, S. W. (1965). Facilitation effect of a background light on target detection: a test of theories of absolute threshold. *Vision Research*, **5**, 299–312.

Behar, I. and Bevan, W. (1961). The perceived duration of auditory and visual intervals: cross-modal comparison and interaction. *American Journal of Psychology*, **74**, 17–26.

Berscheid, E. and Walster, G. W. (1968). Liking reciprocity as a function of perceived basis of proferred liking. Unpublished manuscript. Department of Psychology, University of Minnesota.

Bevan, W. and Pritchard, F. J. (1963). The anchor effect and the problem of relevance in the judgement of shape. *Journal of General Psychology*, **69**, 147–161.

Beyle, H. C. (1932). A scale of measurement of attitude toward candidates for elective governmental office. *American Political Science Review*, **26**, 527–544.

Bieri, J., Atkins, A. L., Briar, S., Leaman, R. L., Miller, H. and Tripodi, T. (1966). "Clinical and Social Judgment". John Wiley, New York.

Black, R. W. and Bevan, W. (1960). The effect of subliminal shock upon judged intensity of a weak shock. *American Journal of Psychology*, **73**, 262–267.

Bonarius, J. C. J. (1965). Research in the personal construct theory of George A. Kelly: role construct repertory test and basic theory, *in* "Progress in Experimental Personality Research" (Ed. B. Maher), vol. 2. Academic Press, New York and London.

Boucher, J. and Osgood, C. E. (1969). The Polyanna Hypothesis. *Journal of Verbal Learning and Verbal Behavior*, **8**, 1–8.

Brown, D. R. (1953). Stimulus-similarity and the anchoring of subjective scales. *American Journal of Psychology*, **66**, 199–214.

Bruner, J. S. and Goodman, C. C. (1947). Value and need as organizing factors in perception. *Journal of Abnormal and Social Psychology*, **42**, 33–44.

Bruner, J. S. and Postman, L. (1948). Symbolic value as an organizing factor in perception. *Journal of Social Psychology*, **27**, 203–208.

Bruner, J. S. and Rodrigues, J. S. (1953). Some determinants of apparent size. *Journal of Abnormal and Social Psychology*, **48**, 17–24.

Bruner, J. S., Shapiro, D. and Tagiuri, R. (1958). The meaning of traits in isolation and in combination, *in* "Person Perception and Interpersonal Behavior" (Eds R. Tagiuri and L. Petrullo). Stanford University Press, Stanford.

Campbell, D. T. (1956). Enhancement of contrast as composite habit. *Journal of Abnormal and Social Psychology*, **53**, 350–355.

Campbell, D. T., Lewis, N. A. and Hunt, W. A. (1958). Context effects with judgmental language that is absolute, extensive, and extra-experimentally anchored. *Journal of Experimental Psychology*, **55**, 220–228.

Cantril, A. (1946). The intensity of an attitude. *Journal of Abnormal and Social Psychology*, **41**, 129–136.

Carter, L. F. and Schooler, K. (1949). Value, need, and other factors in perception. *Psychological Review*, **56**, 200–207.

Cartwright, D. and Harary, F. (1956). Structural balance: a generalization of Heider's theory. *Psychological Review*, **63**, 277–293.

Cohen, R. (1971). An investigation of the diagnostic processing of contradictory information. *European Journal of Social Psychology*, **1**, 475–492.

Cohen, R. and Schümer, R. (1968). Eine Untersuchung zur sozialen Urteilsbildung: I. Die Verarbeitung von Informationen unterschiedlicher Konsonanz. *Archiv für die gesamte Psychologie*, **120**, 151–179.

Cohen, R. and Schümer, R. (1969). Die diagnostische Verarbeitung widersprüchlicher Informationen in Abhängigkeit vom Ausmass des Widerspruchs. *Diagnostica*, *KV/1*, 3–13.

Coombs, C. H. (1964). "A Theory of Data". John Wiley, New York.

Cromwell, R. L. and Caldwell, D. F. (1962). A comparison of ratings based on personal constructs of self and others. *Journal of Clinical Psychology*, **18**, 43–46.

Davidon, R. S. (1962). Relevance and category scales of judgement. *British Journal of Psychology*, **53**, 373–380.

Deutsch, M. and Solomon, L. (1959). Reactions to evaluations of others as influenced by self-evaluations. *Sociometry*, **22**, 93–112.

Dukes, W. F. and Bevan, W. (1952). Accentuation and response variability in the perception of personally relevant objects. *Journal of Personality*, **20**, 457–465.

Eiser, J. R. (1971a). Enhancement of contrast in the absolute judgment of attitude statements. *Journal of Personality and Social Psychology*, **17**, 1–10.

Eiser, J. R. (1971b). Comment on Ward's "Attitude and involvement in the absolute judgment of attitude statements". *Journal of Personality and Social Psychology*, **17**, 81–83.

Eiser, J. R. (1972). Judgement of attitude statements as a function of judges' attitudes and the judgemental dimension. *British Journal of Social and Clinical Psychology* (in press).

Eiser, J. R. and Mower White, C. J. (In preparation). Evaluative consistency and social judgment.

Eiser, J. R. and Smith, A. J. (1972). Preference for accuracy and positivity in the description of oneself by another. *European Journal of Social Psychology*, **2**, 199–201.

Eiser, J. R., Aiyeola, C. N., Bailey, S. M. and Gaskell, E. J. (1972). Attributions of intention to a simulated partner in a mixed-motive game. *British Journal of Social and Clinical Psychology* (in press).

Eriksen, C. W. and Hake, H. W. (1957). Anchor effects in absolute judgments. *Journal of Experimental Psychology*, **53**, 132–138.

Ertel, S. and Stubbe, D. (1970). Grössenakzentuierung ein Lernprodukt? Eine theoretische Auseinandersetzung über die Bedingungen der sozialen Wahrnehmung. *Zeitschrift für Sozialpsychologie*, **1**, 225–233.

Eysenck, H. J. and Crown, S. (1949). An experimental study in opinion-attitude methodology. *International Journal of Opinion and Attitude Research*, **3**, 47–86.

Fechner, G. T. (1860). "Elemente der Psychophysik". Breitkopf & Hartel, Leipzig.

Feffer, M. and Suchotliff, L. (1966). Decentering implications of social interactions. *Journal of Personality and Social Psychology*, **4**, 415–422.

Fehrer, E. (1952). Shifts in scale values of attitude statements as a function of the composition of the scale. *Journal of Experimental Psychology*, **44**, 179–188.

Felipe, A. I. (1970). Evaluative and descriptive consistency in trait inferences. *Journal of Personality and Social Psychology*, **16**, 627–638.

Ferguson, L. S. (1935). The influence of individual attitudes on construction of an attitude scale. *Journal of Social Psychology*, **6**, 115–117.

Fishbein, M. and Hunter, R. (1964). Summation versus balance in attitude organization and change. *Journal of Abnormal and Social Psychology*, **69**, 505–510.

Festinger, L. (1957). "A theory of Cognitive Dissonance". Row, Peterson, Evanston, Ill.

Grice, H. H. (1934). The construction and validation of a generalized scale designed to measure attitude toward defined groups. *Bulletin of the Purdue University Studies in Higher Education*, **26**, 37–46.

Hardy, R. K. (1949). Construction and validation of a scale measuring attitudes towards the L.D.S. Church. Unpublished Master's Thesis, University of Utah.

Harvey, O. J. (1964). Some cognitive determinants of influencability. *Sociometry*, **27**, 208–221.

Harvey, O. J. (1965). Some situational and cognitive determinants of dissonance resolution. *Journal of Personality and Social Psychology*, **1**, 349–355.

Harvey, O. J. (1967). Conceptual systems and attitude change, *in* "Attitude, Ego-Involvement and Change" (Eds C. W. Sherif and M. Sherif). John Wiley, New York.

Harvey, O. J. and Campbell, D. T. (1963). Judgments of weight as affected by adaptation range, adaptation duration, magnitude of unlabelled anchor, and judgmental language. *Journal of Experimental Psychology*, **65**, 12–21.

Harvey, O. J., Hunt, D. E. and Schroder, H. M. (1961). "Conceptual Systems and Personality Organization". John Wiley, New York.

Hays, W. L. (1958). An approach to the study of trait implication and trait similarity, in "Person perception and interpersonal behavior" (Eds R. Taqiuri and L. Petrullo). Stanford University Press, Stanford.

Heider, F. (1946). Attitudes and cognitive organization. *Journal of Psychology*, **21**, 107–112.

Heider, F. (1958). "The Psychology of Interpersonal Relations". John Wiley, New York.

Helson, H. (1947). Adaptation-level as frame of reference for prediction of psychophysical data. *American Journal of Psychology*, **60**, 1–29.

Helson, H. (1948). Adaptation-level as a basis for a quantitative theory of frames of reference. *Psychological Review*, **55**, 297–313.

Helson, H. (1959). Adaptation-level theory, in "Psychology: A Study of a Science (Ed. S. Koch) "Vol. 1. Sensory, Perceptual, and Physiological Foundations. McGraw-Hill, New York.

Helson, H. (1964). "Adaptation-Level Theory". Harper & Row, New York.

Helson, H. and Kozaki, A. (1968). Anchor effects using numerical estimates of simple dot patterns. *Perception and Psychophysics*, **4**, 163–164.

Helson, H. and Michels, W. C. (1948). The effect of adaptation on achromaticity. *Journal of the Optical Society of America*, **38**, 1025–1032.

Hinckley, E. D. (1932). The influence of individual opinion on construction of an attitude scale. *Journal of Social Psychology*, **3**, 283–296.

Hinckley, E. D. (1963). A follow-up study on the influences of individual opinion on the construction of an attitude scale. *Journal of Abnormal and Social Psychology*, **67**, 290–292.

Hinckley, E. D. and Rethlingshafer, D. (1951). Value judgments of heights of men by college students. *Journal of Psychology*, **31**, 257–269.

Holzkamp, K. (1965). Das Problem der "Akzentuierung" in der sozialen Wahrnehmung. *Zeitschrift für experimentelle und angewandte Psychologie*, **12**, 86–97.

Holzkamp, K. and Keiler, P. (1967). Seriale und dimensionale Bedingungen des Lernens der Grossenakzentuierung: Eine experimentelle Studie zur sozialen Wahrnehmung. *Zeitschrift für experimentelle und angewandte Psychologie*, **14**, 407–441.

Holzkamp, K. and Perlwitz, E. (1966). Absolute oder relative Grossenakzentuierung? Eine experimentelle Studie zur sozialen Wahrnehmung. *Zeitschrift für experimentelle und angewandte Psychologie*, **13**, 390–405.

Holzkamp, K., Keiler, P. and Perlwitz, E. (1968). Die Umkehrung der Akzentuierungsrichtung unter serialen Lernbedingungen: Theoretische und experimentelle Beitraege zum Problem der sozialen Wahrnehmung. *Psychologische Forschung*, **32**, 64–68.

Hovland, C. I. and Sherif, M. (1952). Judgmental phenomena and scales of attitude measurement: Item displacement in Thurstone scales. *Journal of Abnormal and Social Psychology*, **47**, 822–832.

Hovland, C. I., Harvey, O. J. and Sherif, M. (1957). Assimilation and contrast effects in reactions to communication and attitude change. *Journal of Abnormal and Social Psychology*, **55**, 244–252.

Jacobs, L., Berscheid, E. and Walster, E. (1971). Self-esteem and attraction. *Journal of Personality and Social Psychology*, **17**, 84–91.

Jaspars, J. M. F. (1965). "On social perception". Unpublished Ph D dissertation. University of Leiden.

Johnson, C. S. (1941). "Growing up in the Black Belt". American Council of Education, Washington.

Johnson, D. M. (1944). Generalization of a scale of values by averaging of practice effects. *Journal of Experimental Psychology*, **34**, 425–436.

Johnson, D. M. (1955). "The Psychology of Thought and Judgment". Harper & Row, New York.

Johnson, T. J., Feigenbaum, R. and Weibey, M. (1964). Some determinants and consequences of the teacher's perception of causality. *Journal of Educational Psychology*, **55**, 237–246.

Jones, E. E. and Davis, K. E. (1965). From acts to dispositions, in "Advances in Experimental Social Psychology" (Ed. I. Berkowitz), Academic Press, New York and London. Vol 2, pp. 219–266.

Jones, E. E., Worchel, S., Goethals, G. R. and Grumet, J. F. (1971). Prior expectancy and behavioral extremity as determinants of attitude attribution. *Journal of Experimental Social Psychology*, **7**, 59–80.

Jordan, N. (1953). Behavioral forces that are a function of attitudes and of cognitive organization. *Human Relations*, **11**, 239–254.

Kelley, H. H. (1967). Attribution theory in social psychology. *Nebraska Symposium on Motivation*, **15**, 192–238.

Kelley, H. H. and Stahelski, A. J. (1970). Social interaction basis of cooperators' and competitors' beliefs about others. *Journal of Personality and Social Psychology*, **16**, 66–91.

Kelly, G. A. (1955). "The Psychology of Personal Constructs". Norton, New York.

Kite, W. R. (1964). Attributions of causality as a function of the use of reward and punishment. Unpublished Ph D dissertation, Stanford University Press, Stanford.

Klein, G. S., Schlesinger, H. J. and Meister, D. E. (1951). The effect of values on perception: an experimental critique. *Psychological Review*, **58**, 96–112.

Krantz, D. L. and Campbell, D. T. (1961). Separating perceptual and linguistic effects of context shifts upon absolute judgments. *Journal of Experimental Psychology*, **62**, 35–42.

Lambert, W. W., Solomon, R. L. and Watson, P. D. (1949). Reinforcement and extinction as factors in size estimation. *Journal of Experimental Psychology*, **39**, 637–641.

Landfield, A. W. (1968). The extremity rating revisited within the context of personal construct theory. *British Journal of Social and Clinical Psychology*, **7**, 135–139.

Larsen, K. S. (1971). Affectivity, cognitive style, and social judgment. *Journal of Personality and Social Psychology*, **19**, 119–123.

Levine, R. I., Chein, I. and Murphy, G. (1942). The relation of the intensity of a need to the amount of perceptual distortion. *Journal of Psychology*, **13**, 283–293.

Lilli, W. (1970). Das Zustandekommen von Stereotypen über einfache und komplexe Sachverhalte: Experimente zum klassifizierenden Urteil. *Zeitschrift für Sozialpsychologie*, **1**, 57–79.

Lysak, W. and Gilchrist, J. C. (1955). Value equivocality and goal availability. *Journal of Personality*, **23**, 500–501.

Manis, M. (1960). The interpretation of opinion statements as a function of recipient attitude. *Journal of Abnormal and Social Psychology*, **60**, 340–344.

Manis, M. (1961). The interpretation of opinion statements as a function of message ambiguity and recipient attitude. *Journal of Abnormal and Social Psychology*, **63**, 78–81.

Manis, M. (1964). Comment on Upshaw's "Own attitude as an anchor in equal-appearing intervals". *Journal of Abnormal and Social Psychology*, **68**, 689–691.

Marchand, B. (1970). Auswirkung einer emotional wertvollen und einer emotional neutralen Klassifikation auf die Schätzung einer Stimulusserie. *Zeitschrift für Sozialpsychologie*, **1**, 264–274.

Marks, E. (1943). Skin color judgments of Negro college students. *Journal of Abnormal and Social Psychology*, **38**, 370–376.

McArthur, L. A. (1970). Luck is alive and well in New Haven: a serendipitous finding on perceived control of reinforcement after the draft lottery. *Journal of Personality and Social Psychology*, **16**, 316–318.

McCurdy, H. G. (1956). Coin perception studies and the concept of schemata. *Psychological Review*, **63**, 160–168.

Mehrabian, A. and Reed, H. (1968). Some determinants of communication accuracy., *Psychological Bulletin*, **70**, 365–380.

Michels, W. C. and Helson, H. (1949). A reformulation of the Fechner law in terms of adaptation-level applied to rating scale data. *American Journal of Psychology*, **62**, 355–268.

Miller, G. A., Galanter, E. and Pribram, K. H. (1960). "Plans and the Structure of Behavior". Holt, Rinehart & Winston, New York.

Murdock, B. B. Jr. (1960). The distinctiveness of stimuli. *Psychological Review*, **67**, 16–31.

Naatz, T. (1970). Untersuchung zur Lebensraum-repräsentanz der Grosse-Valenz-Verknüpfung. Eine bedingungs-analytischer Beitrag zum Problem der sozialen Wahrnehmung. *Zeitschrift für experimentelle und angewandte Psychologie*, **17**, 277–295.

Naatz, T. and Hümmelink, W. (1971). Zur Realisation einer kognitiven Akzentuier-ungstheorie: Experimentelle Entscheidung zwischen dem serialen Ansatz (Tajfel) und dem modifizierten absoluten Ansatz (Holzkamp) bei serialer Stimuluskonstell-ation. *Zeitschrift für Sozialpsychologie*, **2**, 361–373.

Neisser, U. (1967). "Cognitive Psychology". Appleton-Century-Crofts, New York.

Nemeth, C. J. (1970). The effects of free versus constrained behavior on attraction between people. *Journal of Personality and Social Psychology*, **15**, 302–311.

Newcomb, T. M. (1953). An approach to the study of communicative acts. *Psychological Review*, **60**, 393–404.

Osgood, C. E. and Tannenbaum, P. H. (1955). The principle of congruity in the prediction of attitude change. *Psychological Review*, **62**, 42–55.

Ostrom, T. M. (1966). Perspective as an intervening construct in the judgment of attitude statements. *Journal of Personality and Social Psychology*, **3**, 135–144.

Parducci, A. (1954). Learning variables in the judgment of single stimuli. *Journal of Experimental Psychology*, **48**, 24–30.

Parducci, A. (1956). Incidental learning of stimulus frequencies in the establishment of judgment scales. *Journal of Experimental Psychology*, **52**, 112–118.

Parducci, A. (1959). Ordinal effects in judgment. *Journal of Experimental Psychology*, **58**, 239–246.

Parducci, A. (1963). Range-frequency compromise in judgment. *Psychological Monographs*, **77**, (2, whole no. 565).

Parducci, A. (1965). Category judgment: a range-frequency model. *Psychological Review*, **72**, 407–418.

Parducci, A. and Hohle, R. (1957). Restriction of range in the judgment of single stimuli. *American Journal of Psychology*, **70**, 272–275.

Parducci, A. and Marshall, L. M. (1961a). Context effects in judgments of length. *American Journal of Psychology*, **74**, 576–583.

Parducci, A. and Marshall, L. M. (1961b). Supplementary report: the effects of the mean, midpoint and median upon adaptation level in judgment. *Journal of Experimental Psychology*, **61**, 261–262.

Parducci, A. and Marshall, L. M. (1962). Assimilation versus contrast in the anchoring of perceptual judgment of weight. *Journal of Experimental Psychology*, **63**, 426–437.

Parducci, A., Calfee, R. C., Marshall, L. M. and Davidson, L. P. (1960). Context effects in judgment: adaptation level as a function of the mean, midpoint, and median of the stimuli. *Journal of Experimental Psychology*, **60**, 65–77.

Peabody, D. (1967). Trait inferences: evaluative and descriptive aspects. *Journal of Personality and Social Psychology Monograph*, **7**, (4, whole no. 644).

Peabody, D. (1970). Evaluative and descriptive aspects in personality perception: a reappraisal. *Journal of Personality and Social Psychology*, **16**, 639–646.

Peeters, G. (1971). The positive-negative asymmetry: on cognitive consistency and positivity bias. *European Journal of Social Psychology*, **1**, 455–474.

Pettigrew, T. F. (1958). The measurement and correlates of category width as a cognitive variable. *Journal of Personality*, **26**, 532–544.

Pintner, R. and Forlano, G. (1937). The influence of attitude upon scaling of attitude items. *Journal of Social Psychology*, **8**, 39–45.

Postman, L. and Miller, G. A. (1945). Anchoring of temporal judgments. *American Journal of Psychology*, **58**, 43–53.

Pritchard, J. F. and Bevan, W. (1966). Anchor effectiveness as a function of stimulus variation on an incidental dimension. *Journal of General Psychology*, **74**, 245–251.

Prothro, E. T. (1955). The effect of strong negative attitudes on the placement of items in a Thurstone scale. *Journal of Social Psychology*, **41**, 11–17.

Prothro, E. T. (1957). Personal involvement and item displacement on Thurstone scales. *Journal of Social Psychology*, **45**, 191–196.

Rokeach, M. (1951). "Narrow-mindedness" and personality. *Journal of Personality*, **20**, 234–251.

Rokeach, M. (1960). "The Open and Closed Mind". Basic Books, New York.

Rosenberg, M. J. and Abelson, R. P. (1960). An analysis of cognitive balancing, *in* "Attitude Organization and Change" (Eds M. J. Rosenberg *et al.*). Yale University Press, New Haven, Connecticut.

Rosenberg, S. and Cohen, B. D. (1966). Referential processes of speakers and listeners. *Psychological Review*, **73**, 208–231.

Rosenberg, S. and Olshan, K. (1970). Evaluative and descriptive aspects in personality perception. *Journal of Personality and Social Psychology*, **16**, 619–626.

Rotter, J. B. (1966). Generalized expectancies for internal versus external control of reinforcement. *Psychological Monographs*, **80**. (1, whole no. 609).

Runkel, P. J. (1956). Cognitive similarity in facilitating communication. *Sociometry*, **19**, 178–191.

Schafer, R. and Murphy, G. (1943). The role of autism in visual figure-ground relationship. *Journal of Experimental Psychology*, **32**, 335–343.

Schroder, H. M., Driver, M. and Streufert, S. (1967). "Human Information Processing". Holt, Rinehart & Winston, New York.

Secord, P. F. (1959). Stereotyping and favorableness in the perception of Negro faces. *Journal of Abnormal and Social Psychology*, **59**, 309–315.

Secord, P. F. and Backman, C. W. (1964). "Social Psychology". McGraw-Hill, New York.

Secord, P. F. and Backman, C. W. (1965). An interpersonal approach to personality, *in* "Progress in Experimental Personality Research" (Ed. B. Maher), Vol. 2. Academic Press, New York and London.

Secord, P. F., Bevan, W. and Katz, B. (1956). The Negro stereotype and perceptual accentuation. *Journal of Abnormal and Social Psychology*, **53**, 78–83.

Seeman, M. (1971). The urban alienations: some dubious theses from Marx to Marcuse. *Journal of Personality and Social Psychology*, **19**, 135–143.

Segall, M. H. (1959). The effect of attitude and experience on judgments of controversial statements. *Journal of Abnormal and Social Psychology*, **58**, 366–372.

Selltiz, G., Edrich, H. and Cook, S. W. (1965). Ratings of favorableness of statements about a social group as an indicator of attitude towards the group. *Journal of Personality and Social Psychology*, **2**, 408–415.

Sherif, M. and Hovland, C. I. (1961). "Social Judgment: Assimilation and Contrast Effects in Communication and Attitude Change". Yale University Press, New Haven.

Sherif, M., Taub, D. and Hovland, C. I. (1958). Assimilation and contrast effects of anchoring stimuli on judgment. *Journal of Experimental Psychology*, **55**, 150–155.

Sherif, C. W., Sherif, M. and Nebergall, R. E. (1965). "Attitude and Attitude Change: The Social Judgment-Involvement Approach". Saunders, Philadelphia and London.

Skolnick, P. (1971). Reactions to personal evaluations: a failure to replicate. *Journal of Personality and Social Psychology*, **18**, 62–67.

Smith, G. H. (1966). "In the Imagicon". Galaxy Publishing Corporation, New York.

Solley, C. M. and Lee, R. (1955). Perceived size: closure versus symbolic value. *American Journal of Psychology*, **68**, 142–144.

Stevens, S. S. (1957). On the psychophysical law. *Psychological Review*, **64**, 153–181.

Stevens, S. S. (1958). Adaptation-level versus the relativity of judgment. *American Journal of Psychology*, **71**, 633–646.

Streufert, S. and Streufert, S. C. (1969). Effects of conceptual structure, failure, and success on attribution of causality and interpersonal attitudes. *Journal of Personality and Social Psychology*, **11**, 138–147.

Stroebe, W. (1968). An experimental and theoretical study of social judgment. Unpublished doctoral dissertation. University of London.

Stroebe, W. (1971). The effect of judges' attitudes on ratings of attitude statements: a theoretical analysis. *European Journal of Social Psychology*, **1**, 419–434.

Stroebe, W., Thompson, V. D., Insko, C. A., and Reisman, S. R. (1970). Balance and differentiation in the evaluation of linked attitude objects. *Journal of Personality and Social Psychology*, **16**, 38–47.

Suchman, E. A. (1950). The intensity component in attitude and opinion research, *in* "Measurement and Prediction" (Eds S. A. Stouffer *et al.*), chapter 7, pp. 213–276. Princeton University Press, Princeton.

Tajfel, H. (1957). Value and the perceptual judgment of magnitude. *Psychological Review*, **64**, 192–204.

Tajfel, H. (1959a). Quantitative judgment in social perception. *British Journal of Psychology*, **50**, 16–29.

Tajfel, H. (1959b). The anchoring effects of value in a scale of judgements. *British Journal of Psychology*, **50**, 294–304.

Tajfel, H. and Wilkes, A. L. (1963). Classification and quantitative judgement. *British Journal of Psychology*, **54**, 101–114.

Tajfel, H. and Wilkes, A. L. (1964). Salience of attributes and commitment to extreme judgements in the perception of people. *British Journal of Social and Clinical Psychology*, **3**, 40–49.

Tajfel, H. and Winter, D. G. (1963). The interdependence of size, number and value in young children's estimates of magnitude. *Journal of Genetic Psychology*, **102**, 115–124.

Tajfel, H., Sheikh, A. A. and Gardner, R. C. (1964). Content of stereotypes and the interference of similarity between members of stereotyped groups. *Acta Psychologica*, **22**, 191–201.

Thomas, L. E. (1970). The I-E scale, ideological bias, and political participation. *Journal of Personality*, **38**, 273–286.

Thurstone, L. L. and Chave, E. J. (1929). "The Measurement of Attitude". University of Chicago Press, Chicago, Illinois.

Torgerson, W. S. (1959). "Theory and Methods of Scaling". John Wiley, New York.

Tresselt, M. E. (1948). The effect of the experience of contrasted groups upon the formation of a new scale. *Journal of Social Psychology*, **27**, 209–216.

Tresselt, M. E. and Volkmann, J. (1942). The production of uniform opinion by non-social stimulation. *Journal of Abnormal and Social Psychology*, **37**, 234–243.

Triandis, H. C. (1960a). Cognitive similarity and communication in a dyad. *Human Relations*, **13**, 175–183.

Triandis, H. C. (1960b). Some determinants of interpersonal communication. *Human Relations*, **13**, 279–287.

Tripodi, T. and Bieri, J. (1963). Cognitive complexity as a function of own and provided constructs. *Psychological Reports*, **13**, 26.

Upshaw, H. S. (1962). Own attitude as an anchor in equal appearing intervals. *Journal of Abnormal and Social Psychology*, **64**, 85–96.

Upshaw, H. S. (1964). A linear alternative to assimilation-contrast: a reply to Manis. *Journal of Abnormal and Social Psychology*, **68**, 691–693.

Upshaw, H. S. (1965). The effect of variable perspectives on judgments of opinion statements for Thurstone scales: equal-appearing intervals. *Journal of Personality and Social Psychology*, **2**, 60–69.

Upshaw, H. S. (1969). The personal reference scale: an approach to social judgment, *in* "Advances in Experimental Social Psychology" (Ed. L. Berkowitz), Vol. 4. Academic Press, New York.

Vannoy, J. S. (1965). Generality of cognitive complexity-simplicity as a personality construct. *Journal of Personality and Social Psychology*, **2**, 385–396.

Volkmann, J. (1951). Scales of judgment and their implications for social psychology, *in* "Social Psychology at the Crossroads" (Eds J. H. Rohrer and M. Sherif), pp. 273–294. Harper & Row, New York.

Ward, C. D. (1965). Ego-involvement and the absolute judgment of attitude statements. *Journal of Personality and Social Psychology*, **2**, 202–208.

Ward, C. D. (1966). Attitude and involvement in the absolute judgment of attitude statements. *Journal of Personality and Social Psychology*, **4**, 465–476.

Warr, P. B. and Coffman, T. L. (1970). Personality, involvement and extremity of Judgment. *British Journal of Social and Clinical Psychology*, **9**, 108–121.

Warr, P. B. and Smith, J. S. (1970). Combining information about people: comparisons between six models. *Journals of Personality and Social Psychology*, **16**, 55–65.

Wever, E. G. and Zener, K. E. (1928). The method of absolute judgment in psychophysics. *Psychological Review*, **35**, 466–493.

White, B. J. and Harvey, O. J. (1965). Effects of personality and own stand on judgment and production of statements about a central issue. *Journal of Experimental Social Psychology*, **1**, 334–347.

Zajonc, R. B. (1960). The process of cognitive tuning in communication. *Journal of Abnormal and Social Psychology*, **61**, 159–167.

Zavalloni, M. and Cook, S. W. (1965). Influence of judges' attitudes on ratings of favorableness of statements about a social group. *Journal of Personality and Social Psychology*, **1**, 43–54.

Zimbardo, P. G. (Ed.) (1969). "The Cognitive Control of Motivation". Scott, Foresman & Co., Glenview, Illinois.

Author Index

Numbers in italics indicate the pages on which the references are listed.

A

Abelson, R. P., 174, 175, 177, 185, *224*

Adorno, T. W., 104, 105, *218*

Ager, J. W., 90, 103, *218*

Aiyeola, C. N., 198, *220*

Allport, F. H., 217, *218*

Anderson, N. H., 161, 187, 192, *218*

Asch, S. E., 187, *218*

Ashley, W. R., 64, 68, 69, *218*

Atkins, A. L., 107, 108, *218*

B

Backman, C. W., 59, 177, *225*

Bailey, S. M., 198, *220*

Bannister, D., 203, 208, *218*

Baumgardt, E., 22, *218*

Behar, I., 19, *218*

Berscheid, E., 179, 181, *218, 221*

Bevan, W., 19, 21, 44, 45, 46, 47, 48, 60, 69, *218, 218, 224, 225*

Beyle, H. C., 89, 102, 103, *218*

Bieri, J., 107, 108, 208, *218*, 226

Black, R. W., 21, *218*

Bonarius, J. C. J., 206, 208, 210, *219*

Boucher, J., 181, *219*

Briar, S., 107, 108, *218*

Brown, D. R., 44, 45, 47, 144, *219*

Bruner, J. S., 4, 54, 62, 63, 64, 65, 66, 68, 69, 71, 76, 77, 78, 191, *219*

C

Caldwell, D. F., 208, *219*

Calfee, R. C., 20, 30, *224*

Campbell, D. T., 22, 23, 24, 25, 148, *219, 220, 222*

Cantril, A., 130, *219*

Carter, L. F., 62, 63, 64, 65, 67, 76 *219*

Cartwright, D., 175, 182, 204, *219*

Chave, E. J., 88, 89, 91, 97, 102, *226*

Chein, I., 90, *222*

Coffman, T. L., 106, 108, 109, 208, *227*

Cohen, B. D., 205, *224*

Cohen, R., 192, 193, 195, 213, *219*

Cook, S. W., 92, 93, 95, 96, 98, 101, 102, 105, 120, 121, 128, 136, 137, 142, 143, *225, 227*

Coombs, C. H., 182, 206, *219*

Cromwell, R. L., 208, *219*

Crown, S., 90, 102, 103, *220*

D

Davidon, R. S., 211, *219*

Davidson, L. P., 20, 30, *224*

Davis, K.E., 196, 197, *222*

Dawes, R. M., 90, 103, *218*

Deutsch, M., 178, *219*

Driver, M., 106, 108, *225*

Dukes, W. F., 69, *219*

Subject Index

A

Absolute judgement, 6, 8
  relativity of, 9ff, 13ff, 171
Accentuation theory, 53ff, 144ff
  and assimilation-contrast, 146ff
  and effects of value, 4, 54, 65ff, 81ff
  and interval properties of scale,
    149ff
  and judgements of attitude state-
    ments, 144ff
  and person perception, 59ff
  interclass and intraclass differences,
    55ff
  interserial and intraserial
    effects, 70ff
  see also Incidental stimulus variation
Adaptation-level theory, 4, 9ff, 39ff,
    144, 214, 217
  and effects of judge's attitude, 110ff,
    128, 166ff
  and effects of scale composition,
    112ff, 118, 127ff
  and interval properties of scale,
    17ff
  and order of stimulus presentation,
    25ff, 113ff, 122ff
  and "perceptual" versus "seman-
    tic" shifts, 10, 17, 20ff, 33, 117
  and sensory processes, 9, 13ff, 21ff,
    43
  and stimulus distinctiveness, 11,
    35ff

and stimulus relevance, 42ff
and the Weber-Fechner law, 18
applications to social judgement,
  110ff, 117ff, 127ff, 142ff, 166ff
focal, background and residual
  stimuli, 11ff, 19
Anchor stimulus, 12, 16, 21, 28, 34,
  37ff, 110, 144ff, 166, 211
  and central tendency, 39ff
  and stimulus relevance, 44ff
  end-anchoring, 34, 41ff, 115ff, 121,
    165
  judge's attitude as an anchor, 110ff,
    115ff, 131ff, 145, 166, 211
  see also Subjective standards
Assimilation, 38ff, 83ff, 129, 142ff,
  165, 167
Assimilation-contrast model, 37,
  128ff, 145, 149, 166ff, 211
  and involvement, 130ff, 137ff, 211
  and latitudes of acceptance, non-
    commitment and rejection,
    129ff, 146, 211
  as related to psychophysical judge-
    ment, 37ff, 132
  see also Assimilation, Contrast, and
    Judgement of attitude state-
    ments
Attribution, 174, 186ff, 212
  attribution theory, 175, 187, 196ff
  and distinctiveness, 196
  and individual differences, 199ff